iPhone Games Projects

DAVE MARK, SERIES EDITOR

PJ CABRERA
JOACHIM BONDO
AARON FOTHERGILL
BRIAN GREENSTONE
OLIVIER HENNESSY
MIKE KASPRZAK
MIKE LEE
RICHARD ZITO
MATTHEW AITKEN
CLAYTON KANE

Apress®

iPhone Games Projects

ISBN-13 (paperback): 978-1-4302-1968-2

ISBN-13 (electronic): 978-1-4302-1969-9

Printed and bound in the United States of America 9 8 7 6 5 4 3 2 1

Lead Editor: Clay Andres
Developmental Editor: Douglas Pundick
Lead Author and Technical Reviewer: PJ Cabrera
Editorial Board: Clay Andres, Steve Anglin, Mark Beckner, Ewan Buckingham, Tony Campbell, Gary Cornell, Jonathan Gennick, Jonathan Hassell, Michelle Lowman, Matthew Moodie, Duncan Parkes, Jeffrey Pepper, Frank Pohlmann, Douglas Pundick, Ben Renow-Clarke, Dominic Shakeshaft, Matt Wade, Tom Welsh
Project Manager | Production Director: Grace Wong
Copy Editors: Kim Wimpsett, Marilyn Smith
Associate Production Director: Kari Brooks-Copony
Production Editor: Laura Esterman
Compositor | Interior Designer: Diana Van Winkle
Proofreader: Nancy Bell
Indexer: BIM Indexing & Proofreading Services
Cover Designer: Kurt Krames
Manufacturing Director: Tom Debolski

Distributed to the book trade worldwide by Springer-Verlag New York, Inc., 233 Spring Street, 6th Floor, New York, NY 10013. Phone 1-800-SPRINGER, fax 201-348-4505, e-mail orders-ny@springer-sbm.com, or visit http://www.springeronline.com.

For information on translations, please contact Apress directly at 2855 Telegraph Avenue, Suite 600, Berkeley, CA 94705. Phone 510-549-5930, fax 510-549-5939, e-mail info@apress.com, or visit http://www.apress.com.

Apress and friends of ED books may be purchased in bulk for academic, corporate, or promotional use. eBook versions and licenses are also available for most titles. For more information, reference our Special Bulk Sales–eBook Licensing web page at http://www.apress.com/info/bulksales.

The source code for this book is available to readers at http://www.apress.com. You will need to answer questions pertaining to this book in order to successfully download the code.

To my parents, Pedro and Cecilia: LQM
—PJ Cabrera

To my brother Adam, who does 50% of the work and gets 0.01% of the mentions ;)
—Aaron Fothergill

To my teammates, past and present, who have made me the engineer I am
—Mike Lee

Contents at a Glance

Contents

JOACHIM BONDO

PJ CABRERA

AARON FOTHERGILL

BRIAN GREENSTONE

OLIVIER HENNESSY
AND CLAYTON KANE

RICHARD ZITO
AND MATTHEW AITKEN

Foreword

iPhone games are hot, hot, hot! As I write this, there are more than 40,000 apps on the App Store, of which nearly 9,000 are in the Games category, the largest category by far. The next largest category is Entertainment, at just over 5,000 apps. There are nearly 40% more games on the App Store than any other kind of app.

Games is not only the biggest category on the App Store, but it is also the best-selling category. During the promotion of its one billionth download, Apple provided a list of all-time most popular apps. Of the top-20 all-time paid apps, more than 14 were games. Many of these apps were on the top-10 paid apps list at one time or another during the nine months the App Store had been in business. Many are still on the top-100 list. These sold thousands of copies a day in their time, with daily revenue between a few thousand to tens of thousands of dollars.

With such great numbers, it is understandable why the interest in developing iPhone games is so high. It is probably the reason you are reading this foreword. You couldn't have picked up this book at a better time. If you want to get in on the fun and potential profit of making iPhone games, the time to get started is now, and this book is your ticket there!

This book contains lots of information from master independent iPhone game developers—information that is hard to find anywhere else. Some of the authors of this book are responsible for all-time popular games:

- Brian Greenstone developed Enigmo and Cro-Mag Rally.

- Aaron Fothergill developed Flick Fishing.

- Mike Lee developed the original Tap Tap Revolution, the most downloaded game in App Store history.

This book also features a chapter by award-winning game developer Mike Kasprzak, finalist for Best Mobile Game in the Game Developers Conference's Independent Games Festival Mobile 2009. Other authors, including Richard Zito, Joachim Bondo, and Olivier Hennessy, have received glowing reviews and accolades for their games.

The content in this book is phenomenal. The authors provide a variety of points of view and different approaches to iPhone development, showing you how iPhone games are made with various technologies. You will gain knowledge of how to optimize your game using iPhone SDK tools such as Instruments and Shark, as well as optimization tricks that the masters have learned through the crucible of experience. You will also get invaluable insight into game design, arguably the most important aspect of game creation. If your game is not properly designed, all the technical prowess in the world isn't going to help it be popular.

I am honored to have worked with the independent game development professionals in the creation of this book. I have learned from their experience thanks to the chapters they have written. And with this book, you, too, can acquire the know-how and insight to make the next generation of all-time most popular and award-winning games.

Now, pick up this book and get started!

PJ Cabrera

FoneGears Systems LLC founder and lead developer

About the Lead Author and Technical Reviewer

PJ Cabrera is a software engineer with more than 12 years of experience developing information systems in various industries, programming in C, C++, Java, PHP, Python, and Ruby. But his real passion for many years has been hacking gadgets (i.e., turning a Sega Dreamcast into a NetBSD router, or running Android and Debian GNU/Linux on a Palm TX) and making home-brewed games for consoles such as Dreamcast, PlayStation 2, GameBoy Advance, and PSP. He is very excited that he can finally share his creative side on iPhone and XBox 360 with the general public through the App Store and XNA Community Games.

Acknowledgments

Special thanks to Glenn Cole who reviewed every chapter, provided quality control, and contributed the introduction.

I would like to acknowledge the support of my family as I worked on this book. Thanks for putting up with my absence every evening and weekend I had to work on my chapters, and for your unreserved love.

And thanks to my friends Ronada Wanner, Lenny Ramirez, Cesar Otero, and Luis Pulido, for cheering me on and believing in me.

This book would not have been possible without the tireless professionalism of many staff at Apress. Many thanks go out to Clay Andres, for believing in me; our project manager Grace Wong, for her gentle reminders of my looming immutable deadlines; Caroline Rose, Kim Wimpsett, and Marilyn Smith for editing and copy editing duties (my chapter is much improved because of their efforts); Laura Esterman, Douglas Pundik, and Glenn Cole in production editing (the chapters look awesome!). To everyone else at Apress, thanks for everything you did to make this book a reality.

PJ Cabrera

Introduction

First, the obvious: the iPhone rocks. Less obviously, so does the iPod touch—no phone, no cellular network (and the associated monthly fee), just a wonderful game-playing, application-downloading, insanely great Cocoa touch machine. Consumers love them both for their stability, ever-present network access, ineffable coolness, and (as we developers know firsthand) all of those great third-party apps.

Apple's App Store rocks, too, and as the owners of these devices have made it clear, games rock the most! The *Wall Street Journal* reported data from Mobclix showing that over a quarter of the applications in Apple's App Store are games (see http://blogs.wsj.com/digits/2009/03/23/no-recession-for-iphone-game-apps/). Venture capitalists are getting in on the action as well, financing game developer Ngmoco to the tune of $10 million. There has even been a conference devoted to gaming on the iPhone (see http://www.igsummit.com/).

Think of this book as a guide and companion through your personal journey of game development for the iPhone and iPod touch. And like any good travel guide, it's full of tips, highlights, and invaluable suggestions for avoiding the costly and time-consuming mistakes of the early explorers who have gone before you.

But the life of the game developer is not all fun and, well, games, so there's more. After all, games development requires knowledge of the same basic coding and language skills as any form of app development. So we've loaded the book with code you can reuse as building blocks for your own apps. Even those developers who don't have game development as their highest priority will find a lot of solid information here for use in their applications.

Who This Book Is For

This book is for everyone writing game applications for iPhone and iPod touch. It's assumed that you already have some development experience, both in general and specifically with Objective-C and Cocoa on the iPhone. We have made no attempt to cover every aspect of every API for every sort of game imaginable. We have left a lot of room for your imagination, and have instead filled the book with key concepts and compelling stories we hope you will find both useful and inspirational.

We're able to do this because this book is part of Apress's comprehensive road map of Mac and iPhone developer titles. So, if you have experience with Objective-C and Cocoa, but not specifically for the iPhone, *Beginning iPhone Development* by Dave Mark and Jeff LaMarche is a great way to fill in the gaps. If you have experience with an object-oriented language like C++, C#, or Java, a glance through the first few chapters of Apple's free online reference "The Objective-C 2.0 Programming Language" (available from `http://developer.apple.com`) may be sufficient before moving to *Beginning iPhone Development*. Otherwise, you'll want to begin either with *Learn Objective-C on the Mac* by Mark Dalrymple and Scott Knaster, if you have experience with C but not with Objective-C, or *Learn C on the Mac* by Dave Mark, if you're starting from scratch or have not used a C-like language like PHP, ASP, or JavaScript.

Just as some portions of the iPhone SDK are based on standard C rather than on the Cocoa frameworks, so, too, do some portions of this book use standard C pointers and structs. If you are not comfortable with these, *Expert C Programming* by Peter van der Linden (published by Prentice Hall) will help to bring you up to speed.

What's in the Book

The journey begins by giving serious consideration to the user experience. We've all heard that an application should be well polished before being released, but what does that really mean? Joachim Bondo, author of the elegant chess application Deep Green, shares his thoughts on what makes a great user interface, and how he decides which features to add and which to leave out. Seeing all of the thought that went into Deep Green will show you what polish really means.

In Chapter 2, PJ Cabrera shares his ideas on bringing back the social aspect of games. He backs this up with code to show how to call a web service, how to parse the resulting XML, how to post data back to the web service, and for truly RESTful web services, how to simplify the task with a drop-in library. As a bonus, you will also see how to prototype a RESTful web service using Ruby on Rails, so you can get started quickly.

Long-time developers will appreciate how the old text game Star Trek has evolved into using OpenGL ES in the game Space Hike. Aaron Fothergill explains the process in Chapter 3, and also shares a nifty technique for saving struct-based data.

Chapter 4 finds "rock star" Brian Greenstone of Pangea Software—makers of Bugdom, CroMag Rally, and more—sharing his "must-do" list for iPhone action games. Brian also guides you through performance analysis using both Instruments and Shark. The first time I read this chapter, I was exhausted by the end.

In Chapter 5, Olivier Hennessy and Clayton Kane share some of their tricks of the trade in the form of the game design document (think of it as a plan for success). They also provide an overview of the available game engines and why you should consider using one.

Are you thinking about other platforms as well as the iPhone? In Chapter 6, Mike Kasprzak shares his techniques for writing an OpenGL ES–based game for the iPhone that can also run on Windows and on Linux with minimal changes. Also included are techniques for "frame skipping" and physics simulation.

Mike Lee—previously of Delicious Monster, cofounder of Tapulous, and now at Apple—shares his insights on the code optimization process in Chapter 7. Mike goes into the thought process behind optimization, including key observations that help drive toward a solution. He also makes a strong argument for embracing the vendor's frameworks, even when you're tempted to roll your own.

The book concludes with Richard Zito and Matthew Aitken writing about multiplayer gaming. They explore the various techniques for networking, demonstrating the pros and cons of each. Low-level sockets are covered, both with and without Bonjour. You'll learn how to "publish" the game's availability on the network, and how to allow users to join in.

We've also added a special online bonus chapter by Jamie Gotch on how to implement a clone of the game Puyo, a falling blocks game, using the A* (A-star) path-finding algorithm. A* is typically used to implement artificial intelligence for unit movement in genres such as real-time strategy, adventure, and role-playing games. This chapter shows how to use A* to find adjacent blocks of the same color in the game. Jamie's game Fieldrunners was the winner of the Game Developers Conference's Independent Games Festival Mobile 2009 competition.

There is something here for everyone, from experienced OpenGL developers, to enterprise software developers, to those who have completed only an introductory text. I know, because I've read every chapter and checked every line of code. It has been an illuminating journey through applications so diverse and rich with experience that I kept finding new surprises and deeper insights. I hope you get as much out of this book as I have.

Glenn Cole

Joachim Bondo

Company: *Cocoa Stuff (one-man shop)*

Location: *Copenhagen, Denmark*

Former Life As a Developer: *I have 27 years of experience in starting up and running smaller software development companies and developing software using a wide range of programming languages, such as BASIC, COMAL 80, Pascal, C, C++, Objective-C, SQL, NewtonScript, PHP, JavaScript, and Bash. I've worked in many environments, such as THINK C and Think Class Library (TCL), Macintosh Programmer's Workshop (MPW), Metrowerks CodeWarrior and PowerPlant, 4th Dimension, Newton Toolkit (NTK), Sybase, MySQL, TextMate, Xcode, Cocoa, and Cocoa Touch. Platforms include Mac OS 3–8, Newton OS, Palm OS, Unix (FreeBSD and Mac OS X), Mac OS X Panther and Leopard, and iPhone OS.*

Life As an iPhone Developer: *I created Deep Green, a chess game, using the official iPhone SDK from Apple (since the day it was released).*

What's in This Chapter: *With the focus on creating a beautiful, elegant, and powerful user interface, and in a noncode language, the chapter covers the key areas that made Deep Green a successful application in the App Store, featured by Apple in several sections such as What's Hot and Staff Favorites.*

Key Technologies:

- *User interface design*
- *Simplicity*
- *Product statement*

Chapter 1

Simplify the User Interface for Complex Games: Chess, the Deep Green Way

On the day Deep Green was released, John Gruber of Daring Fireball quoted me for saying this:

> When I compare the various iPhone chess apps (I bought them all), Deep Green offers pretty much the same functionality as the rest, and sometimes more, but with a fraction of the UI. Achieving this is why I'm four months later than the rest.

Creating a successful application requires intelligent design from the very beginning, or you may walk down the wrong path. In this chapter, I'll share some of my design decisions that ended up making Deep Green a success—ten years ago as well as today.

More specifically, I'll cover simplicity from a user interface (UI) perspective more than dealing with the underlying code. In fact, you won't see a single line of code in this chapter.

Code is the foundation of your application, but even more important, your application will be judged by its user interface. If it fails to deliver a phenomenal user experience, your application won't likely be a success.

It's my belief that simplicity and success go hand in hand in general—and even more so in the context of iPhone application development.

Once Upon a Time . . .

When I bought my first Newton in 1996, I soon realized that a portable device like that was the perfect companion for playing chess. It was always at hand, always ready, and ever patient.

This was back when Apple didn't enjoy the mass adoption of its products and when developers were counted by the dozens, not the thousands. At the time, three years after the Newton was launched, there existed only one chess application. It was expensive, feature-poor, and slow. From a UI perspective, it was even unattractive.

In the summer of 1997, I made the first sketches for my own chess application. The year before, IBM's Deep Blue chess computer became the first machine to win a chess game against a reigning world champion (Garry Kasparov). With Newton's green enclosure and screen, the name for Deep Green was obvious.

In early 1998, I released the first public beta, as shown in Figure 1-1.

Figure 1-1. *Deep Green for the Newton*

Users were enthusiastic, praising Deep Green for its simple, yet powerful, implementation.

Here was a type of application, often implemented in a very complicated and clumsy way, made appealing and fun—maybe even like Apple would have done it. Moves were being animated, Newton OS–native gestures were deeply integrated, and the application looked great by the standards of the time. Games could be played back and forth and set up as desired (see Figure 1-2).

Figure 1-2. *Deep Green in Playback and Setup modes on the Newton*

In a matter of days thereafter, Steve Jobs terminated the Newton project altogether.

It didn't seem to have much impact on the interest in Deep Green. However, I knew it wouldn't last, and I probably wouldn't get to implement the many ideas I had for future versions.

The only real complaint I got from users was that Deep Green was simply too hard to beat, even at the lowest level. The Newton MessagePad 2000/2100 with its screaming 160 MHz StrongARM processor gave users an especially hard time. The engine was written in C++, and the user interface was written in NewtonScript. I had to implement what I ended up calling Concentration in order to have the engine choose among lesser moves at lower concentrations (see Figure 1-3).

Figure 1-3. *Deep Green's New Game "slip" on the Newton*

When Steve Jobs unveiled the iPhone ten years later at the Macworld conference of 2007, I knew right away I had to make Deep Green for my soon-to-be favorite handheld device. And this time, I reckoned, he wouldn't pull the carpet underneath my feet.

It took me a year of all my spare time, and a good bit of goodwill from my family, to finish Deep Green for the iPhone and iPod touch. The result, I think, is a fine testament to its predecessor, based on the same underlying design goal: *simplicity* (see Figure 1-4).

Figure 1-4. *Deep Green on the Newton (left) and on the iPhone (right)—a decade apart*

In the following sections, I'll talk exactly about that—simplicity. For reasons I'll explain herein, I believe simplicity is the most important feature you can add to your application. Read on.

Why Should We Care About Simplicity?

I'll be talking a lot about simplicity because simplicity was, and still is, the overall design goal of Deep Green. In the context of software development, I define simplicity as follows:

simplicity = beauty (how things look) + elegance (how things work)

That is, a high degree of simplicity requires a high degree of beauty and elegance. You can develop a beautiful application without it being elegant, and vice versa, but in order to create a truly *simplistic* application, you need to maximize and marry both beauty and elegance.

So, why is simplicity important, why should we developers care, and why do our users care? Well, we should care exactly for *that* reason: because our users care.

They may not know they do, however. In fact, I'll argue that most users think they want features. Features can be quantified, measured, and compared. And that's what users can express their need for. But underneath the desire for features is something bigger. *Control.* I believe what we all want as software users is the feeling of being in control. If we're in control, we'll be able to focus on what's important. We'll have more time with pure enjoyment. Simplicity is the means for creating the feeling of control.

A good example of the opposite, in my opinion, is Microsoft Word. It offers an amazing amount of features, out of which I'm guessing the average user may use 10 percent. You find yourself frustrated over and over, because you can't find the feature you want—it's buried in that 90 percent you don't use. Which few buttons in the countless numbers of toolbars are relevant to you at any given moment? It's very hard to tell. You often find yourself browsing around for the relevant functionality. You're out of control. You're having a bad user experience.

How Simplicity Was Achieved

In order to being able to develop a simplistic application, you need to find out what's important in your application. And to do this, you need to have a *product statement*. The product statement describes in one sentence what your product is. In Deep Green's case, the product statement is as follows:

A simplistic chess application for the casual player

The product statement is my guiding principle during the entire process from idea through design and development to release and maintenance. It's the beacon I'm relentlessly steering toward for every decision I make through the entire process. If I'm uncertain whether to include a feature or where to place it in the application, I go back to this statement and see whether and where the feature fits in.

If I lose track of the product statement, I lose control of the entire process, and Deep Green with it, and it's up to forces beyond my control what happens to my application.

With this in mind, I'll take you through some of the main areas of Deep Green and explain my motivations for doing what I did, which ultimately led to the application I'm so proud of (see Figure 1-5).

Distilling the Essence

The keywords of the product statement are *chess*, *casual*, and *simplistic*. This leads to defining the primary and secondary, and possibly tertiary, func-

Figure 1-5. *Deep Green's application icon*

tionality. The primary functionality should be supported by the most prominent user interface elements and be available to the user at all times, where the secondary functionality should be one gesture away. The tertiary functionality should probably not even make it to an iPhone application, but if so desired, it should be hidden away from the rest, and more important part, of the user interface. In Deep Green, I defined the primary functionality as follows:

- Displaying board and pieces

- Moving pieces

- Making a new game

- Taking back moves

- Showing the last move

- Getting a hint from the engine

- Seeing whose turn it is

This functionality is what chess boils down to when you play it casually. I wanted to create the sense of playing over the board with a friend, where Deep Green is the friend.

I defined the secondary functionality as follows:

- Setting up a position

- Playing back the game one move at a time

- Seeing captured pieces

- Swapping sides

In Deep Green all of this is one gesture away with a tap, a swipe or flick, or a multifinger gesture.

If you're successful in defining these areas and you keep them in mind when designing and developing your application, chances for a truly simplistic application are much higher than if you uncritically squeeze all functionality into the UI at once.

Pushing the Pixels

First, I have to dwell a bit on the graphics because that's what immediately meets the eye when launching Deep Green. Unfortunately, I'm not capable of producing graphics that satisfy my own preposterously high standards for looks and quality. Fortunately, others are, and I was lucky enough to get the chance to work with Japan's Mikio Inose on Deep Green's graphics. In him I met a person who would follow me to the very last pixel—and often even further.

Deep Green, as what I would call an application of high quality, will always be priced at the higher end. In order to give users value for money, this had to be reflected at every level of the application—from the quality of the underlying code all the way up to the "materials" used to depict the objects in the user interface, such as pieces and board.

In Deep Green, the pieces are supposed to be ebony and ivory, and the board is noble wood. If you look closely at the icon in Figure 1-5, you'll see the grains of the ebony. You can even see it in the smaller pieces on the

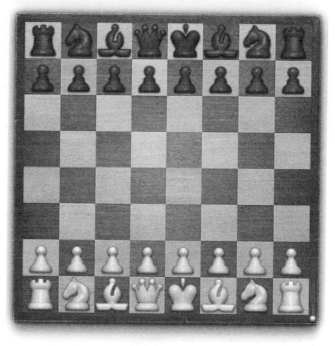

Figure 1-6. *Deep Green's ebony and ivory pieces on noble wood*

board. The ivory pieces even feature the perhaps not-so-well-known Schreger lines that are used by connoisseurs to distinguish real ivory from fake (see Figure 1-6).

Do you notice the resemblance to the Newton version? The pieces are based on the same font, Adobe's Cheq—or, rather, its freeware derivative, Chess Regular by Alastair Scott. I wanted to continue on the same path of branding that I started ten years earlier.

The board is worn and has dents from years of use. Yes, even just playing casually can cause its wear and tear. The board can be flipped on its back, just like a real board, and on the backside you'll see the engine and other elements depending on the context (see Figure 1-7).

Notice the engravings on the main gear. It says "Cocoa Stuff, DENMARK." Above the visible gears there's an engraving in the wood saying "Manufactured by Cocoa Stuff." I'll go into even more detail with the engine in the "Making the User Smile" section.

Letting the User Focus

Figure 1-7. *The backside of the board showing the engine and splash ornaments*

Going back to the product statement, Deep Green is about playing chess. Nothing more, nothing less. It doesn't have the bells and whistles of more capable desktop applications. When you launch Deep Green, you are taken directly to the main view showing the board with pieces and the toolbar. It's very clean and pleasing and ready to play (see Figure 1-8).

I even contemplated sliding the toolbar out of the way, to make the experience even more secluded, but I figured the user would be more puzzled about not finding anything anywhere than relieved by the simplicity. Remember, I want my primary functionality exposed.

Contrary to any of the other chess applications I have downloaded from the App Store, Deep Green lets you move pieces via both tap-tap and drag-and-drop gestures. Tapping a piece makes it wiggle like when moving the icons in the home screen. If you've started a tap-tap move, you can still move the piece or any other piece simply by starting to drag or by tapping it. You don't have to set a preference as I've seen in some apps. You just go ahead and do what's most natural. I tend to drag and drop for shorter distances and tap-tap for longer. It's not entirely trivial to implement (it's certainly not rocket science either), but this is something the user will be doing repeatedly. As a developer, you *have* to spend that extra time polishing that experience.

Figure 1-8. *Main view of Deep Green in Play mode*

Since the user's finger will cover and obscure the destination square when moving the finger around on the board, I wanted to help identify both the piece that's currently being dragged and where it would go should the finger be lifted. I did that by enlarging the piece, offsetting it slightly upward, and making it semitransparent so that the board can be seen underneath. At the same time, I'm leaving a semitransparent copy of the dragged piece on its original square so that it's obvious what piece is currently being dragged and where it would go back to if released on an illegal square.

Finally, I'm displaying horizontal and vertical guides to give feedback on what square the finger is currently over. If the current square represents a legal move, the guides will highlight in green. They will highlight in red on an illegal move (see Figure 1-9).

Figure 1-9. *Dragging a piece over a legal (left) and illegal (right) square*

Notice the second and third buttons from the left in the toolbar. They are for taking back your last move and for showing the last move, respectively. The buttons feature a miniature piece that denotes which type of piece the given move involves. In Figure 1-9, it shows that if you tap the Take Back button, you'll take back your last move, which was a bishop move.

Tapping the Show Last button—Deep Green's last move in this case—will show a queen's move. Just by looking at the buttons, you may be able to figure out what will happen if you take back a move or what Deep Green's last move was. By incorporating a primary feature this way, I can save an ugly move list somewhere. Keep in mind, I'm targeting the casual player, not the type of player who wants to look at a list of algebraic move notations.

The fourth button in the toolbar is the Engine button. When it's Deep Green's turn and the engine is working, the gear spins. When it's your turn, tapping it will make it suggest a move (while also spinning because the engine is hard at work).

Drilling Down

There are *application settings*, and there are *game settings*. Application settings are rarely changed, probably only once, and should be maintained via the general Settings application. In Deep Green these are settings such as how to notify the player about events such as check, checkmate, and stalemate (they could be via callouts, sounds, and vibration), whether to display coordinates on the board, whether to prevent the iPhone from going to sleep, and so on, as shown in Figure 1-10.

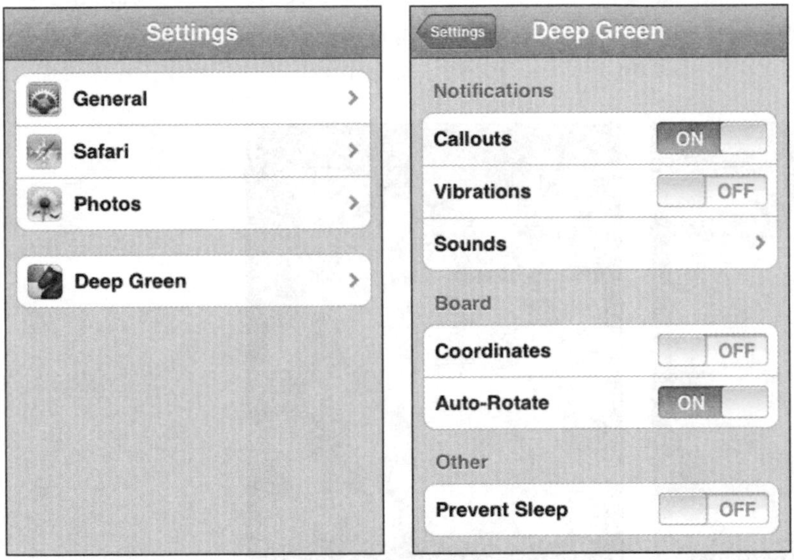

Figure 1-10. *Deep Green application settings displayed in the Settings application*

Game settings, on the other hand, will be changed much more often, perhaps as often as each game. As a secondary feature, these settings are only a tap away—and within the application.

The screen real estate on the iPhone is very limited compared to desktop and laptop computers, and Apple designed the iPhone user interface with this in mind. It allows you to drill down to the information you seek very easily by initially being presented with the high-level information, allowing you to tap to the lower-level information. This is how the Settings application works, and I've implemented the Game Info view the very same way. Initially, it shows the high-level information such as the players and captured pieces (see Figure 1-11), and from there you can drill down to tertiary information such as game state, current castling availability, full-move number, half-move clock, and so on.

I chose to adopt the same implementation as that of the Settings application so that the user would feel at home with the user interface right away, even to the extent that it looks exactly like the table views in Settings. Unfortunately, these elements are not available in Apple's Cocoa Touch framework, so I had to reverse-engineer them to pixel perfection.

My point in all this is to say that this way of hierarchically structuring views and information is another way of achieving simplicity. Instead of presenting the user with everything at once, I'm simplifying or summarizing the information in such a way that the user controls what areas he or she wants to explore, and only then do I present that particular subset of information.

Figure 1-11. *The highest-level Game Info view (left) showing secondary information and Game State (right) showing tertiary information*

Less Is More

My goal with the initial version of Deep Green for the iPhone was to at least match the feature set of the Newton version. In that, I had three game modes: *Play mode*, *Setup mode*, and *Playback mode*. These modes would offer the functionality to play a game, set up a given position (taken from the newspaper or a chess book, for example), and step back and forth in the current game.

The solution for setting up a position that many chess applications for the iPhone seem to implement is to squeeze in another view, in an already very tight view, that displays all the pieces and little arrows or widgets to specify the game state such as castling availability, en passant square, color to move, and other information needed to fully specify a legal game position (see Figure 1-12).

Figure 1-12. *A constructed example of the easy solution*

Figure 1-13. *Deep Green with the simplistic solution*

Although this is a very straightforward, and possibly even intuitive, solution, it's not very user friendly. Even though everything is there, it's up to the user to figure out what it all means. There are pieces everywhere, and it's all very confusing. It's not clear what to do and how to do it.

The solution I ended up implementing in Deep Green was to introduce the *drawer*. The drawer resides under the board and slides out when needed. When switching to Setup mode, it slides out with the different pieces, as shown in Figure 1-13.

What this solution perhaps suffers from in straightforwardness, it more than compensates for in simplicity and power. When seeing the drawer for the first time, the user will invariably ask herself, where are the white pieces? But how long does it take her to guess it's under the white color switch button? My guess is, not very long.

By stimulating the user's curiosity, I'm not only engaging her, but I'm also allowing myself to get rid of a bunch of clutter. The user doesn't need to drag both white and black pieces from the drawer onto the board simultaneously.

And here's the interesting part; by hiding the UI, I'm making it even more powerful. In this context I've done that by allowing the user to double-tap a piece to toggle its color. So if you have a black knight on the board and you want it to be white, simply double-tap it. So, you could easily place all the pieces in just one color and then double-tap the pieces that need to be the opposite color. If you double-tap a piece in the drawer, all drawer pieces swap color (just like tapping the color switch button), as shown in Figure 1-14.

The power is in what's *not* there, rather than in what *is* there. That's my simplistic solution.

My solution for setting the game state is to reuse the UI that's already there in the form of the Game Info view under the *i*-button (shown earlier in Figure 1-11). Once again, I've eliminated unneeded UI by implementing a design that can be used for both displaying and setting the game state and information while both playing the game and setting up a given position.

Figure 1-14. *Drawer pieces in the process of toggling from white to black in a chain reaction type of animation*

NOTE

The ultimately simplistic way of setting up a position is of course the FEN string, which, by the way, is one of the options Deep Green offers in its internal API. The FEN string lets you specify the position by listing the pieces on each rank and appending the game state. The position shown in Figure 1-14 would be `r4rk1/pppn3p/3b2p1/3b1Bq1/3P4/2P4P/P1Q2Pp1/RR4K1 w - - 0 20`. Using this method in the user interface on the iPhone would perhaps be challenging the user too much, I think.

Empowering the User

The last of the three game modes, besides Play mode and Setup mode, is Playback mode. This is where you can step back and forth in the game and resume playing from any position.

Here, also, I've taken a somewhat different approach than the other chess applications currently available for the iPhone and iPod touch. Where these applications don't seem to offer an explicit mode, they let you rather implicitly undo and redo moves. On one side, this is very straightforward, but on the other, it's rather constraining.

A big part of learning chess, besides simply playing it, of course, is studying others' games. As a user, you'd want to step through a game in order to learn from it—without taking back moves. There's a big difference between *taking* back and forth moves and *stepping* back and forth. Where taking back and forth modifies the game, stepping doesn't.

I took this even further in Deep Green by letting the user single-step back and forth, jump to the beginning and to the end of the game, and *auto-replay* a game by animating the moves in sequence—just like playing a movie for the user to sit back and enjoy. All these operations animate the pieces smoothly (see Figure 1-15).

The slider in the familiar drawer even lets you *scrub* back and forth with instant feedback. So when you drag the slider, the position on the board updates itself immediately to reflect the given position. This way you can quickly jump to a certain stage in the game and fine-tune the position on the back and previous buttons.

I find myself doing this all the time, and the feedback is extremely rewarding. You feel in total control, and you get a sense of a very powerful device and application because Deep Green reacts immediately.

Figure 1-15. *Playback mode with an intuitive user interface*

To summarize, playing back a game belongs to the group of secondary functions and shouldn't be confused with the primary function of undoing a move, for which there is a button in the toolbar in Play mode. And because it's a secondary function, it's one gesture away.

The easiest way of entering Playback mode is to flick right with your finger below the board where the drawer will come out. In the built-in Photos application, flicking right on a photo animates to the previous photo—it goes back in time. Going to Playback mode in Deep Green is also like going back in time because it lets you explore the historic moves.

Left-flicking in Photos goes forward in time by showing the next photo. And so does doing it in Deep Green, because a left-flick takes you to Setup mode, where you can set up a position to play next.

Making the User Smile

Like a real-life chessboard, and so many other things in real life, the chessboard in Deep Green has a backside. When making a horizontal flick from one of the board edges toward the center, the board flips around on its back in the direction of the flick (see Figure 1-16).

When in Play mode, the backside shows the captured pieces and a representation of the *chess engine*. The board backside with the engine is really just a gimmick. It doesn't have much of a function. At best, it duplicates existing functionality from the Game Info view in that it shows the captured pieces.

UI that doesn't have a function can be categorized as bloat or clutter, and that's what I've been advocating against in the whole chapter. So, why on Earth did I choose to spend half the graphics designer budget on bloat? I don't know either. Or, that's not entirely true. I do know, because I spent a lot of time and effort thinking about it before asking the designer to make the engine for me.

Figure 1-16. *Board backside with captured pieces. The graphics file for the engine consisted of about 600 layers, and the gears can actually turn.*

One of the many things I like about the Macintosh platform is the odd little things the creative developers are adding to their software in order to surprise us and make us smile—just some day, perhaps after months of use. If you haven't already, you'd be surprised what can happen when clicking around in your installed applications while holding the Alt key down, for example.

I wanted the same for Deep Green, because I like these hidden features myself, especially if they're useful in some way or another. And although you can see the captured pieces in the Game Info view, I personally prefer to quickly flip the board around and then flip it back to continue the game. Again, this is a secondary function, one gesture away, that I don't want to spoil the aesthetics with in the main layout.

So, besides being semi-useful, it also makes sense that you can actually touch and affect the board. I mean, you can with the pieces.

The design of the mechanical engine, which obviously doesn't have anything to do with the artificial intelligence of Deep Green's chess engine, was constructed in a 3D application and rendered into bitmaps, resulting in a Photoshop file with almost 600 layers of gears, shadows, and other effects. From there it was pixel-perfected by hand. As a result of its 3D model origins, the gears can actually turn—and they do. Try flipping the board while Deep Green is "thinking." The gears will animate. While having a Deep Green vs. Deep Green game, you can flip the board around and watch the gears spin, and the captured pieces appear as the game progresses.

I hope it makes you smile when you encounter this. It sure makes me.

Summary

These were my words on how I developed a successful application, ten years ago as well as today. I'm sure this also explains at least part of the reason why Deep Green has been featured on the App Store in several sections such as What's Hot and Staff Favorites. To me, simplicity is the single most important feature you can add to your application. It's the prerequisite for delivering a superior user experience.

I hope I've inspired you to dare leave out features that are secondary and tertiary to your product statement and that spending a large amount of time, and even money, on the user interface is a clever investment.

PJ Cabrera

Company: *FoneGears Systems LLC*

Location: *Vega Baja, Puerto Rico*

Former Life As a Developer: I have more than 12 years of experience in computer programming and software engineering, working with C, C++, Python, PHP, Java, and Ruby on Rails. I've consulted in a wide range of industries, such as textiles manufacturing, goods distribution, commercial insurance, communications, pharmaceuticals, and finance, as well as government agencies at the state level in the United States.

Life As an iPhone Developer: A couple games and a utility application are under development, and should be released by the time this book is published.

I use Inkscape, GIMP, Pixelmator, and Blender to create graphics and icons. To program games for the iPhone, I use the cocos2d and SIO2 Interactive gaming libraries.

What's in This Chapter: This chapter makes the case for games that use social networking features to engage users beyond the moment of play, to create a community by allowing users to share their game experience with others. It gets into the nitty-gritty details of integrating high-score leaderboards and achievement web services natively on the iPhone.

Key Technologies:

- *REST web services*
- *NSURLConnection*
- *NSXMLParser*
- *ObjectiveResource*

Responsive Social Gaming with RESTful Web Services

W hen I played my first video game in 1978, it was a very social experience. My neighbors, the Reyes family, had bought an Atari 2600 console for Christmas. One night, they invited my family to play with them. I remember vividly those early games of Pong, Combat, Backgammon, and Othello. This transformative experience was ingrained in my memory forever. (Other, earlier transformative experiences are probably lost due to faulty RAM.)

I was only eight years old, but I remember thinking, "This must be one of those computers I heard about on TV. I want to know how they work! I want to know how to make games like these!" I became obsessed, like only an eight-year-old boy can be, with computers and how they worked. While other kids dreamed of dinosaurs and heavy-duty construction equipment, I dreamed of CPUs and algorithms implemented in BASIC and hexadecimal. (I was a weird kid.) Thus began a hobby that later turned into a career in computer programming and software engineering.

While the Atari sounds and graphics are quaint by today's standards, they obviously had an impact on me. No one had seen anything like it at the time—well, maybe in sci-fi movies, but not for real, right in their living rooms. Yet what I remember most of those late 1970s nights isn't what was on the TV screen, but the Reyes family playing and enjoying this electronic miracle together.

Over time, video games lost some of this social factor. As time passed, gamers were often thought of as lonely, antisocial creatures. Yet every so often, games with social factors are reborn, either as MUDs, MMOs, or more recently, as games on social networking sites.

In this chapter, we will examine how to create a native iPhone game with social networking features. You'll see what is possible, which should help get ideas flowing for your own games.

Social Networking Games and the iPhone

In the past decade, Internet use has expanded into the mainstream as Internet-ready computers and broadband access have become more affordable. Leading the charge are so-called social networking sites, where users can share links, notes, photos, music, and videos with family, friends, acquaintances, and colleagues. The more innovative social networks provide an extensible API through which other application providers can extend the social experience further. Many of these third-party extensions fall into the category of games.

The iPhone, with its always-on connectivity to the mobile data network, takes users to a new level of network use, as they are no longer restricted to their desks, living rooms, dens, or kitchens. This enables iPhone owners to be engaged with their lives on the Web at all times, if they choose to go that route.

Sure, other phones have been able to connect to the Web. Some even let you install apps to go beyond the built-in functionality. The difference is that while previous smartphone owners could use their phones to get on the Web if the wished, with the iPhone, users *love* to get on the Web all the time. And the iPhone App Store provides iPhone owners with tens of thousands of applications that reach almost every part of the Web with an iPhone-optimized experience.

But iPhone games have been the exception to this expanded reach. Very few iPhone games offer an experience that goes beyond the game itself on your phone. Once you play a round of most iPhone games, the experience is over until you start another round. Nothing else happens with the score you made. And unless you tell someone, no one knows you played for five consecutive levels without losing a life. Your iPhone certainly doesn't care.

But what if it did?

In creating my own iPhone games, I wanted to do something different. I knew that I was just a programmer, not a graphic design expert. I wasn't going to create a category killer with gorgeous graphics—at least, not without a lot of help and a bigger budget than I have right now. And perhaps I'll never invent some clever, unique game-play element that gives my games an edge over the rest.

Thinking back to my memories of my earliest encounter with video games with the Reyes family, I decided the differentiating factor in my games would be the implementation of a social factor right into the game. When playing my games, your iPhone will notice whether you have played five consecutive levels without losing a life, and give you the tools to tell the whole World Wide Web about it!

Most iPhone games provide users with a high-score leaderboard, where users can see how they and other players are doing with the game. A very few games provide a forum where iPhone users can share their game experiences with other players, share tips on how to beat specific levels, and just generally have fun talking about the game with others. This is nice, but we could be doing much more.

Just for starters, you could reward users for accomplishing specific objectives in your games, and let users share these accomplishments with others. Figure 2-1 shows Trism, a popular iPhone game that features an achievements display.

Playing for a certain number of levels straight without losing a life is difficult in some games. It would be great if you could reward players for that. If you implement social networking features into your game, you can not only give your users awards, but perhaps they could put a widget on their MySpace or Facebook profile, telling the world what their latest highest score is and what achievements they have earned.

You can accomplish this by setting up a web service, and having your iPhone game connect to and send requests to that web service to record high scores and achievements awarded to players. Then, separately from that, you make a JavaScript or Flash widget that connects to your web service and displays the user's latest highest score and earned achievements.

Figure 2-1. *The game Trism by Steve Demeter is a unique variation of match-three games, which award players when they accomplish specific goals in the game. There are very few iPhone games with a feature like this.*

This is an iPhone book, so I will not go into the details of making JavaScript or Flash widgets. But we can get started with a simple web service, including the iPhone code to connect to it, and submit information to the web service directly from your game. In the following sections, I will describe how to implement a simple high-score web service and native iPhone code to connect to this web service and retrieve the top-100 high scores.

Creating the Prototype High-Score Web Service

Rather than reinventing the wheel with a custom network protocol and writing a high-speed server in C or C++, I decided to make a RESTful web service to store user names, high scores, and all the other information I needed for the social networking features of my games. I accomplished this quickly and easily by using Rails.

With Rails, I can create a prototype RESTful web service in a matter of minutes, and then incrementally polish and improve it to its final form. I know that it won't be just a throwaway, toy web service. That said, the focus of this book is on iPhone implementation details; this isn't a Rails book.

Here, I will cover only the basic steps necessary to create the web service. This simple high-score web service will just take the user's name and the current high score, and store that information in a big fat list. It won't concern itself with logins and other security trappings.

Creating the High-Scores Rails App

Rails and a supported database are all you need to get started developing Rails apps. If you are developing with the iPhone SDK, you must have Mac OS X 10.5.5 (Leopard) or later, and thankfully, Leopard comes with Rails and SQLite 3 installed. With some basic knowledge of using the Unix command line from the Mac OS X Terminal app, you can get started with Rails.

First, update RubyGems and Rails to the latest version. Open Terminal and type in the following commands (you will be prompted for your Mac OS X password):

```
sudo gem install rubygems-update
sudo update_rubygems
sudo gem install -y rails
```

This will update RubyGems and Rails and their dependency packages, if you don't already have them.

Next, change directory to where you usually store your projects. Enter the following to create a directory to store everything together and change current directory there:

```
mkdir iPhoneGamesProjects; cd iPhoneGamesProjects
```

Then create a skeleton Rails app named simple_high_score_service, as follows:

```
rails simple_high_score_service
```

Change directory to your newly created Rails app:

```
cd simple_high_score_service
```

Now create a Rails controller, view, and model for handling the high score and the name of the user:

```
script/generate scaffold highScore \
score:integer full_name:string
```

Finally, have Rails create the database where your Rails model will be stored:

```
rake db:migrate
```

Believe it or not, with just a few minutes' work, you have a prototype high-scores web service. Run the Rails app by typing the following:

```
script/server
```

Now open your web browser to `localhost:3000/high_scores` to see the product of those strenuous minutes of hard work.

Your web browser should present you with a plain-looking web app where your users can store their name and their latest high score. It will store one record for each name and score pair. The default code generated by Rails lists records in the order in which they are saved in the database, and the navigation is a bit lacking, but it is a good, usable prototype. And the best part is that it implements full XML web services, with no extra work on your part. Figure 2-2 shows the simple high-score web service after I entered a few scores.

Figure 2-2. *The simple high-score web service, after entering some scores*

High-score leaderboards are usually presented as a top-100 list of scores in descending order. Let's make a few changes to the web service code to implement this. In your still-running Terminal session, enter the following command:

```
$ script/generate controller Top100Scores index
```

This creates a skeleton controller called Top100Scores, with a single empty action and view called index.

Open your new controller file, *simple_high_score_service/app/controllers/top100_scores_controller.rb*, in your favorite text editor, and then replace the entire contents with the code in Listing 2-1.

Listing 2-1. New Content of top100_scores_controller.rb

```
class Top100ScoresController < ApplicationController
  # GET / top100_scores
  # GET /top100_scores .xml
  def index
    @high_scores = HighScore.find(:all, :limit => 100,
        :order => 'score desc')

    respond_to do |format|
      format.html # index.html.erb
      format.xml  { render :xml => @high_scores }
    end
  end
end
```

This code grabs up to 100 high scores in descending order from the database, and displays them either as HTML or XML, depending on the requested format. When no format is specified in the request URL, the default is HTML.

Next, open the file *simple_high_score_service/app/views/top100_scores/index.html.erb* in your text editor, and then replace the entire contents with the code in Listing 2-2.

Listing 2-2. New Contents of index.html.erb

```
<h1>Top 100 high scores</h1>

<table>
  <tr>
    <th>Score</th>
    <th>Full name</th>
  </tr>

<% for high_score in @high_scores %>
  <tr>
```

```
      <td><%=h high_score.score %></td>
      <td><%=h high_score.full_name %></td>
    </tr>
  <% end %>
  </table>
```

```
<br />
```

This code simply displays each high score in the top 100 in a simple HTML table, along with the score and the player's full name.

Finally, open the file *simple_high_score_service/config/routes.rb* in your text editor, and add the code marked in bold in Listing 2-3, right after the second line. Don't touch or erase anything else; just insert the four lines of code in bold after the resource mapping for high_scores.

Listing 2-3. *Modifications to routes.rb*

```
ActionController::Routing::Routes.draw do |map|
  map.resources :high_scores
  map.connect 'top_100_scores', :controller => 'top100_scores',
    :action => 'index'
  map.connect 'top_100_scores.xml', :controller => 'top100_scores',
  :action => 'index', :format => 'xml'
```

If you now visit localhost:3000/top100_stores with your browser, you will see the scores listed in descending order.

There's really not much to this prototype web service at this point, but since this isn't a web or Rails development book, you will leave it like that. Now, let's discuss how this Rails app works in terms of RESTful XML web services.

Using RESTful XML Web Services

The moniker *REST*, short for representational state transfer, refers to a way of architecting distributed systems such as web services. RESTful XML web services use the simplicity of the HTTP protocol to communicate between the client and the server. Objects are transmitted serialized as XML (JavaScript Object Notation, or JSON, has become quite popular lately, but that's a subject for another book). Using REST simplifies the implementation, as there is no need to reinvent the wheel. Why drive ourselves insane creating complex networking code when simple HTTP and XML can serve our needs?

You query a RESTful web service by sending an HTTP GET request to the URI representing the entity you want to retrieve. For example, you can issue a GET request for http://localhost:3000/high_scores.xml, and the server responds by sending an XML representation of all the high scores in the database, as shown in Listing 2-4.

Listing 2-4. Sample Result of an http://localhost:3000/high_scores.xml Request on the High-Scores Web Service

```
<high-scores type="array">
    <high-score>
        <created-at type="datetime">
                2009-01-12T23:45:18Z
        </created-at>
        <id type="integer">1</id>
        <full_name type="string">
                Billy
        </full_name>
        <score type="integer">10002</score>
        <updated-at type="datetime">
                2009-01-12T23:45:18Z
        </updated-at>
    </high-score>
    <high-score>
        <created-at type="datetime">
                2009-01-12T23:48:03Z
        </created-at>
        <id type="integer">2</id>
        <full_name type="string">
                Suzie
        </full_name>
        <score type="integer">10008</score>
        <updated-at type="datetime">
                2009-01-12T23:48:03Z
        </updated-at>
    </high-score>
</high-scores>
```

If you want the details for just one high-score record, you send an HTTP GET request indicating that record's ID. For example, if you issue a request for `http://localhost:3000/high_scores/1.xml`, the server responds with a representation of the high-score record with an ID of 1 in XML, as shown in Listing 2-5.

Listing 2-5. Sample Result of an http://localhost:3000/high_scores/1.xml Request on the High-Scores Web Service

```
<high-score>
    <created-at type="datetime">
            2009-01-12T23:45:18Z
    </created-at>
    <id type="integer">1</id>
    <full_name type="string">
            Billy
```

```
        </full_name>
        <score type="integer">10002</score>
        <updated-at type="datetime">
              2009-01-12T23:45:18Z
        </updated-at>
</high-score>
```

REST supports the operations that are needed by most database applications. Along with getting values from the web service, REST also provides "verbs" for posting new data, making updates, and deleting records. You can manage the records as follows:

Create a new high-score record: Send an HTTP POST request to `http://localhost:3000/high_scores.xml`, with the data representation of the new high score in XML format. The server replies with the high-score data representation in XML, including the ID for the new record and `created_at` and `updated_at` date and time stamps.

Update the data for a high-score record: Send an HTTP PUT request that includes the ID of the record to update. For example, to update the record with an ID of 1, send `http://localhost:3000/high_scores/1.xml`, with the data representation of the modified record in XML format. The server responds with the modified record representation in XML, including the `updated_at` date and time stamp.

Delete a high-score record: Send an HTTP DELETE request to the URI associated with the representation of that record (an XML representation of the record to be deleted isn't necessary). For example, to delete the high-score record with an ID of 1, send an HTTP DELETE request to `http://localhost:3000/high_scores/1.xml`. The server simply responds with a report of whether the DELETE operation was successful, with an HTTP response status code of 200.

Again, since this isn't a web services book, I've just provided a brief introduction to RESTful web services. Next, let's discuss the iPhone SDK side of things.

Displaying High Scores on the iPhone

The goal is to implement a small sample application to display the top-100 high scores from the prototype web service you created in the previous section. This involves four main steps:

- Create the user interface (UI). You create the Xcode project, assemble the UI in Interface Builder, organize the code to work with your UI, and declare any variables needed by the code.

- Connect to web services. You use NSURLConnection to download the top-100 high scores from the web service.

- Parse the XML. You use NSXMLParser to parse the XML.

- Notify the table that displays the scores that you have fresh data for it to process, which makes the UI send a message to its data source and query the data model.

Now let's get started creating the UI to display the high scores.

Creating the User Interface

I will not go into every detail of creating the UI. I assume you have used Xcode to create a few simple iPhone applications.

NOTE

If you need more information about creating UIs for your iPhone apps, refer to a book like *Beginning iPhone Development* (Apress, 2008) or any of the tutorials available on the various iPhone development blogs. Go through at least two tutorials that create and connect some UI elements in Interface Builder before continuing here.

Open Xcode, create a new project, and choose the Navigation-Based Application template, as shown in Figure 2-3 (my New Project dialog box includes a few custom project templates, so yours won't look exactly like the one in the figure). When Xcode asks you what to call your project, name it ViewHighScores.

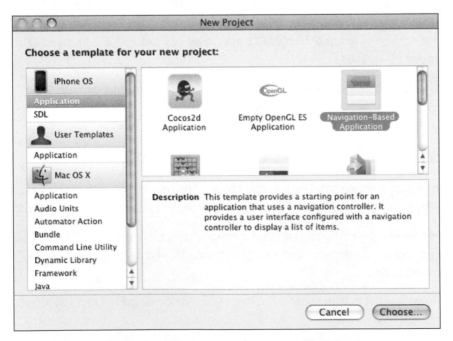

Figure 2-3. *Open Xcode and create a new navigation-based application.*

Once you have created the project, you need to make some modifications to the application controller and delegate files.

Modifying the App Controller and Delegate

Select the Classes group under ViewHighScores in the Groups and Files section of Xcode. Above the text editor area, you will see the *ViewHighScoresAppDelegate.h*, *ViewHighScoresAppDelegate.h*, *RootViewController.h*, and *RootViewController.m* files.

In the files list, select *RootViewController.h* to begin editing it in the editor area below the list. The code marked in bold in Listing 2-6 shows the changes to make to this file. Make sure to insert the code into the correct place in *RootViewController.h*, and then save the file when you're finished.

Listing 2-6. *Changes to the Interface Code for RootViewController.h*

```
#import <UIKit/UIKit.h>

@interface RootViewController : UITableViewController {
    UITableView *myTableView;
}

@property (nonatomic, retain) IBOutlet UITableView *myTableView;

- (void)reloadData;

@end
```

This code creates an instance variable called myTableView in the RootViewController class, and sets up an IBOutlet property for this variable. This is the Xcode way to connect code elements like variables with GUI objects in Interface Builder. You also declare a message called reloadData, which will be used to cause the UITableView to reload its data from its data source.

Now that you have changed the interface of the RootViewController class, you need to change the implementation to match. Select the *RootViewController.m* file in the file list to load it in the editor pane, carefully insert the code in bold in Listing 2-7 into the proper place in the file, and then save it.

Listing 2-7. Changes to the Implementation Code for RootViewController.m

```
#import "RootViewController.h"
#import "ViewHighScoresAppDelegate.h"

@implementation RootViewController

@synthesize myTableView;

- (void)reloadData {
    [myTableView reloadData];
}

- (void)viewDidLoad {
    [super viewDidLoad];
    self.title = @"View High Scores";
}
```

This code synthesizes the property declared in Listing 2-6, defines the code for the reloadData message, and sets up the title of the RootViewController.

Once you have modified the *RootViewController.m* file, open the *ViewHighScoresAppDelegate.h* file and modify it with the code marked in bold in Listing 2-8.

Listing 2-8. Changes to the Interface Code for ViewHighScoresAppDelegate.h

```
#import <UIKit/UIKit.h>

@class RootViewController;

@interface ViewHighScoresAppDelegate : NSObject <UIApplicationDelegate> {

    UIWindow *window;
    UINavigationController *navigationController;

    NSMutableData *responseData;
    NSXMLParser *highScoresParser;
    NSMutableArray *highScores;
    NSMutableDictionary *newScore;
    NSString *currentKey;
    NSMutableString *currentStringValue;

    RootViewController *rootViewController;
}

@property (nonatomic, retain) IBOutlet UIWindow *window;
@property (nonatomic, retain) IBOutlet
    UINavigationController *navigationController;
```

```
@property (nonatomic, retain) NSMutableArray *highScores;
@property (nonatomic, retain) IBOutlet
    RootViewController *rootViewController;

- (void)getHighScores;
- (void)getHighScoresFromWebService:(NSString *)URLstr;
- (void)parseHighScores:(NSData *)highScoresXMLData;

@end
```

The code in Listing 2-8 declares a few internal variables for use inside your app delegate instance messages. It also declares the messages getHighScores, getHighScoresFromWebService:, and parseHighScores:. Among the internal variables are the following:

- responseData: This variable will be used to store the downloaded XML from the high-scores web service.

- highScoresParser: This will hold an object that will parse the high scores from the XML data.

- highScores: This is an array of NSDictionary instances. Each instance holds the full-name and high-score elements parsed from the XML data.

- newScore: This is an NSMutableDictionary, which holds a single high-score record during XML processing.

- currentKey and currentStringValue: These hold values used during XML process-ing, to add high scores to the newScore dictionary.

Now that you have modified the interface to the app delegate, you need to make matching changes to the implementation. Open the *ViewHighScoresAppDelegate.m* file and modify it with the code marked in bold in Listing 2-9.

Listing 2-9. *Changes to the Implementation Code for ViewHighScoresAppDelegate.m*

```
#import "ViewHighScoresAppDelegate.h"
#import "RootViewController.h"

@implementation ViewHighScoresAppDelegate

@synthesize window;
@synthesize navigationController;

@synthesize highScores;
@synthesize rootViewController;
```

```
- (void)applicationDidFinishLaunching:(UIApplication *)application {
    // Configure and show the window
    [window addSubview:[navigationController view]];
    [window makeKeyAndVisible];

    [self getHighScores];
}
```

The code in Listing 2-9 synthesizes the highScores and rootViewController properties declared in Listing 2-8, and modifies the applicationDidFinishLaunching: message, by calling the message getHighScores as the last step in the application's launch.

Now that you have modified the RootViewController and ViewHighScoresAppDelegate source code, you must make some connections in Interface Builder.

Connecting the myTableView Property to the Table View Object

First, you need to connect the myTableView property to the Interface Builder Table View object. Follow these steps:

1. In Xcode, select the Resources group from the Groups and Files list. Above the text editor area, you will see *the RootViewController.xib* and *MainWindow.xib* files. Double-click the *RootViewController.xib* file to open the file in Interface Builder.

2. Select File's Owner from the main list.

3. From the Interface Builder menu, select **Tools ➤ Inspector** to open an inspector window (which actually might be open already, currently titled "Root View Controller attributes" or something similar).

4. Click the second tab of that window to change the window title to "Root View Controller connections."

5. In the inspector window, you will see an item named myTableView, with a small open circle to the right of its name. This is the myTableView IBOutlet property created in the source code in Listing 2-6. Press and hold down the mouse button on this circle, and a blue line will extend from the circle and follow your mouse pointer as you move it around. Drag your pointer over to the Table View object, either on the main list or the actual view, and release the mouse button to make the connection, as shown in Figure 2-4.

6. Save and close the *RootViewController.xib* file in Interface Builder.

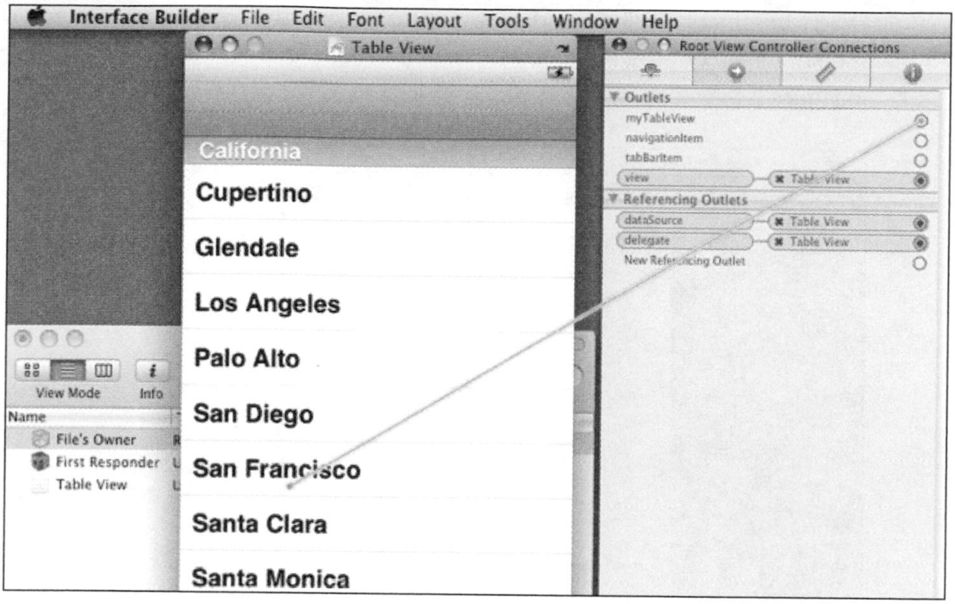

Figure 2-4. *Connecting the property myTableView to the Table View object in Interface Builder*

Connecting the rootViewController Property to the Root View Controller Object

Now you need to connect another property between Interface Builder GUI elements—this time, between the `rootViewController` property and the View High Scores App Delegate object. Here are the steps:

1. In Xcode, select the Resources group in the Groups and Files list, and double-click the *MainWindow.xib* file.

2. In Interface Builder, select the View High Scores App Delegate object in the main list.

3. Select the second tab in the inspector window. You will see an item named `rootViewController`, with a small open circle to the right of its name. This is the `rootViewController IBOutlet` property created in the source code in Listing 2-8.

4. Drag from the open circle, and release the mouse button when the pointer is over the Root View Controller object, either in the main list or in the view itself, as shown in Figure 2-5.

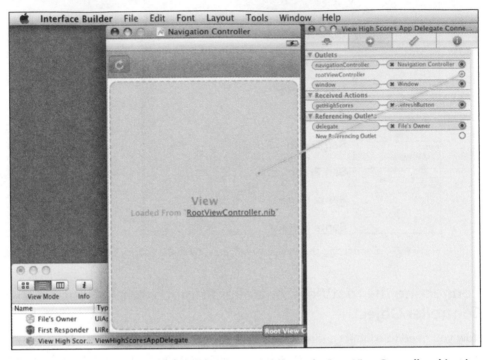

Figure 2-5. *Connecting the property rootViewController to the Root View Controller object in Interface Builder*

5. Save and close the *MainWindow.xib* file.

Now that you have created your Xcode project and made GUI connections in Interface Builder, you can start creating the code to load high scores from the simple high-score web service.

Connecting to Web Services

Since the subject of this chapter is a social networking feature for iPhone games, web service connections are important. Here, I will give you a very thorough walk-through of the code to implement retrieving of the top-100 high scores from the sample web service.

The good news is that this sample code is applicable to communicating with any web service or application, not just Rails web services. Whether you need to talk to a PHP or .NET server, or you are downloading some static files like MP3s and PDFs, you will use pretty much the same code.

Creating NSURL, NSURLRequest, and NSURLConnection Objects

The iPhone SDK provides a very comprehensive way to connect to web resources using the NSURL, NSURLRequest, and NSURLConnection classes. These classes let you send a request to a web service, and receive notification of a successful response or failure. The API allows your UI to be updated to reflect what is happening with the download, without dealing with multiple threads. This happens without too much of an impact on performance.

To make requests to a web service with these classes, you begin creating an NSURL object by passing in a string holding the URL, and then create an NSURLRequest. Listing 2-10 shows the implementation of loading high scores. Open the file *ViewHighScoresAppDelegate.m* in Xcode and add the code marked as bold. As you can see, the code goes directly after the last brace for (void)dealloc, but before the line with @end at the very end of the file.

Listing 2-10. Creating the NSURL, NSURLRequest, and NSURLConnection Objects

```
- (void)dealloc {
    [navigationController release];
    [window release];
    [super dealloc];
}

#pragma mark web service connection methods

#define HIGH_SCORES_URL @"http://localhost:3000/top_100_scores.xml"

- (void)getHighScores
{
    [self getHighScoresFromWebService: HIGH_SCORES_URL];
}

- (void)getHighScoresFromWebService:(NSString *)URLstr
{
    [rootViewController setTitle: @"Getting High Scores ..."];
    [[UIApplication sharedApplication]
        setNetworkActivityIndicatorVisible:TRUE];

    NSURL *theURL = [NSURL URLWithString:URLstr];
    NSURLRequest *theRequest = [NSURLRequest
        requestWithURL:theURL
        cachePolicy:NSURLRequestUseProtocolCachePolicy
        timeoutInterval:10.0];

    NSURLConnection *theConnection = [[NSURLConnection alloc]
        initWithRequest: theRequest delegate: self];

    if (theConnection) {
```

```
            responseData = [[NSMutableData data] retain];
    } else {
        // The connection request is invalid; malformed URL, perhaps?
        [rootViewController setTitle: @"Error Getting High Scores"];
        [[UIApplication sharedApplication]
            setNetworkActivityIndicatorVisible:FALSE];
    }
}

@end
```

The code in Listing 2-10 defines a preprocessor constant called HIGH_SCORES_URL and assigns it the address to the simple high-scores web service. This example is going to run in the iPhone simulator that comes with the SDK, so it is OK to use localhost. To deploy this to an iPhone or iPod touch, change localhost to the IP address of the computer where you run your simple high-scores web service.

After defining this constant, the code defines a method named getHighScores, which calls another method, getHighScoresFromWebService, with the URL constant as parameter. It is in this second method that work begins in loading the URL.

First, you set a title to rootViewController, indicating you are getting the high scores, and then you make the network activity indicator visible. Next, you allocate an NSURL object with the high-scores web service URL, and use that to allocate the NSURLRequest object.

```
NSURL *theURL = [NSURL URLWithString:URLstr];
NSURLRequest *theRequest = [NSURLRequest
    requestWithURL:theURL
    cachePolicy:NSURLRequestUseProtocolCachePolicy
    timeoutInterval:10.0];
```

The NSURLRequest takes the NSURL instance created previously, a timeout interval in seconds, and a cache policy constant. For this particular example, the policy is set to respect the caching done by the operating system behind the scenes, and any caching by the web service provider itself. When you set this policy, the iPhone SDK's URL loading process is smart enough to download data only when the cache is deemed older than the fresh data or when the cache has expired the limit set by the web service provider.

The best part is that you don't have to do anything unless your application has special caching needs. This particular caching policy is good enough for most cases.

Note that in order for this automatic caching to work properly, you need to make sure your Rails web service is set up with proper caching procedures. That is a subject for a whole book on Rails application server configuration and deployment, so I won't get into it here.

NOTE

> Setting this caching policy is important when your game downloads the high scores often; for example, if your users like to check the high scores each time they finish a game. The player's score may not have landed in the top 100, which means the top-100 list may not have changed since the player's previous game. If you're caching things properly on the server, it makes no sense to ignore the server's caching and force the iPhone to download the high scores again. With over 30 million iPhone and iPod touch owners worldwide at the time of this writing, and apparently growing by at least a million more every month, trust me when I say that you want to limit the amount of unnecessary downloads from your web services. This is even more important if you're going to be offering a free trial version of your games. No one likes to get billed for server bandwidth overage fees.

Once you have created the NSURLRequest instance, you create an NSURLConnection instance. Then you check that you were returned a valid (not null) NSURLConnection instance. If you are returned a null NSURLConnection instance, you inform the user by changing the title of the rootViewController, and turn off the network activity indicator.

```
NSURLConnection *theConnection = [[NSURLConnection alloc]
    initWithRequest: theRequest delegate: self];

if (theConnection) {
    responseData = [[NSMutableData data] retain];
} else {
    // The connection request is invalid; malformed URL, perhaps?
    [rootViewController setTitle: @"Error Getting High Scores"];
    [[UIApplication sharedApplication]
        setNetworkActivityIndicatorVisible:FALSE];
```

Once you have determined that the connection object is not null, you allocate a mutable data object to hold the data as it is received by the system.

Then you . . . What? Huh? Is that all?

It looks like the code to get the high scores ends here, but in fact, we're just getting started.

Setting Up the Connection Delegate

The NSURLConnection message initWithRequest:delegate: takes a parameter for the delegate, which is an instance of a class that implements the NSURLConnectionDelegate category. The NSURLConnectionDelegate category defines delegate methods that receive informational callbacks about the status of a URL connection. In Listing 2-10, the application delegate is the connection delegate, so you pass self as the delegate parameter. To process the connection properly, the app delegate must implement all methods defined by the NSURLConnectionDelegate category.

For instance, the `connection:didFailWithError:` message is called if the connection fails, either because of a timeout or an address not found error. Listing 2-11 shows the implementation of `connection:didFailWithError:`. Add this code into the file *ViewHighScoresAppDelegate.m*, immediately after the code you added from Listing 2-10. (Add all of the code shown in Listing 2-11.)

Listing 2-11. *Implementation of connection:didFailWithError*

```
-(void)connection:(NSURLConnection *)connection
        didFailWithError:(NSError *)error
{
    [rootViewController setTitle: @"Error Getting High Scores"];
    [[UIApplication sharedApplication]
        setNetworkActivityIndicatorVisible:FALSE];

    NSLog(@"Error connecting - %@", [error localizedFailureReason]);
    [ connection release];
    [ responseData release];
}
```

As when the creation of the connection returns a null `NSURLConnection` instance, you change the title of the `rootViewController` to inform the user an error occurred, and turn off the network activity indicator. Then you write the error to the log and release the connection and the `responseData` created in Listing 2-10.

> **NOTE**
>
> HTTP error codes such as 404 and 500 are not connection failures. When you receive these error codes, the server has already received the request, and it is the server that has responded with the 404 or 500 error code. The server could not have responded if the connection had failed.

If there is no connection error, the URL loading system continues, and eventually the delegate message `connection:didReceiveResponse:` is called once the URL loading system has received sufficient load data to construct an `NSURLResponse` object. This message is where you are notified of error codes such as 404 and 500. You must examine the response error code, determine if there has been an error at the server, and if so, cancel the transfer and notify your user.

The `connection:didReceiveResponse:` message can be called multiple times if the server responds with a series of redirects, or when the content type being returned is a MIME multipart document. Each time the method is called, you should check the status and set to zero the length of the mutable data object that will hold the received data. This is to ensure that MIME multiparts are handled correctly, and that the data object is not holding data from previous requests or redirects. Listing 2-12 shows the

implementation of the connection:didReceiveResponse: message. Once again, add this
to *ViewHighScoresAppDelegate.m*, immediately after the code in Listing 2-11.

Listing 2-12. *Implementation of connection:didReceiveResponse*

```
-(void)connection:(NSURLConnection *)connection
       didReceiveResponse:(NSURLResponse *)response
{
    NSHTTPURLResponse *HTTPresponse = (NSHTTPURLResponse *)response;
    NSInteger statusCode = [HTTPresponse statusCode];
    if ( 404 == statusCode ||  500 == statusCode ) {
        [rootViewController setTitle: @"Error Getting High Scores"];
        [[UIApplication sharedApplication]
            setNetworkActivityIndicatorVisible:FALSE];

        [connection cancel];

        NSLog(@"Server Error - %@", [ NSHTTPURLResponse
                localizedStringForStatusCode: statusCode ]);
    } else {
        [ responseData setLength:0 ];
    }
}
```

In a similar fashion, the connection:didReceiveData: message will be called at least
once, and should be coded with the assumption that it will be called multiple times before
the data transfer from the server is finished. The message should simply append the data
parameter to the data object in which all the received data is held. Listing 2-13 shows the
implementation, which also goes in *ViewHighScoresAddDelegate.m*. Add this code directly
after the connection:didReceiveResponse: message from Listing 2-12.

Listing 2-13. *Implementation of connection:didReceiveData*

```
- (void)connection:(NSURLConnection *)connection
       didReceiveData:(NSData *)data
{
    [ responseData appendData:data ];
}
```

Finally, once the URL request has finished and all the data has been retrieved, the URL loading system will call the connectionDidFinishLoading: message. After this message is
called, you have received all the data sent from the server, and can finally process it. In this
case, the requests are made to a web service that returns data in XML format. You must parse
the data returned and perform the necessary action: update the table of high scores that the
user requested to see. Listing 2-14 shows the implementation of this message. As with previous listings, add this directly beneath the code from Listing 2-13.

Listing 2-14. *Implementation of connectionDidFinishLoading*

```
- (void)connectionDidFinishLoading:(NSURLConnection *)connection
{
    [ self parseHighScores: responseData ];
    [ connection release ];
    [ responseData release ];
}
```

This is how you request data from a URL and retrieve the data.

All the URL loading code up to this point is generic and will work regardless of what type of data you are retrieving. You could be downloading an image to display, a PDF document, or an MP3 podcast—anything, really.

Parsing XML

Another subject that isn't given the attention it deserves in most iPhone books is XML processing. Some give it a passing mention; others ignore the subject completely. So guess what? Since XML parsing is ultra-important when dealing with web services, you get another in-depth walk-through. Ain't I nice?

In the implementation of connectionDidFinishLoading: in Listing 2-14, you call the message parseHighScores to process the XML data you got from the URL loading process. This went in another message to keep the URL loading code separate from the XML processing code. The parseHighScores message creates an instance of the NSXMLParser class and sets self again as the delegate to receive callbacks for the different XML parsing events, as shown in Listing 2-15. Add this code after the code in Listing 2-14.

Listing 2-15. *Implementation of parseHighScores*

```
- (void)parseHighScores:(NSData *) highScoresXMLData
{
    if (highScoresParser)
        [ highScoresParser release ];
    highScoresParser = [[ NSXMLParser alloc]
        initWithData: highScoresXMLData ];
    [ highScoresParser setDelegate:self ];
    [highScoresParser setShouldResolveExternalEntities:NO];
    [ highScoresParser parse ];
}
```

Like the NSURLConnection delegate, the NSXMLParser delegate receives several messages as it goes through the necessary processing steps. NSXMLParser processes the XML from the top, one line at a time, and as different events happen, it sends messages to the delegate to handle these events. If you have done XML processing before in C/C++, Java, or .NET, you may notice that NSXMLParser is most similar in concept to SAX (Simple API for XML) parsing.

The parser sends the parser:didStartElement:namespaceURI:qualifiedName: attributes: message when it finds start tags. Listing 2-16 shows the implementation of this message in the high-scores application. Add this code right after the code from Listing 2-15.

Listing 2-16. *The parser:didStartElement:namespaceURI:qualifiedName:attributes: Message Used by the NSXMLParser Delegate*

```
- (void)parser:(NSXMLParser *)parser
        didStartElement:(NSString *)elementName
        namespaceURI:(NSString *)namespaceURI
        qualifiedName:(NSString *)qName
        attributes:(NSDictionary *)attributeDict
{
    currentKey = nil;
    [currentStringValue release];
    currentStringValue = nil;

    if ( [elementName isEqualToString:@"high-scores"])
    {
        if (highScores)
            [highScores removeAllObjects];
        else
            highScores = [[NSMutableArray alloc] init];

        return;
    }

    if ( [elementName isEqualToString:@"high-score"] )
    {
        newScore = [[NSMutableDictionary alloc]
            initWithCapacity: 2];
        return;
    }

    if ( [elementName isEqualToString:@"score"] )
    {
        currentKey = @"score";
        return;
    }

    if ( [elementName isEqualToString:@"full-name"] )
    {
        currentKey = @"full-name";
        return;
    }

}
```

The code in Listing 2-16 works as follows:

- If the parser finds the start tag `<high-scores>`, you create an `NSMutableArray` to hold the high scores. If the array is already created, you empty it of any items it might hold, presumably from a previous high-scores download.

- If the parser finds the start tag `<high-score>` (note that, this time, it's the singular noun), you create an `NSMutableDictionary` called `newScore` to hold the high-score record, specifically the values of the `score` and `full-name` tags.

- If the parser finds the start tags `<score>` and `<full-name>`, you put the appropriate key in a variable called `currentKey`, which you will use in another delegate message to store the tag value in the `newScore` dictionary.

The `parser: foundCharacters:` message is sent to the parser delegate when the parser finds text between the start and end tags. If the text between the tags spans several lines, the message is called more than once. Listing 2-17 shows the implementation. This code goes right after the code from Listing 2-16.

Listing 2-17. *The parser:foundCharacters: Method Used by the NSXMLParser Delegate*

```
- (void)parser:(NSXMLParser *)parser
        foundCharacters:(NSString *)string
{
    if (currentKey) {
        if (!currentStringValue) {
            currentStringValue = [[NSMutableString alloc]
                initWithCapacity:50];
        }
        [currentStringValue appendString:string];
    }
}
```

In Listing 2-17, first you check if the variable `currentKey` is not nil. If it is nil, you return immediately and do nothing else in this message. If `currentKey` is not nil, you check if the variable `currentStringValue` is nil. If `currentStringValue` is nil, you create an `NSMutableString` object. Finally, you append the text for the tag in `currentStringValue`.

The `parser:didEndElement:namespaceURI: qualifiedName:` message is sent to the parser delegate when the parser finds end tags. Listing 2-18 shows the implementation of this delegate message. Add this code right after the code from Listing 2-17.

Listing 2-18. *The parser:didEndElement:namespaceURI:qualifiedName Method Used by the NSXMLParser Delegate*

```
- (void)parser:(NSXMLParser *)parser
        didEndElement:(NSString *)elementName
        namespaceURI:(NSString *)namespaceURI
```

```
                qualifiedName:(NSString *)qName
{
    if (( [elementName isEqualToString:@"high-scores"]))
    {
        // reaching this end tag means we've finished parsing everything
        [rootViewController setTitle: @"View High Scores"];
        [[UIApplication sharedApplication]
            setNetworkActivityIndicatorVisible:FALSE];
        return;
    }

    if ( [elementName isEqualToString:@"high-score"] )
    {
        // add the new score to the table model and
        // force the table to update
        [ highScores addObject: newScore ];
        [rootViewController reloadData];
        return;
    }

    if ( [elementName isEqualToString:@"score"] ||
            [elementName isEqualToString:@"full-name"])
    {
        [ newScore setValue: currentStringValue forKey: currentKey ];
    }

    currentKey = nil;
    [currentStringValue release];
    currentStringValue = nil;
}
```

This implementation does the following:

- If the end tag </high-scores> is found, that means you are finished processing
  everything. In that case, you change the title of the rootViewController to "View
  High Scores" (during processing, it reads "Getting High Scores …") and turn off the
  network activity indicator.

- If the end tag </high-score> (again note this is the singular noun) is found, you add
  the newScore dictionary to the highScores array and notify the rootViewController
  to update the display of the table view.

- If the end tag </score> or </full-name> is found, you take the values of currentKey
  and currentStringValue, and store them in the newScore dictionary.

Along with the messages implemented in the preceding code, there are also notification
messages for parsing errors because of invalid data, for parsing DTD declarations internal to

the XML object itself, and for external DTD references. Our implementation was simple because it had no external DTD references or internal DTD declarations.

The end result of all this XML processing is to store the high scores in an array of a dictionary with two keys: `score` and `full-name`. This array is named `highScores` in the app delegate. You notify the root view controller that it should refresh the display of the table view each time you process a high-score record; that is, after you add a `newScore` dictionary to the `highScores` array.

At this point, if you were to run the project through the iPhone simulator, the app would show an empty table with a title bar of "Getting High Scores ...," as shown in Figure 2-6, before changing back to "View High Scores" a few seconds later. Meanwhile, the network activity indicator would spin to indicate some type of network activity was happening. But the table would display nothing. That's because you haven't modified the root view controller table view data source messages to display the high scores.

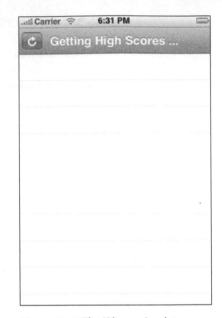

Figure 2-6. *The iPhone simulator running the View High Scores app after the connection and XML parser delegate implementation, but with the dummy data source implementation*

Displaying the High Scores in the Table View

To display the high scores, you need to modify a few methods in the *RootViewController.m* file. Open *RootViewController.m* in Xcode and add the code marked in bold in Listing 2-19.

Listing 2-19. *Changes to the Implementation Code for RootViewController.m*

```
/*
// Override to allow orientations other than
// the default portrait orientation.
- (BOOL)shouldAutorotateToInterfaceOrientation:
        (UIInterfaceOrientation)interfaceOrientation {
    // Return YES for supported orientations
    return (interfaceOrientation == UIInterfaceOrientationPortrait);
}
*/
```

```
- (void)didReceiveMemoryWarning {
    // Releases the view if it doesn't have a superview
    [super didReceiveMemoryWarning];

    // Release anything that's not essential, such as cached data
    ViewHighScoresAppDelegate *appDelegate =
        (ViewHighScoresAppDelegate *)[
            [UIApplication sharedApplication] delegate];
    [[appDelegate highScores] removeAllObjects];
}


#pragma mark Table view methods

- (NSInteger)numberOfSectionsInTableView:(UITableView *)tableView {
    return 1;
}



// Customize the number of rows in the table view.
- (NSInteger)tableView:(UITableView *)tableView
        numberOfRowsInSection:(NSInteger)section {
    ViewHighScoresAppDelegate *appDelegate =
        (ViewHighScoresAppDelegate *)
            [[UIApplication sharedApplication] delegate];
    return [[appDelegate highScores] count];
}



// Customize the appearance of table view cells.
- (UITableViewCell *)tableView:(UITableView *)tableView
        cellForRowAtIndexPath:(NSIndexPath *)indexPath
{
    static NSString *CellIdentifier = @"Cell";

    UITableViewCell *cell =
        [tableView dequeueReusableCellWithIdentifier:CellIdentifier];
    if (cell == nil) {
        cell = [[[UITableViewCell alloc] initWithFrame:CGRectZero
            reuseIdentifier:CellIdentifier] autorelease];
    }
```

```
    // Set up the cell...
    ViewHighScoresAppDelegate *appDelegate =
        (ViewHighScoresAppDelegate *)[[UIApplication sharedApplication]
        delegate];
    NSDictionary *row = [[appDelegate highScores]
        objectAtIndex:indexPath.row];

    NSString *full_name = [row objectForKey:@"full-name"];
    NSString *score = [row objectForKey:@"score"];
    cell.text = [NSString stringWithFormat:@"%@ - %@",
        full_name, score];

    return cell;
}
```

This didReceiveMemoryWarning method is called when memory is low. So, first, although
this method is not part of the data source messages, it is important to handle it correctly.
The code in Listing 2-19 modifies this method to empty the highScores array. This array is
in the app delegate, so you use the UIApplication sharedApplication object in Cocoa to
obtain a reference to the app delegate, and then access the highScores array and empty it.

The code modifies the method numberOfSectionsInTableView to always return 1, because
there is only one section of data in the high-scores table. This table is not displayed in
grouped mode anyway.

NOTE

If you're not sure what *grouped mode* means in relation to Cocoa Touch table views, do a Google search for
"iPhone table view tutorials" or check out the book *Beginning iPhone Development* (Apress, 2008).

Similarly, the method tableView: numberOfRowsInSection: always returns the number
of rows in the highScores array, disregarding the section, because there is only one section and the table is not in grouped mode. In this method, you use the UIApplication
sharedApplication object to get a reference to the app delegate, in the same manner as in
the didReceiveMemoryWarning method. With the reference to the app delegate, the code
then obtains the count from the highScores array.

Finally, the method tableView:cellForRowAtIndexPath: creates or dequeues a reusable
UITableViewCell instance, as is the standard practice for table view cells. Then, once again,
you use the UIApplication sharedApplication object to get a reference to the app delegate. After you have the app delegate, you obtain the NSDictionary instance from the
highScores array row corresponding to the index path passed as parameter indexPath.
You modify the cell text to display the full name and score stored in the dictionary.

If you run the project now on the iPhone simulator, the UI changes just as before: the title bar lets you know the code is getting high scores, and the network activity indicator spins. However, this time, high-score records actually appear in the table, as shown in Figure 2-7. Neat!

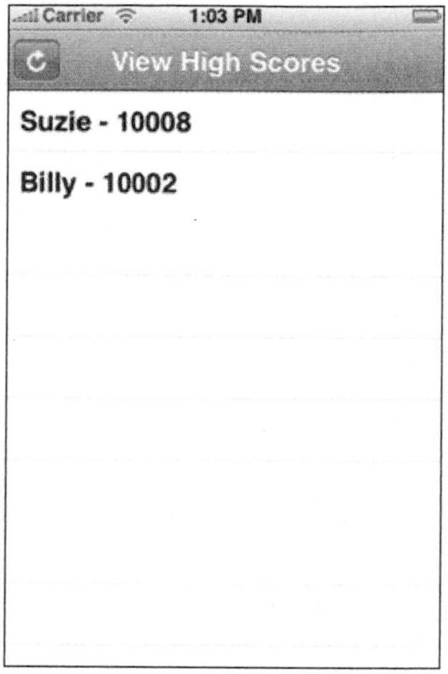

Are you thinking that displaying things in a table is not all that exciting? I agree. The point of this exercise was to walk you through the code for URL loading and XML parsing. The table view part was just to bring it all together in a visual way, to show that all the other code works.

Submitting High Scores to the Web Service

So far, you have learned about RESTful web services, URL loading, and XML parsing. You have a web app where you can enter some high-score records by hand, and you can display those high scores on your iPhone.

Figure 2-7. *The iPhone simulator running the View High Scores app and actually displaying high scores*

That's all fine and dandy, but that's not how it's done in games, right? The users don't remember their high scores, go to a web site, and enter them by hand. It is your job as the game developer to write code to submit the user's high score to the server. What does that code look like?

Uploading high scores is almost like downloading high scores. You prepare a URL, create a request with it, and make a connection. Then the URL loading process calls messages in your connection delegate when the server responds to say the high score was submitted successfully. The difference is that you use HTTP POST instead of the default HTTP GET (which you used to download the scores), and you send your data to the server in XML format. Let's look at an example of that in Listing 2-20.

Listing 2-20. *Submitting a New High Score Record to the Simple High-Score Server*

```
NSData *highScoreData =  [[NSString stringWithFormat:
    @"<high-score> \
        <full-name>%@</full-name> \
        <score>%@</score> \
    </high-score>",  "Bobby", "10005", nil]
    dataUsingEncoding:NSASCIIStringEncoding];
```

```
NSString *URLstr = HIGH_SCORES_URL;
NSURL *theURL = [NSURL URLWithString:URLstr];

NSMutableURLRequest *theRequest = [NSMutableURLRequest
    requestWithURL:theURL];

[theRequest setHTTPMethod:@"POST"];
[theRequest setValue:@"text/xml" forHTTPHeaderField:@"Content-type"];
[theRequest setHTTPBody: highScoreData];

[[UIApplication sharedApplication]
    setNetworkActivityIndicatorVisible:TRUE];

NSURLConnection *theConnection =   [[NSURLConnection alloc]
    initWithRequest:theRequest delegate:self];

if (!theConnection) {
    // the connection request is invalid; malformed URL, perhaps?
}
```

In the code in Listing 2-20, first you put your data in an XML format similar to the high scores you parsed earlier. The difference is that because this is a new record, you can leave out the <id>, <created_at>, and <updated_at> tags—just the full name and score are sufficient. In the listing, I broke up the string into several lines for readability, not because it must go on separate lines.

After you create the XML data, you create an NSURL instance with your URL string, and then create an NSMutableURLRequest with it. *Mutable* means changeable, indicating you are going to change some settings in this request from their defaults. In this case, you are making the following changes:

- Change the HTTP method from GET to POST.

- Set the Content-type header to let the web service know what kind of data you are sending.

- Put the data in the request body.

When you were getting the top-100 scores, you used an NSURLRequest, rather than an NSMutableURLRequest, because you didn't need to change the request from the default settings.

After you create the request, you need to submit it to the simple high-score service. As with the previous top-100 high scores processing, you create an NSURLConnection and set your delegate, and then the delegate is called as different URL loading events take place. As you learned in the earlier discussion of RESTful web services, the service will respond with the high-score record in XML format, with the <id>, <created_at>, and <updated_at> tags set appropriately.

But you just want to know that your high-score submission worked! You don't generally need to examine your submitted data again with all the tags that the web service returns.

You can simplify the connection delegate for submitting high scores by just checking for connection errors and whether the response status has a status code of 200, which means everything went OK. This is why in this example of creating an NSURLConnection, you only check if it is nil, and don't bother to create a data object to hold the data that is returned. You just want to know if there was an error connecting, if there was an error at the server, and the value of the response status code. Let's see how that works in Listing 2-21.

Listing 2-21. *The Delegate Methods for Checking If High Score Submission Was Successful*

```
-(void)connection:(NSURLConnection *)connection
      didFailWithError:(NSError *)error
{
    [[UIApplication sharedApplication]
        setNetworkActivityIndicatorVisible:FALSE];

    // alert the user there has been an error submitting the high score

    NSLog(@"Error connecting - %@", [error localizedFailureReason]);
    [connection release];
}


-(void)connection:(NSURLConnection *)connection
      didReceiveResponse:(NSURLResponse *)response
{
    NSHTTPURLResponse *HTTPresponse = (NSHTTPURLResponse *)response;
    NSInteger statusCode = [HTTPresponse statusCode];

    if ( 404 == statusCode || 500 == statusCode ) {

        [[UIApplication sharedApplication]
            setNetworkActivityIndicatorVisible:FALSE];

        // alert the user there has been an error submitting the high score

        [connection cancel];

        NSLog(@"Server Error - %@", [ NSHTTPURLResponse
            localizedStringForStatusCode:statusCode ]);

    } else if ( 200 == statusCode) {
        // the high score submission was successful!
```

```
        // do whatever other processing you need here
        [[UIApplication sharedApplication]
            setNetworkActivityIndicatorVisible:FALSE];
    }
}
```

If you wanted to have the web service modify a record, you could reuse the code from List-ings 2-20 and 2-21. Instead of setting the HTTP method to POST, you would use the HTTP method PUT. As the URI, you would use the address of the representation of the record you want to modify, such as `localhost:3000/high_scores/1.xml`. Then you would just make sure that the record was modified properly by checking the response for status code 200.

To delete a record, you would use the HTTP method DELETE, and use the URI for the specific record you want to delete. You could omit the Content-type header and the body, because you don't need to send any data to request a deletion. You just need to send the DELETE request to `localhost:3000/high_scores/1.xml` and check the response for status code 200.

Submitting User Achievements

Now that you know how to create records in a RESTful web service, retrieve, update, and delete them, you'll find that working with achievements is similar. Somewhere in your game logic, you determine that the player has earned an achievement, and send a POST request to the right resource and check the response for status code 200. Listing 2-22 shows an example.

Listing 2-22. *Sample Game Loop Code for Checking If the User Has Not Died for Five Levels in a Row*

```
// relevant portion of an example game loop
if (playerDead) {
    levelsFinishedSinceLastDeath = 0;
}
if (levelFinished) {
    currentLevel++;
    levelsFinishedSinceLastDeath += !playerDead;
    if (levelsFinishedSinceLastDeath >= 5 &&
            ![user hasAchievement:FIVE_LEVELS_NO_DEATH] )
    {
        [user earnAchievement: FIVE_LEVELS_NO_DEATH];
    }
}
```

This is just a portion of code I made up to give you an idea. Take it as inspiration and not as working code.

The gist is that you keep track of whether the player has died and how many levels in a row the player has finished without dying. You also track whether the player has finished the level. You then check an object called `user` to determine whether the player has already earned a particular achievement. If not, you call a method on `user` called `earnAchievement:`. This method could update the UI to notify the user she has earned an achievement, and make the new user achievement request to the web service.

Introducing ObjectiveResource

ObjectiveResource, available from `http://iphoneonrails.com`, is an Objective-C port of the ActiveResource library for Ruby, made popular by Rails 2.0. ActiveResource makes it easy for Rails apps to connect to RESTful web services. Similarly, ObjectiveResource makes it easy for iPhone and Mac OS X apps to connect to RESTful web services. All the complexity discussed in the previous sections is abstracted away by ObjectiveResource.

When I began writing this chapter, ObjectiveResource was incomplete and unstable. That is why I've concentrated on URL loading and XML parsing, and the specifics of communication with RESTful web services. This knowledge will come in handy if ever you need to connect to a web service with very complicated XML or that implements non-RESTful APIs. And it certainly doesn't hurt to know what's going on behind the scenes!

Now that ObjectiveResource is more stable, it is a very worthy alternative to implementing web service connections from scratch.

CAUTION

ObjectiveResource works with only "real" RESTful web services. If you're going to roll your own XML web service with PHP or .NET, you will not be able to use ObjectiveResource on the iPhone side of your app. The introduction to RESTful web services earlier in this chapter should help get you started if you want to do it the RESTful way in your choice of language.

Using ObjectiveResource

To use ObjectiveResource, download the library from `http://iphoneonrails.com`, unzip it, and then drag and drop the folder into your project in Xcode. Make sure to tell Xcode to copy the folder into your project (there's a check box at the top of the dialog box to select to make this happen).

Once the ObjectiveResource code is copied to your project, you can begin coding classes for your resources. As an example, Listing 2-23 has some of the changes to the sample View High Scores app needed for using ObjectiveResource.

Listing 2-23. *Using ObjectiveResource with the simple_high_scores_service Web Service*

```objc
// contents of HighScores.h
#import "ObjectiveResource.h"
@interface HighScores : NSObject
{
    NSString *fullName;
    NSNumber *score;
     //this maps to the Rails "id" property
    NSString *highScoreId;
    NSDate *createdAt;
    NSDate *updatedAt;
}
@property (nonatomic , retain) NSString *fullName;
@property (nonatomic , retain) NSNumber *score;
@property (nonatomic , retain) NSString *highScoreId;
@property (nonatomic , retain) NSDate *createdAt;
@property (nonatomic , retain) NSDate *updatedAt;
@end

// contents of HighScore.m
#import "HighScore.h"

@implementation  HighScore
@synthesize fullName, score, highScoreId , createdAt , updatedAt;

+ (NSArray *)getTop100Scores {
    NSString *top100ScoresPath = [NSString stringWithFormat:@"%@%@",
                        [self getRemoteSite],
                        @"top_100_scores.xml"];

    Response *res = [Connection get: top100ScoresPath];
    return [self allFromXMLData:res.body];
}

- (void) dealloc
{
    [createdAt release];
    [updatedAt release];
    [highScoreId release];
    [fullName release];
    [score release];
    [super dealloc];
}
```

```objc
// changes to ViewHighScoresAppDelegate.h
#import <UIKit/UIKit.h>

@class RootViewController;

@interface ViewHighScoresAppDelegate :
        NSObject <UIApplicationDelegate> {

    UIWindow *window;
    UINavigationController *navigationController;

    NSArray *highScores;

    RootViewController *rootViewController;
}

@property (nonatomic, retain) IBOutlet UIWindow *window;
@property (nonatomic, retain) IBOutlet UINavigationController
    *navigationController;

@property (nonatomic, retain) NSArray *highScores;
@property (nonatomic, retain) IBOutlet RootViewController
    *rootViewController;

- (void)getHighScores;

@end

// changes to ViewHighScoresAppDelegate.m
#import "ViewHighScoresAppDelegate.h"
#import "RootViewController.h"
#import "ObjectiveResourceConfig.h"

@implementation ViewHighScoresAppDelegate

@synthesize window;
@synthesize navigationController;

@synthesize highScores;
@synthesize rootViewController;

#define HIGH_SCORES_URL @"http://localhost:3000/"

- (void)applicationDidFinishLaunching:(UIApplication *)application {
    // Configure and show the window
    [window addSubview:[navigationController view]];
    [window makeKeyAndVisible];
```

```objectivec
    [ObjectiveResourceConfig setSite: HIGH_SCORES_URL];

    [self getHighScores];
}

- (void)applicationWillTerminate:(UIApplication *)application {
    // Save data if appropriate
}

- (void)dealloc {
    [navigationController release];
    [window release];
    [super dealloc];
}

#pragma mark web service connection methods

- (void)getHighScores {
    highScores = [HighScore getTop100Scores];
}

// you can delete all the URL loading and XML parsing code
// you won't need it!
@end

// changes to RootViewController.m
// Customize the appearance of table view cells.
- (UITableViewCell *)tableView:(UITableView *)tableView
        cellForRowAtIndexPath:(NSIndexPath *)indexPath
{
    static NSString *CellIdentifier = @"Cell";

    UITableViewCell *cell =
        [tableView dequeueReusableCellWithIdentifier:CellIdentifier];
    if (cell == nil) {
        cell = [[[UITableViewCell alloc] initWithFrame:CGRectZero
            reuseIdentifier:CellIdentifier] autorelease];
    }

    // Set up the cell...
    ViewHighScoresAppDelegate *appDelegate =
        (ViewHighScoresAppDelegate *)[[UIApplication sharedApplication]
            delegate];
    HighScore *highScore =
        [[appDelegate highScores] objectAtIndex:indexPath.row];
```

```
    cell.text = [NSString stringWithFormat:@"%@ - %@",
        highScore.full_name, highScore.score];

    return cell;
}
```

As you can see, the code to use ObjectiveResource is substantially simpler and shorter than the version that uses URL loading and XML parsing.

Submitting High Scores with ObjectiveResource

Listing 2-24 shows how to submit a high-score record to the web service.

Listing 2-24. *Using ObjectiveResource to Submit a High Score*

```
HighScore newScore = [[[HighScore alloc] init] autorelease];
newScore.full_name = "Bobby";
newScore.score = 10002;
[newScore saveRemote];
```

And that is really it! If you've used Hibernate on Java or NHibernate on .NET, you'll find that using ObjectiveResource is similar. The difference is that there is no mindless XML configuration, and you're dealing with a web service, rather than a database.

ObjectiveResource simplifies communications with RESTful web services significantly. All the URL loading and XML parsing take place behind the scenes. Your objects will inherit code from the ObjectiveResource category to make simple methods calls for creating, retrieving, updating, and deleting records on your RESTful web services.

Summary

This chapter walked you through how to use URL loading and XML parsing to create a high-score server. It was very code-heavy, but to be honest, at the time of this writing, very few resources, online or in book form, deal with the subject in this much detail. And this detail is important to get social networking implemented the right way for your iPhone games.

When push comes to shove, and you're trying to get a social networking feature built into your app, are you going to be glad I dug in deep, or would you rather I had stuck to pleasing platitudes, all mom and apple pie, about the wonderful dream of social networking built into native iPhone games? Yeah, that's what I thought.

In the end, I hope I was successful in getting you excited about the possibility of adding social networking features directly into your game. Perhaps I've made you think about spending a bit more development time doing more than just a high-score server. Wouldn't it be cool to give players at least a "My highest score" widget? It may help promote your game!

Letting your users share their gaming experience with others can help grow a community around your games, which can lead to strong sales.

But, for me, it all goes back to being social, playing in groups, with friends and family hovering around the TV and having a good time. With the ubiquitous connectivity in the iPhone and social networking, we may be able to bring some of those good times back to gaming.

Aaron Fothergill

Company: *Strange Flavour Ltd.*

Location: *Newcastle, UK*

Former Life As a Developer: I started my career on the Apple][in the 1980s, including writing tools for a radio station on the first Macs. More games on the ST and Amiga followed, including Jitterbugs, the cult hits SkyStrike and Jetstrike, and tools for the STOS and AMOS programming environments. Later, I worked at other game companies, including Electric Spectacle, Cranberry Source, and Argonaut Games, where we created Croc 2, Aladdin Nazira's Revenge, and Harry Potter, among other console games. In 2004, I left to start Strange Flavour with my brother Adam. We have created ToySight and Airburst for the Mac, which have won the Apple Design Award, as well as TotemBall and Spyglass Boardgames.

Life As an iPhone Developer: For the iPhone, I've written Plank, Flick Fishing, and SlotZ Racer. Our next game is due out as this book is being published. Our development environment includes a bunch of Macs, Xcode, Cinema 4D, Photoshop, and TextWrangler.

What's in This Chapter: The chapter covers how to create an OpenGL ES game from scratch. It also explains how to implement automatic game save functionality, and how the game loop works. The focus is on using straightforward C code, rather than Objective-C, for accessibility and simplicity.

Key Technologies:

- *Game saving from a system notification*
- *Texture loading for OpenGL sprites*
- *OpenGL-based sprite drawing*
- *Creating an OpenGL ES project and setting up a render loop for a game*

Chapter 3

Rapid Game Development Using (Mostly) Standard C

Why don't you get a proper job?" is something you'll hear a lot if you say you work in the games industry. I've been writing video games since the early 1980s, and I still get asked that one.

Writing games is something you do because it's fun. If it's something you do because It also makes a profit, that's a good thing, but there are better-paying jobs for computer programmers in boring industries,[1] so enjoying writing games is the most important thing about the work.

I started iPhone programming as a spare-time project while working on Strange Flavour's Xbox Live Arcade game Airburst. Initially our first iPhone project, Plank, was a project to teach my brother, Adam, who normally does all our art and sound, to code. So, Adam did most of the initial R&D work and learned all the fun new features of Xcode 3, because I'd been away from Xcode for at least a version or two. He updated me, and we used our first iPhone game, Plank, as a learning project and a bit of an experiment. Since then, we've written the best-selling games Flick Sports Fishing and SlotZ Racer, and we should have our fourth game in the App Store by the time you read this book. Figure 3-1 shows some screen shots of SlotZ Racer, Flick Sports Fishing, and Plank.

---

1   When it's 5 a.m. on a Saturday morning and I'm still hunting down an obscure bug, these other jobs seem more exciting.

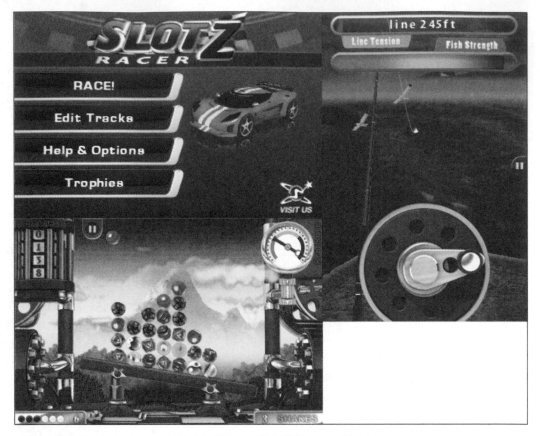

Figure 3-1. *Clockwise from top left: SlotZ Racer, Flick Fishing, and Plank*

TIP

> Teaming up with another coder, even someone who's just learning to code, can be a massive benefit to
> you because you can take turns being clever. More often than not, one of you will remember some critical
> element of the documentation that the other has forgotten.

What I've found about writing iPhone games is that they appeal to the part of me that
likes writing games just for fun; they are just like console games but are in nice small packets. Because of the nature of the iPhone's features, games for it tend to be played in short
bursts as players find themselves with a free moment, so short and simple pickup games
are rewarding. Longer games that can be played in short goes can also work well, as long as
they autosave when you get incoming calls or have to quit to get off the bus, for example.

The iPhone also suits elements of some of my favorite old-school-style game play and is rather
practical for my game-writing code style, allowing rapid prototyping of a game idea and simple development and debugging without having to fight with the operating system too much.

For this chapter, I'll show how easy it is to develop an iPhone game primarily using straight C for the code, combining it with only essential Objective-C to set the app up and handle playing nicely with OS X. If you're an old-schooler like myself or just starting on the iPhone after working on other platforms, you might not have gotten the hang of Objective-C just yet or want to get straight into writing games. Objective-C is a great language, but it doesn't make any difference to the resulting game whether the main code is C, C++, or Objective-C, so why not just write with whatever you're familiar with and get into writing the game you want to do instead of sitting down and learning another language? So, for the game we're going to write here, I'll mostly be using C and showing where Objective-C bits are more convenient. As you work more on the iPhone, you'll probably find yourself using more Objective-C where you find it to be more useful, especially if you're using the OS X UI in your game.

The game I'll show how to write is a version of a classic type of game that was on pretty much every 8-bit computer in some form or another and inspired whole genres of modern gaming. Back then it was called Star Trek and had you warping around a small sector of space-fighting Klingons, restocking at star bases, and generally going where no geek had gone before. That, of course, was before all the *Next Generation* stuff and also before copyright lawyers worked out how to switch their computers on and found out they had a whole new potential revenue stream.

So, this game will be similar in game play to those games of old, but to keep the lawyers happy, It will be called Space Hike, and you'll battle in the space cruiser Expendable to halt the incursion of evil Mingon battleships into Empire Space. Space Hike was specifically written for this book. The actual game play for Space Hike is really about resource management because the aim is to destroy all the enemy ships without running out of energy or vending machine supplies. Because each star base or colony planet can give you only one reload of supplies, you have to manage them carefully if you're going to eliminate all the Mingon battleships. Figure 3-2 shows the finished game after my brother, Adam, created the final artwork.

This type of game is relatively simple to describe and explain in code, but it also is a game that benefits from being able to be quickly saved and exited as required. That

Figure 3-2. *The finished Space Hike game*

gives me an excuse to show you a simplified version of the code required to save game data on the iPhone so that you can read it back and continue the game the next time it starts up.

Breaking games up into bite-sized chunks like this is ideal for the iPhone. iPhone gaming is showing a trend of being "opportunistic" gaming. Gamers tend to fire up a game when they have some spare time while doing other things, such as when on a bus or in a lunch break at work or school. This means that it's a good idea for a game to work well in short bursts and save progress automatically whenever the user hits the home button as he sees the boss coming!

Getting Started

Knowing what you want the game to do and what will be fun is the most important part of writing your game. Everything else is just problem solving. With Space Hike, I'm following an age-old game design, so I have a good idea of how it will work and what would be in the game, but adapting it to the iPhone means there will be some novel problems, especially with the interface.

Initially, it's a good idea to write a short design document and note any resources that this game design requires such as graphics and sound effects. It should also show you something of how the game will flow and how you might need to structure some of the code. This can be very different for each game. Plank started as an adaptation of a mini-game Adam and I wrote in our Mac game ToySight, so most of the design document involved deciding which elements should be kept from the original and how Adam wanted to change the graphical style. Flick Fishing had a big critical features list, such as game modes required, effects, "tricks" we wanted in the game, and a list of fish! SlotZ was more technical because the whole game hinged around my writing a track system that would let us design tracks in-game and race on them.

With Space Hike, it was pretty obvious that the game had two main modes to its game play: navigating around space and fighting the Mingon ships. Both are pretty much single screen elements,[2] which made our job easier.

One other element that shows early in the design is that the game involves a lot of text for buttons and alerts. If it were going to be a larger game, we'd have to consider writing a font system,[3] but for Space Hike it was simpler to just handle all the text as graphics with a short routine to handle drawing numbers with the digits 0–9 as sprites, as you can see in Figure 3-3.

At this stage, it's best to get a rough idea of the size of the graphics you'll be using. Remember to stick to sizes that are powers of two for OpenGL ES to handle them efficiently.

---

2   Expanding the navigation mode to a full 3D space simulator and combat screen to a real-time multiweapon shooter are left as an exercise for the reader.

3   When drawing with OpenGL, it's generally more practical to create your own font drawing system that uses sprites for each character than to use system fonts. Apart from practicality and speed in drawing the characters on the screen, it also gives your artist more flexibility in how the characters can be drawn and styled.

This means that we're going to have to dive into the realms of coder art! When you need to get on with the game and don't want to be bogged down in creating artwork, knock 'em out fast, and focus on technical elements such as their size and basic content rather than making them a masterpiece. When you have them working, you can come back to them and rework them or use them as a threat to make sure your artist does them properly so that they don't get left in the game he has the art credit on! Figure 3-4

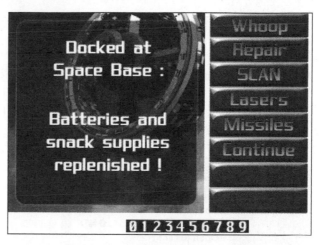

Figure 3-3. *Text in Space Hike is predrawn as images so we don't have to create a font system. The digits 0–9 are loaded as individual sprites to display numbers.*

shows you the contrast between the original coder art that I quickly hacked together to get the game working and the final art that Adam produced to stop people laughing at it.

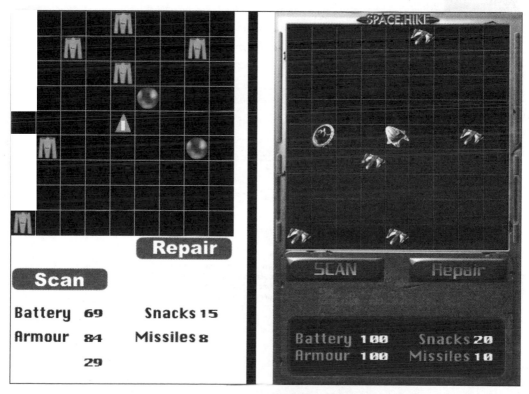

Figure 3-4. *My original coder art and the considerably less eye-damaging final art for Space Hike.*

Creating the Project

For iPhone apps, it's not too bad an idea to start with one of the Apple sample apps and rework it to suit your needs when starting your game. However, as an exercise for this chapter (and because it gives us shorter and simpler code), I'll show how to start Space Hike from scratch with the New OpenGL ES project option. Select **File ➤ New Project** in Xcode, and select OpenGL ES Application, as shown in Figure 3-5.

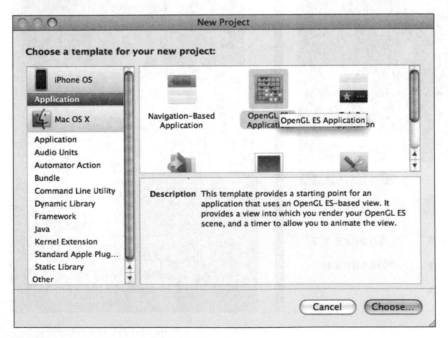

Figure 3-5. *Creating a new OpenGL ES project*

Call your project Space Hike, and Xcode will create a basic OpenGL ES app for you to work from. If you run it in the simulator, you get a nice spinning square. Shiny!

The good news is, this gives you the basic functionality you need to open a full-screen OpenGL window to draw in and run an app with a rendering loop. It's ideal for bolting on the code for your game with relatively minimal fuss.

There are a few functions we don't need in the code, so we'll do a bit of trimming. In the Classes folder, find the *SpaceHikeAppDelegate.m* file, and scrub out the contents of the following function:

```
-(void)applicationDidFinishLaunching:(UIApplication *)application {
}

-(void)applicationWillResignActive:(UIApplication *)application {
}
```

as well as the following:

```
-(void)applicationDidBecomeActive:(UIApplication *)application {
}
```

Then add the following at the top after the #import "EAGLView.h" line:

```
#import "Texture2D.h"
```

In the *EAGLView.m* file, delete the following functions:

```
-(void)startAnimation
```

```
-(void)stopAnimation
```

```
-(void)setAnimationTimer:(NSTimer *)newTimer
```

```
-(void)setAnimationInterval:(NSTimeInterval)interval
```

In the -(void)dealloc function, delete the following line:

```
[self stopAnimation];
```

Most of this is code to draw the spinning square, so for the moment we're actually taking a step backward and reducing functionality! Not to worry, though. With a bit more trimming, you'll have a lean, mean core machine on which to build the Space Hike (or any other) game.

Next up in *EAGLView.m*, replace the -(void)drawView function with the following:

```
- (void)startDrawing {
```

```
    [EAGLContext setCurrentContext:context];

    glBindFramebufferOES(GL_FRAMEBUFFER_OES, viewFramebuffer);
    glViewport(0, 0, backingWidth, backingHeight);

    glMatrixMode(GL_PROJECTION);
    glLoadIdentity();
    glOrthof(-160.0f, 160.0f, -240.0f, 240.0f, -1.0f, 1.0f);
    glMatrixMode(GL_MODELVIEW);
//  glRotatef(3.0f, 0.0f, 0.0f, 1.0f);

    glClearColor(0.5f, 0.5f, 0.5f, 1.0f);
    glClear(GL_COLOR_BUFFER_BIT);

}


- (void)endDrawing {

    glBindRenderbufferOES(GL_RENDERBUFFER_OES, viewRenderbuffer);
    [context presentRenderbuffer:GL_RENDERBUFFER_OES];
}
```

This is where you will still be using Objective-C functions but in a different way from the way the new project does it. Rather than putting the whole frame drawing in a single function in *EAGLView.m*, you split it into two functions that you call on either side of the drawing. I'm keeping them as Objective-C because they're referring to the EAGLContext, so it's generally easier to do them this way, even if most of the code in them is straight C OpenGL calls.

You could, in fact, move a good chunk of this out into the general drawing routine (particularly if you're using different GL views like we did in Flick Fishing and SlotZ Racer), but for Space Hike the screen is pretty simple, so you can leave it as is.

TIP

One thing to note from the `startDrawing` function is that the orthographic view is set to –160,160 and –240, 240, which gives us a vertical screen with a range of screen coordinates: –160 to 160 in X and –240 to 240 in Y. This makes the screen center 0,0 and is generally pretty simple for positioning items on the screen. I made the mistake of having it set to 0 to 480 and 0 to 320 in Plank, which was pretty simple at first but made aligning new objects on the fly a bit of a pain, especially because Adam had started the project and written a lot of the menus without using the following tip.

TIP

If you want to use this to write a game in landscape format, add the following after `glLoadIdentity();`:

```
glRotatef(270,0,0,1);
```

Next, modify the `glOrthof` command to the following:

```
glOrthof(-240.0f,240.0f,-160.0f,160.0f,-1.0f,1.0f);
```

All your GL drawing will now be in landscape mode!

Next you edit the *EAGLView.h* file to match the trimmed set of functions. Delete the three function declarations listed there (`startAnimation`, `stopAnimation`, and `drawView`) along with these variables:

```
NSTimer *animationTimer;
```

and

```
NSTimeInterval animationInterval;
```

Return to *SpaceHikeAppDelegate.m*, and then go ahead and add the following line to `applicationDidFinishLaunching`, which will set up a timer to call the frame-rendering function:

```
mTimer = [NSTimer scheduledTimerWithTimeInterval:(1.0/FPS) target:self
        selector:@selector(renderScene) userInfo:nil repeats:YES];
```

Adding the following after the `#import` lines sets the frame rate at 30 FPS based on this timer calling once every 1/30th of a second:

```
#define FPS 30
```

You can now add the following function to *SpaceHikeAppDelegate.m*, and it will be called at 30fps:

```
-(void)renderScene
{
    [glView startDrawing];

// draw lots of stuff with OpenGL commands in here

    [glView endDrawing];
  }
```

Again, it's another bit of code where it's more convenient to use the Objective-C functionality because you're using NSTimer.

Other than the calls to the start/end Drawing functions, pretty much everything in renderScene can be straight C. I've created simple sprite-drawing functions to avoid having a listing full of sequences of OpenGL commands, but that's more for readability than anything else.

Depending on what you're drawing with OpenGL, you may find it easier to create functions that handle all the OpenGL calls or mix OpenGL translate, scale, and rotate calls with DrawSprite or DrawModel type functions. For Flick Fishing and SlotZ, we use straight DrawSprite() and DrawModel() functions that handle the calls to do the drawing and typically call the OpenGL commands to position the sprite outside of that call. For example:

```
glPushMatrix();
glTranslatef(x,y,0);
glRotatef(90,0,0,1);
DrawSprite(spr[SPR_ICON]);
glPopMatrix();
```

Each time we came across a special case where a slightly different drawing function was needed, I'd just do a modification. For instance, in Flick Fishing, I needed to dynamically modify the model for the fishing rod based on the amount of pull on the line. So, I ended up with a DrawBendyModel() function that took the model data I would normally be feeding to the DrawModel() function and modified it before drawing it. If your drawing functions are simple and straightforward, it's easy to quickly add to them and create new ones on the fly to add unique capabilities that suit your game. Don't get bogged down in creating multipurpose drawing routines for all eventualities; just add extra variants of your drawing routines as you need them.

For Space Hike, you'll be creating sprites by loading textures (more on that later) with their vertex and texture vertex data stored in an array of structures and using simple functions for DrawSpriteAt and DrawSpriteScaledAt to easily draw sprites. Again, this is a way of simplifying things so you can get on with sticking things on the screen and writing the game.

Let's leave the drawing loop and SpaceHikeAppDelegate for the moment and take a look at how you're going to load the textures and use them as sprites.

For this, we've added the *Texture2D.m* and *Texture2D.h* files. These originally started way back as edited versions of Apple's source code but have since been rewritten to make the texture loading more suitable for use with OpenGL, to add the sprite creation and drawing functions, and to make the whole thing straight C rather than an Objective-C class.

As with the rest of the code, it's all on the Apress web site, but here are the pertinent bits.

Essentially, you have two elements: the textures you're loading into OpenGL from disk and the sprites, which are square models with a texture attached.

For the sprites, you have a sprite_type structure defined as follows:

```
typedef struct {
    GLuint       name;  // OpenGL ID of texture used for this sprite
    GLfloat    verts[12]; // array of vertices
(2 triangles, scaled to the size of the texture)
    GLfloat    tverts[8]; // texture vertices to match
} sprite_type;
```

And for the textures themselves, you have the following:

```
typedef struct {
    GLuint name; // OpenGL ID this texture gets stored as
    CGSize size; // size of the image as it was loaded in, w/h
    NSUInteger    width,height; // actual height of the texture stored
for OpenGL, rounded up to nearest power of 2
    Texture2DPixelFormat format; // pixel format of texture
    GLfloat maxS,maxT; // U/V coordinate modifiers.

} texture_type;
```

With these two structures, you create global arrays for the sprites and textures:

```
sprite_type      gSprite[64];
texture_type     gTexture[64];
```

Why use global arrays instead of being nicely OOP and using storage classes? It's actually another convenience thing. It's generally a lot easier to poke around and look at data in a global variable because you have only one instance of it in memory and It's a nice block; it's also easier for a cross reference to be used elsewhere in the game if you need. The downside is that you lose some of the protective features of classes, so you have to make sure you're not doing anything stupid with them. For larger projects with more than a couple of coders, this becomes a big worry, and looking toward a more object-oriented approach becomes sensible; however, for an iPhone game, you save far more time with this simplification than you'd lose through the odd silly mistake that classes might have shielded you against.

The texture-loading routine pulls the image in from disk, makes sure it's a suitable power-of-two size, and then creates a sprite with it (you use the gNumSprites counter to keep track of the number of sprites you've loaded). This is split across a few functions,

LoadTextureImage() is the one we actually call to do all the work that first calls CreateNamedImage() with the filename to make a CFImageRef.[4] The image is pulled into memory, and its width and height are checked to make sure they're a power of two (OpenGL ES 1.1 allows only power-of-two textures) and that they're under the maximum size. It then calls the InitTexture() function with that data to create the OpenGL image. The OpenGL texture name generated, along with the relevant texture sizes, is returned into the next available gTexture[] (gNumTextures is our count of these) and the current sprite number is stored in the spr[] array, which lets you specify which sprites you're loading the texture for.

The InitTexture() function also calls the CreateSprite() function to make a new sprite model to display the texture.

The upshot of this is that you end up with a gSprite[] array with all your textures loaded as sprites with suitable vertex data to draw them at their normal size. You also have a gTexture[] array with just the texture information, which we don't use in Space Hike directly, but it's useful if you want to use the textures for drawing 3D models or any other OpenGL drawing.

To load an image as a sprite, you call it like this:

```
LoadTextureImage(CFSTR("ViewScreen"),CFSTR("png"),SPR_VIEWSCREEN);
```

which we've done in the applicationDidFinishLaunching part of *SpaceHikeAppDelegate.m*.

SPR_VIEWSCREEN is part of an enumeration of the sprite numbers, which we've kept in *SpaceHikeAppDelegate.h*. To add a new sprite to the game, you add its name to the enumeration list and add a new LoadTextureImage line for it.

The LoadTextureImage function stores the sprite name you've requested it to load the texture for in the spr[] array, which is just a handy lookup table of the sprites you've loaded.

It's pretty much one for one with the gNumSprites count in Space Hike, but doing this slight indirection allows you to insert sprite loads, creating textureless sprites or sprites that can be reused anywhere in the list without having to completely redo the sprite name enumeration list.

This is particularly handy with the GrabSpriteSet() function, which takes a single texture that you've loaded as a sprite and defines a whole set of sprites using the same texture. We use this for our buttons, icons, and the 0–9 digits in Space Hike, for instance.

---

4   The original Apple samples used UIImage and CGImage, which can cause memory problems when used with OpenGL because they cache the image in memory, thus keeping a duplicate of it along with the OpenGL copy even after you release it. If you're doing a game with a lot of graphics, that can be a bit of an issue.

The sprite-drawing functions are added as follows:

```
DrawSpriteAt(spritenum, x,y)
```

```
DrawSpriteScaledAt(spritenum,x,y,sx,sy)
```

and

```
DrawNumberAt(number,x,y)
```

which give you enough basic drawing functions to handle Space Hike.

TIP

Note in the sprite-drawing routines that I use `glPushMatrix()` and `glPopMatrix()` around the GL calls. This technique is pretty much second-nature to most seasoned OpenGL coders, but essentially it stores the current drawing matrix on the stack so that any translating, rotating, or scaling is done only on the object we are drawing and not subsequent ones.

So, you can start cramming all the game play code in there. You have enough of a basic drawing toolkit to write pretty much any 2D sprite-based game. Plank, for instance, was based almost entirely on very similar code because it was partially a teaching project to allow Adam to learn some game programming.

By working with such simple code, you can get your game up and running quickly. Thus, you don't lose the momentum of the great game idea that inspired the coding session and can get into the fun part of making it all play (Figure 3-6).

Of course, rapid prototyping like this also means we bump into any game design problems nice and early in the development process. For instance, when I first wrote out the design for Space Hike, I imagined the map display that shows the sector of space around you as an 11×11 grid, which looked fine on the iPhone simulator and worked OK when you use the mouse but became fiddly to use on an actual device when you're trying to tap a small square with your finger. To be honest, I expected this might be the case because I've found anything smaller than 24×24 pixels in size is an awkward area to hit with a normal human finger without risking

Figure 3-6. Combat!

tapping anything around it. Ideally you need to go 32×32 or more. So, Space Hike's scanner map got redefined to 9×9 squares, giving us a whole 35 pixels per grid square to play with (or 32×32 with an artistic surround).

Originally I also had an option to switch on your shields, which was in the original Star Trek games and reduced damage at the expense of constantly draining power when they were on, but with the simplified Space Hike game, they didn't really gel and added an extra layer of complexity that wasn't needed. Besides, Star Trek just pinched them from E. "Doc" Smith anyway!

The first builds of Space Hike controlled your movement by requiring you to tap the location you wanted to whoop to (the Expendable uses the experimental "Whoop" drive, so-named after the sound it makes despite all laws of physics about sound in a vacuum). Then press the Whoop button to activate it. After a bit of play, I simplified this to just tapping the location you want to jump to, making the Whoop button useless.

Addressing the Save Game Problem

As I mentioned earlier, iPhone game players have a tendency of playing in short bursts when time is available. This means that either your game has to be so simple that someone can play and forget about it in a minute or you need to save the game's progress and state immediately when the player hits the home button or answers an incoming call like in Figure 3-7.

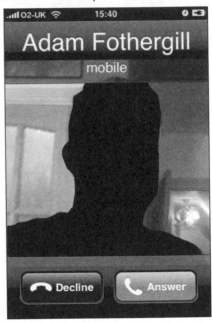

Figure 3-7. If your game doesn't autosave, answering this phone call will lose all your game's data!

How to Save

Fortunately, OS X lets you know this is about to happen by sending a notification to your delegate, which triggers the applicationWillTerminate function:

```
-(void)applicationWillTerminate:(UIApplication *)application
{
    // save our game here
}
```

This notification is particularly useful because it is called whenever your game is going to be forced to quit by the OS because of an incoming call or the user hitting the home button. The downside is that you have to save the data quickly (within five seconds), or the OS will just kick your app out without bothering to save it.

OS X uses the NSUserDefaults system to let you save a set of preferences in the current user's profile for your app. It uses the NSDictionary system, and in the Apple example, you would register the dictionary after creating it as a sequence of pairs of objects and keys, with each parameter you're saving having to be named and stashed using the appropriate NSNumber or NSData type and generally ending up with a really nasty-looking list that invariably has way too many square brackets in it to be easy to work with.

How to Save the Easy Way

Kudos goes to Daniel Labriet of DanLabGames for starting me on the following method of handling the data that's a lot more straightforward and much easier to mess with in the context of a game.

You set up the basic dictionary and register it for the user defaults like so:

```
NSDictionary *dict = [NSDictionary dictionaryWithObjectsAndKeys:
                         [NSNumber numberWithFloat:63] ,
                         @"SaveGame",@"dummy",
                         [NSNumber numberWithFloat:1] ,

                         nil ]; // terminate the list
    [[NSUserDefaults standardUserDefaults] registerDefaults:dict];
```

But then you use a structure for the save game that you define in the *AppDelegate.h* file:

```
typedef struct
{
    int check;
    int gameactive;
    int mode;
    int alert;
    int scanactive;
    colony_type colonies[NUM_COLONIES];
    evilspacealien_type mingons[NUM_MINGONS];
    int snacks;
    int batteries;
    int armour;
    int missiles;
    int locationx;
    int locationy;
} savegame_type;
```

You create a gSaveGame variable with that structure, and any data you want to save either as game prefs or save game info, you can put in that structure and do the following in the SaveGame routine:

```
NSData * savedata;
    unsigned char * ptr;
    unsigned char * save;
    save = malloc(sizeof(gSaveGame));

    ptr = (unsigned char *)&gSaveGame;
    for(a = 0; a < sizeof(gSaveGame);a++)
    {
        *(save + a) = *(ptr + a);
    }

    savedata = [[NSData alloc] initWithBytes:save
length:sizeof(gSaveGame)];
    //-----------------------------------------------
    [[NSUserDefaults standardUserDefaults] setObject:savedata
forKey:@"SaveGame"];
    [[NSUserDefaults standardUserDefaults] synchronize];
```

Because this just creates a block of data the size of the gSaveGame structure and stores it in the SaveGame key/object pair, it will adapt to whatever you add to the structure, and you don't have to do a lot of editing of the save game dictionary definition each time you change it.

Loading the prefs back is just as simple (I do this at the start of the game):

```
-(void)LoadPrefs
{

    int check;
    NSData *savedata;
    savedata = [[NSUserDefaults standardUserDefaults]
dataForKey:@"SaveGame"];

//if user is starting game for the first time, set defaults and save them
    if(savedata == NULL || gResetStats)
    {
        //    printf("RESET SCORES\n");
        gResetStats = 0;
        gSaveGame.gameactive = 0;
        [self SavePrefs];
    }
    else
    {
```

```
    [savedata getBytes:&gSaveGame length:sizeof(gSaveGame)];

    // now grab your saved game data from the gSaveGame structure
    check = gSaveGame.check;
  // check to see if our save game is the right version
  if(check != 14020901)
  {
      // barf, bad data
      gResetStats = 1;
  }
  if(gSaveGame.gameactive)
  {
      // grab the save game data and resume
// the game from where we left off
      ResumeGame();
      gSaveGame.gameactive = 0;
  }


    }
}
```

You'll note that you add a check value to the data to confirm the save game you're loading is the same version number as the current game build. You may also want to add a checksum to the data too. That way, you can reject any saves that have broken or old data. Once your game is released, the version number normally won't change, but while you're developing it, you can change the version number to automatically reject old saves that would otherwise give you bad data.

When you're actually saving the game, it's worth having a gameactive flag like in the savegame_ type structure. Set this to 1 while the game is playing and back to 0 after you finish a game and return to the menus. This way, you know whether there is a game to continue when your app launches.

Listing 3-1 shows the full game load and save functions, and Figure 3-8 shows the results of giving the player the ability to autosave.

Figure 3-8. *Now that the game autosaves when you are interrupted, the Mingon Empire doesn't stand a chance!*

TIP

This is more of a style thing, but where a lot of coders are taught to use i, j, k, l as throwaway index variables for counters, I tend to prefer to use a, b, c, d, and so on. There are two reasons for this. One is that i, j, and l are really quite difficult to read and are easy to mistake for the number 1 when you're wading through code, especially when you're a little bit dyslexic or suffering from permanent eye strain like most coders. The second is that when I hit e or f, I know I'm nesting a loop a bit too far!

Listing 3-1. *The Save and Load Game Functions*

```
-(void)SavePrefs
{
    int a;

    // Thanks to Dan for much better save/load code
    // than the Apple hackers :)
    NSDictionary *dict = [NSDictionary dictionaryWithObjectsAndKeys:
                        [NSNumber numberWithFloat:63] ,
                        @"SaveGame",@"dummy",
                        [NSNumber numberWithFloat:1] ,

                        nil ]; // terminate the list
    [[NSUserDefaults standardUserDefaults] registerDefaults:dict];

    // put our game data into our save game structure
    // modify this to suit your game
    gSaveGame.check = 14020901;
    // adding a version number allows you to disregard save data
    // that's from earlier versions of the game
        // our active game save has been copied to gSaveGame
    // by the StashGame() function already
    //-----------------------------------------------

    //    Now actually save it

    NSData * savedata;
    unsigned char * ptr;
    unsigned char * save;
    save = malloc(sizeof(gSaveGame));

    ptr = (unsigned char *)&gSaveGame;
    for(a = 0; a < sizeof(gSaveGame);a++)
    {
        *(save + a) = *(ptr + a);
    }

    savedata = [[NSData alloc]
```

```
initWithBytes:save length:sizeof(gSaveGame)];
    //-------------------------------------------------
    [[NSUserDefaults standardUserDefaults]
setObject:savedata forKey:@"SaveGame"];
    [[NSUserDefaults standardUserDefaults] synchronize];
}

-(void)LoadPrefs
{

    int check;
    NSData *savedata;
    savedata = [[NSUserDefaults standardUserDefaults]
dataForKey:@"SaveGame"];
    //if user is starting game for the first time,
    // set defaults and save them
    if(savedata == NULL || gResetStats)
    {
        //     printf("RESET SCORES\n");
        gResetStats = 0;
        gSaveGame.gameactive = 0;
        [self SavePrefs];
    }
    else
    {


        [savedata getBytes:&gSaveGame length:sizeof(gSaveGame)];

        // now grab your saved game data from the gSaveGame structure
        check = gSaveGame.check;
        // check to see if our save game is the right version
        if(check != 14020901)
        {
            // barf, bad data
            gResetStats = 1;
        }
        if(gSaveGame.gameactive)
        {
            // grab the save game data and resume
            // the game from where we left off
            ResumeGame();
            gSaveGame.gameactive = 0;
        }

    }


}
```

```c
// ResumeGame() : resumes a game that was saved on exit

void ResumeGame()
{
    int a;

    gGameOver = 0;
    gGameMode = gSaveGame.mode;
    gAlert = gSaveGame.alert;
    gScanActive = gSaveGame.scanactive;
    gSnacks = gSaveGame.snacks;
    gBatteries = gSaveGame.batteries;
    gArmour = gSaveGame.armour;
    gMissiles = gSaveGame.missiles;
    gLocationX = gSaveGame.locationx;
    gLocationY = gSaveGame.locationy;

    for(a = 0; a < NUM_COLONIES;a++)
    {
        gColony[a] = gSaveGame.colonies[a];
    }
    for(a = 0; a < NUM_MINGONS;a++)
    {
        gMingon[a] = gSaveGame.mingons[a];
    }



}

// StashGame() : check to see if there's an active game
// (ie not game over) and if so, copy all the data to gSaveGame

void StashGame()
{
    int a;
    if(gGameOver == 0)
    {
        gSaveGame.gameactive = 1;
        gSaveGame.mode = gGameMode;
        gSaveGame.alert = gAlert;
        gSaveGame.scanactive = gScanActive;
        gSaveGame.snacks = gSnacks;
        gSaveGame.batteries = gBatteries;
        gSaveGame.armour = gArmour;
        gSaveGame.missiles = gMissiles;
        gSaveGame.locationx = gLocationX;
```

```
            gSaveGame.locationy = gLocationY;
            for(a = 0; a < NUM_COLONIES;a++)
            {
                gSaveGame.colonies[a] = gColony[a];
            }
            for(a = 0; a < NUM_MINGONS;a++)
            {
                gSaveGame.mingons[a] = gMingon[a];
            }

    }
    else
    {
        gSaveGame.gameactive = 0;
    }
}
```

Space Hike: The App

With game saving and sprite drawing all worked out, you just mix in a little bit of game play, and you have a full game. Let's take a look at how it all fits together.

The Render Loop and Basic Organization

You can download the full code for Space Hike from the Apress web site, but the main game logic is pretty straightforward and is mostly written into the renderScene function with a few support functions.

For a more complicated game, it would make a lot of sense to spread the functionality across several functions to keep the main render loop readable and simple. Just how much you split the code up really depends on your preferred coding style (or that of the team you are working with).

In Space Hike, the renderScene function is called once every frame. So, everything you do in it, you have to consider as being just the code for this particular frame of time. That means that anything you want to happen over more than a single frame, such as timers and waiting for button presses, you have to handle atomically by checking each time you're in the renderScene function.

For instance, each frame you need to see whether a button has been pressed. The system gives you a notification when the screen is first touched, and in the *EAGLView.m* file, you process the notification, check what point of the screen was tapped, and, if it's on one of the button zones, set the gTouched variable to the button number that was hit.

In the render loop, you test gTouched after you've drawn the screen and react accordingly if it's not 0:

```
if(gTouched)
{
    // process the button touched here
    // ..
    // ..
    gTouched = 0; // reset to 0 once handled so we don't keep repeating it
}
```

You also check any game play variables, such as the Expendable's armor or batteries. If either run out, the game sets its state to the relevant defeat status.

Space Hike uses a relatively simple state system to track what it's doing. Depending on the value gGameMode, the game will handle events and game play accordingly, and you simply change between them to display the screen in the relevant mode or halt game play to alert the player.

There are three states, defined in the *SpaceHikeAppDelegate.h* file as follows:

```
enum {
    MODE_MAP = 0,
    MODE_BATTLE,
    MODE_ALERT
};
```

The game mostly switches between MODE_MAP and MODE_BATTLE as its two main screens. The game will jump to MODE_BATTLE when you land on a map square with enemies on it. Switching to MODE_ALERT switches to the dialog screen with the relevant alert message being set in the gAlert variable. This is another advantage of having all the game text as graphics. You simply set gAlert to the graphic panel for the message you want and draw it as a sprite.

My personal preference is to have a separate variable called gGameOver to show when the game has ended rather than having a MODE_GAMEOVER state. This lets me test gGameOver first and ignore all the other game state code if it's set. I can also test gGameOver anywhere else in the code if I need. I could just as easily test gGameMode to see whether it was set to MODE_GAMEOVER, but I just find it easier to remember I have a gGameOver variable.

In Space Hike I set the value of gGameOver depending on just how the game ended. There are four possible endings:

- GO_WON: When the player has wiped out all the Mingon battle cruisers and saved the galaxy

- GO_OUTOFPOWER: When the Expendable has run out of power (see Figure 3-9)

- GO_OUTOFSNACKS: When the Expendable has run out of snack food

- GO_DEFEATED: When the Expendable has been destroyed in battle

If gGameOver is set to any of these values, you draw a suitable end screen and wait for the player to tap the screen.

There are a few more game play variables that show up in the renderScene function, such as gScanActive, which changes the map view to a full scan of the galaxy. So when this is set, you know you have to draw the screen differently in map mode.

If you are in combat mode, the variable gCombatPage tells the game which combat screen to show. If you were writing Space Hike as a live action combat game, this would be a lot more complicated, of course. Fortunately, Space Hike is nice and simple, so the combat simply displays a different screen depending on which weapon you fire and whether you have destroyed your opponent.

Figure 3-9. Oops!

Game Logic Overview

I know you're really reading this and learning how to write an iPhone game only so that you can get your own brilliant game design created. So, Space Hike has been written to keep out of your way and let you see how an iPhone game works, without lots of its own complex game logic getting in your way.

However, just so you can see what it's doing and pick up a few tricks that might help you write Grand Rainbow Fallout Theft 4 for the iPhone, here's a description of the basic game logic for Space Hike.

Space Hike is turn-based and works around a small galaxy map of 25×25 squares. It always starts in map mode, with the player able to see a section of 9×9 squares and buttons for SCAN and Repair.

If the player hits the SCAN button, you set the gScanActive flag variable, and the game draws the whole 25×25 square grid instead of just local space at the cost of a bit of the ship's battery power. Any screen tap clears gScanActive and puts the user back to normal map-viewing mode.

When the player taps a map square, the Expendable's location is moved to that square, and you call the CheckNewLocation() function to see where you've landed. This function checks to see whether you've landed on a colony planet or space station, which would change you to the Alert state and display information on resupply (or not). It also checks to see whether you're now on the same square as a Mingon battle cruiser, switching to battle mode if that's the case.

In battle mode game play is turn-based too. The player can fire lasers or more powerful missiles. Either will always hit, but missiles do twice as much damage. The primary game play is about resource management in that you have to destroy the enemy ship before your own armor or battery power runs out. If things aren't looking too good, there's also an emergency Whoop button to try to escape the battle to a random spot in space.

Depending on which button the player presses, you process the battle (or escape), display the appropriate screen, and possibly change back to map mode or even set the game over state at the end of the battle.

The only other mode is the Alert mode. This is set by various events in the game, such as landing on a colony planet or space station square, and drops back to map mode when the Continue button is hit. Figure 3-10 shows an in-game alert.

Drawing and Handling the Game

Because the renderScene function is roughly split into two sections, drawing and then responding to a button press, most of the code to handle each mode has two components as well.

Figure 3-10. *The Alert mode simply draws a panel with the alert text over the background screen.Drawing a Frame*

The first part of renderScene draws the current frame, so the gGameMode variable is checked to see what background graphic to use from the three you use:

```
GlColor4f(1,1,1,1);
if(gGameMode == MODE_MAP && gScanActive != 0)
{
    DrawSpriteAt(SPR_LONGRANGESCREEN,0,0);
}
else
{
    if(gGameMode == MODE_BATTLE)
    {
        DrawSpriteAt(SPR_COMBATSCREEN,0,0);
    }
    else
    {
        DrawSpriteAt(SPR_VIEWSCREEN,0,0);
    }
}
```

As you can see, you just have three different sprites for the backgrounds, each of which covers the whole screen and clears it for the current frame's information to be drawn on top.

Each is drawn for a different mode; Figure 3-11 shows what they look like.

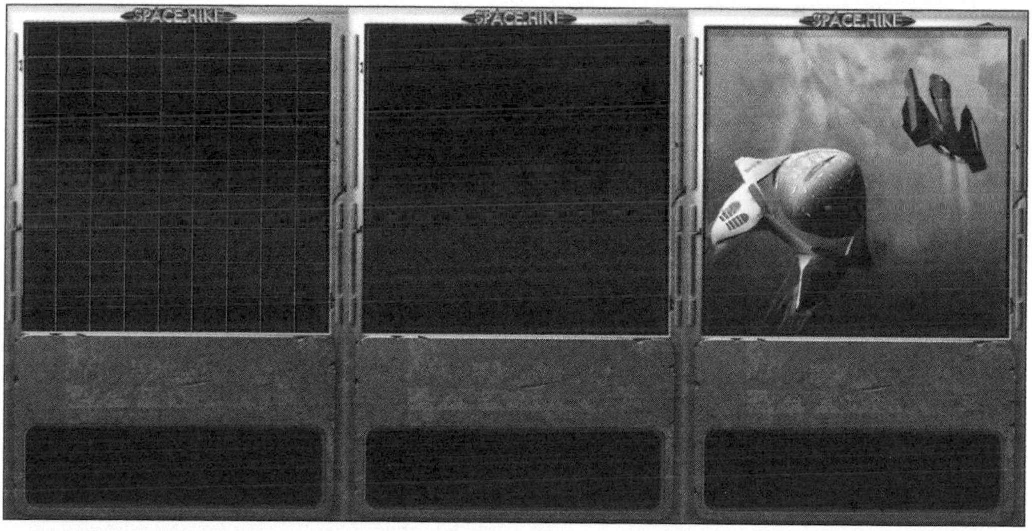

Figure 3-11. *To clear the background, you simply draw a background sprite over the whole screen. Here are the three different background screens for Space Hike that are used: the main view, long-range scan view, and combat mode.*

With the background suitably cleared and drawn, you can process the game state and draw the information for the current mode.

First, the gGameOver variable is checked. If it's greater than 0, the game has ended. That's usually badly for the player!

```
if(gGameOver > 0)
{
    gCombatPage = 0;
    glColor4f(1,1,1,1);
    switch(gGameOver)
    {
        case GO_WON:
            DrawSpriteAt(SPR_WIN,0,0);
            break;
        case GO_OUTOFPOWER:
            DrawSpriteAt(SPR_OUTOFPOWER,0,0);
            break;
        case GO_OUTOFSNACKS:
            DrawSpriteAt(SPR_OUTOFSNACKS,0,0);
            break;
        case GO_DEFEATED:
            DrawSpriteAt(SPR_LOST,0,0);
            break;
    }
}
else // gGameOver > 0
{
    ... handle the non game over game states here
}
```

As with the background drawing, the "game over" state just uses graphic panels as sprites to display each game ending. If gGameOver is 0, the game drops into the else state, and you draw the actual game modes.

If the user is in combat, the gCombatPage variable overrides the drawing and displays the results of the last shot. If not, the game does a switch based on gGameMode and draws the display and buttons for each mode.

```
if(gGameOver > 0)
{
    .. game over state from above
}
else // gGameOver > 0
{
    if(gCombatPage > 0)
    {
        // display combat page for last shot
        DrawSpriteAt(SPR_COMBATSCREEN + gCombatPage,0,0);
    }
    else // gCombatPage > 0
```

```
{
    switch(gGameMode)
    {
        case MODE_ALERT:
            DrawSpriteAt(gAlert,0,80);
            DrawSpriteAt(SPR_BUTTON5,-80,-90);
        break;
        case MODE_MAP:
            if(gScanActive)
            {
                DrawScannedMap(gLocationX,gLocationY);
                    }
            else
            {
                DrawMap(gLocationX,gLocationY); // draw viewscreen map
            }
            // draw buttons
            glColor4f(1,1,1,1);
            // Repair Button
            DrawSpriteAt(SPR_BUTTON1,80,-90);
            // Long range Scan button
            DrawSpriteAt(SPR_BUTTON2,-80,-90);
            // Battery/Armour stats
            DrawSpriteAt(SPR_STATS,-96,-196);
            // Snacks/Missiles stats
            DrawSpriteAt(SPR_STATS2,64,-196
            // draw battery power value
            glColor4f(1,1,1,1);
            // tint the display red if we're on low power
            if(gBatteries < 25)
                glColor4f(1,0,0,1);
            DrawNumberAt(gBatteries,-42,-180);
            // draw armour value
            glColor4f(1,1,1,1);
            if(gArmour < 25)
                glColor4f(1,0,0,1);
            DrawNumberAt(gArmour,-42,-202);
             // draw snacks value
            glColor4f(1,1,1,1);
            if(gSnacks < 4)
                glColor4f(1,0,0,1);
            DrawNumberAt(gSnacks,106,-180);
            // draw missiles value
            glColor4f(1,1,1,1);
            DrawNumberAt(gMissiles,106,-202);
            // for debugging purposes, draw number of Mingons remaining
            //     DrawNumberAt(gMingonCount,-42,-228);
```

```
                break;
                case MODE_BATTLE:
                    // Lasers button
                    DrawSpriteAt(SPR_BUTTON3,-80,-90);
                    // Missiles button
                    DrawSpriteAt(SPR_BUTTON4,80,-90);
                    // emergency whoop button
                    DrawSpriteAt(SPR_BUTTON0,-80,-130);
                    // draw battery and armour stats label
                    DrawSpriteAt(SPR_STATS,-96,-196);
                    // draw Snacks and Missiles stats label
                    DrawSpriteAt(SPR_STATS2,64,-196);
                    // draw batteries value
                    glColor4f(1,1,1,1);
                    if(gBatteries < 25)
                        glColor4f(1,0,0,1);
                    DrawNumberAt(gBatteries,-42,-180);
                    // draw armour value
                    glColor4f(1,1,1,1);
                    if(gArmour < 25)
                        glColor4f(1,0,0,1);
                    DrawNumberAt(gArmour,-42,-202);
                    // draw snacks value
                    glColor4f(1,1,1,1);
                    if(gSnacks < 4)
                        glColor4f(1,0,0,1);
                    DrawNumberAt(gSnacks,106,-180);
                    // draw missiles value
                    glColor4f(1,1,1,1);
                    DrawNumberAt(gMissiles,106,-202);
                break;
            }
        }
    }
}
```

That's all the drawing done! You'll notice that in MODE_MAP you call either the DrawMap() or DrawScannedMap() function to draw the actual map. These functions are mostly the same, other than the area and scale they draw in the view screen.

```
// DrawMap(int locx,int locy) : Draws the current viewscreen (9x9 squares)
area of the map
void DrawMap(int locx,int locy)
{
    int a;
    int x,y;
    // update map icons
    // draw the colony planets and space stations
    for(a = 0; a < NUM_COLONIES;a++)
```

```
    {
        x = gColony[a].x - locx;
        y = gColony[a].y - locy;
        // check to see if colony is within the current scan area
        if(abs(x) < 5 && abs(y)< 5)
        {
            // if colony has been used to restock, draw it shaded
            if(gColony[a].used == 1)
            {
                glColor4f(0.5,0.5,0.5,1);
            }
            else
            {
                glColor4f(1,1,1,1);
            }
            DrawSpriteAt(gColony[a].sprite, x * 32,80 - y * 32);
        }
    }
    // draw Mingons
    glColor4f(1,1,1,1);
    for(a = 0;  a < NUM_MINGONS;a++)
    {
        if(gMingon[a].armour > 0)  // if <=0 it's been destroyed
        {
            x = gMingon[a].x - locx;
            y = gMingon[a].y - locy;
            if(abs(x) < 5 && abs(y)< 5)
            {
                DrawSpriteAt(SPR_ICON1,x * 32, 80 - y * 32);
            }
        }
    }
    // draw the Expendable in the center
    DrawSpriteAt(SPR_ICON0,0,80);
}
```

There are two ways you could have stored and handled the locations of everything on the
map. One method is to have a map array of 25×25 ints and set the map data for the coordinate of an item to that item's code. For instance:

```
gMap[gColony[a].x][gColony[a].y] = MAP_COLONY;
```

This has the advantage that it's very easy to see and draw an object at any specific place on
the map, but it has the disadvantage that only one item can be at any place on the map. It's
also a bit of a pain if objects (such as the Mingons in our case) are moving around, because

you have to clear the old location and change the new location as they move. This method was popular in much older games because it doesn't take a lot of CPU power to process.

The other method, which I used in Space Hike, is simply to iterate through each list of items whenever I want to check them. Technically it means the game is doing a fair bit more each time I test, but the iPhone's CPU is fast enough to do this sort of testing without even blinking, so that's not an issue. More important, it will let the game have multiple objects on one map spot, so Mingon battle cruisers can move over a square occupied by a colony planet or a space station, and I can have multiple Mingon ships on one square.

In the previous DrawMap() function, you simply compare the coordinates of each object to see whether it's within the view screen area. Using the abs(x) function on the offset of an object's coordinate from the view screen's center is a really quick and easy way to test this.

One other thing to note is that the game is running at 30 frames per second (fps) and not waiting each frame for input. So, you can actually animate things on the screen if you want. In the DrawScannedMap() function, I pulse the scale of the player's ship so that it's more visible on the smaller scale map.

Note the use of the fmod(a,b) function to make gShipPulse wrap around 0–360 degrees:

```
// draw the Expendable in the center, pulse its scale so we can see it :)

spritesize = (9.0 / MAP_SIZE) *
(sin(gShipPulse * RAD_DEGREE) * 0.2 + 0.8);

DrawSpriteScaledAt(SPR_ICON0,locx *
tilesize - MAP_SIZE / 2 * tilesize,80 - locy * tilesize +
MAP_SIZE / 2 * tilesize,spritesize,spritesize);

gShipPulse = fmod(gShipPulse + 16.0f,360.0f);
```

Handling the Game Turn

With the current frame drawn, you can check whether the player has hit a button and deal with the game turn. Turn-based games are generally an easier start to game programming, but as long as you remember that you're dealing only with what's happening for this particular frame of time, it's fairly simple to use the same basic code to write a real-time game too.

Because all the buttons in Space Hike are placed in the same spots on the screen, the actual testing for them is easy enough to do in the touch detection code in *EAGLView.m*. On receiving notification of a tap by the system, you process it and set gTouched if a button has been hit.

touchesBegan is the notification you get from the system, and it calls dispatchFirstTouchAtPoint to process the data from each touch:

```
// Handles the start of a touch
```

```
- (void)touchesBegan:(NSSet *)touches withEvent:(UIEvent *)event
{
    // Enumerate through all the touch objects.
    for (UITouch *touch in touches) {
        // Send to the dispatch method, which will make
        // sure the appropriate subview is acted upon
        [self dispatchFirstTouchAtPoint:[touch locationInView:self]];
    }
}

-(void) dispatchFirstTouchAtPoint:(CGPoint)touchPoint
{
    int a,x,y;

    // checks for map position (grid of 11x11 tiles)
    // or which one of 4 buttons
    touchPoint.x = touchPoint.x - 160;
    touchPoint.y = touchPoint.y - 240;
    printf("x %f, y %f\n",touchPoint.x,touchPoint.y);
    // first see if touchPoint is within the bounds
    //  of the map.., -132,-56 to 132,216
    // Map is button 1 and returns gMapX,gMapY as offset coords
    // combat display, tap anywhere to continue,
    // so just return button 1 for any screen hit
    if(gCombatPage > 0 || gGameOver > 0) {
        gTouched = 1;
        return;
    }
    if(fabs(touchPoint.x) < 144 &&
touchPoint.y > -224 && touchPoint.y < 64)
    {
        gTouched = 1; // map
        printf("mapx %f,%f\n",(touchPoint.x + 144) / 32,
(touchPoint.y + 224) / 32);
        gMapX = (touchPoint.x + 144);
        gMapY = (touchPoint.y + 224);
        gMapX = gMapX / 32 - 4;
        gMapY = gMapY / 32 - 4;

        return;
    }

    // now check our 4 buttons
    // returns 2-5
    for(a = 0; a < 4;a++)
    {
        // get the button position
```

```
        x = (a % 2) * 160 - 80;
        y =  (a / 2) * 40 + 90;
        printf("x = %d, y = %d\n",x,y);
        // see if the touch point is within 64,16 of the button center
        if(fabs(touchPoint.x - x) < 64 && fabs(touchPoint.y - y) < 16)
        {
            gTouched = 2 + a;
            printf("gTouched = %d\n",gTouched);
            return;
        }

    }
}
```

The buttons are always in the same place on the screen. Button 1 is the main view screen from –144 to 144 in X and –224 to 64 in Y.

The four button positions are below that—two across and two down. Again, you can use the abs function (in this case the fabs() variant that works with floats) to see whether coordinates are in range to compare the touch position to each button.

The upshot of all that code is that whenever a button is tapped, the gTouched variable gets set to the button number. So, you simply need to test gTouched each frame in renderFrame and react to button presses depending on what mode the game is in.

This gives you a pretty hefty chunk of if statements, but essentially it's most of Space Hike's game logic. It looks nasty, but if you split it up a bit, it's pretty straightforward. You test gTouched after you've done the drawing in the frame:

```
if(gTouched)
{
    // depending on which mode we're in (map, combat or an alert),
    // respond differently to the buttons
    printf("Button %d touched\n",gTouched);
```

First, you test the gGameOver variable. If it's "game over," any button presses restart the game:

```
        if(gGameOver > 0)
        {
            if(gTouched == 1)
            {
                InitGame();

            }
        }
        else
        {
```

Next, you test the gCombatPage variable. If it's set, clear it to dismiss the combat results screen it's showing:

```
if(gCombatPage > 0)
{
    // display combat screens
    gCombatPage = 0;
}
else
{
```

And now the big stuff! Switch is based on the current game mode and handles the various button presses:

```
switch(gGameMode)
{
    case MODE_MAP:
```

Map mode is pretty simple. Button 1 is the view, so if it's in normal view mode, you work out what map square was tapped and jump the player there. As you've moved, you call the CheckNewLocation() function that checks for landing on bases or getting into combat with Mingon ships.

```
switch(gTouched)
{
    case 1: // set jump coordinates
        // if scan is active, switch it off and ignore input
        if(gScanActive)
        {
            gScanActive = 0;
        }
        else
        {
            gDestinationX = gLocationX + gMapX;
            gDestinationY = gLocationY + gMapY;
            // wrap around 25x25 map
            gDestinationX = (gDestinationX
+ MAP_SIZE) % MAP_SIZE; gDestinationY = (gDestinationY
+ MAP_SIZE) % MAP_SIZE;
            printf("destination set to %d,%d\n",
gDestinationX,gDestinationY);
            if(gDestinationX != gLocationX ||
gDestinationY != gLocationY)
            {
                // WHOOP!
                int fuel;
                fuel = fabs(gMapX) + fabs(gMapY);
                if(fuel <= gBatteries)
```

```
                    {
                        gLocationX = gDestinationX;
                        gLocationY = gDestinationY;
                        gBatteries -= fuel;
                        printf("WHOOP! to %d,%d\n",
gLocationX,gLocationY);

                        CheckNewLocation();
// checks to see if we've landed on anything fun
                        gScanActive = 0;
                    }
                }
            }
            break;
```

The long-range scan button is pretty simple. Assuming the player has enough battery power available, set gScanActive to 1. The draw function will handle the rest by using DrawScannedMap() instead of DrawMap().

```
            case 2: // long range scan
                if(gBatteries >= 5 && gScanActive == 0)
                {
                    gBatteries -= 5;
                    gScanActive = 1;

                    printf("long range scan\n");
                }
            break;
```

Repairing armor is just as simple. Again, you check the battery power, and if there's enough, you bolt some extra armor on. CheckNewLocation() is called so that Mingon ships can move while you're repairing the ship. Because CheckNewLocation() deducts one of the snacks, you sneakily add one on before calling it (the Expendable's crew isn't allowed to snack until they get the repairs done):

```
            case 3: // repair armour
                printf("repair armour\n");
                if(gBatteries >= 5)
                {
                    gBatteries = gBatteries -
min(5,(100 - gArmour) / 2);
                    gArmour = min(100,gArmour + 20);
                    gSnacks = min(20,gSnacks + 1);
                    CheckNewLocation(); // so the Mingons move
                }
```

```
            break;
        }
    break;
```

```
    case MODE_BATTLE:
```

Here's where you get to blow stuff up. Or at least show pictures of stuff blowing up!

```
        switch(gTouched)
        {
```

For each combat button, the game does the relevant stat zapping, knocking armor off the enemy ship, and damaging the Expendable's armor from the return fire. It then sets gCombatPage to the correct display for the button pressed. The Whoop button does an emergency jump to a random location to try to get the player out of combat but at the cost of a lot of battery power (see Figure 3-12).

Figure 3-12. *We're outta here!*

```
        case 2: // fire lasers!
            gMingon[gAttacker].armour -= (20 + rnd(20));
            gCombatPage = COMBAT_LASERS;

                // PEW PEW PEW !
                gArmour = max(0,gArmour - 5 - rnd(5));
                gBatteries = max(0,gBatteries - 1);
                printf("PEW PEW PEW!\n");
                break;
        case 3: // fire missiles
            if(gMissiles > 0)
            {
                gMingon[gAttacker].armour -= (50 + rnd(20));
                gArmour = max(0,gArmour - 5 - rnd(5));
                gMissiles--;
                gCombatPage = COMBAT_MISSILES;
            }
            // whoosh!
            printf("WHOOOSH!\n");
            break;
        case 4: // RUN!
            gLocationX = rnd(MAP_SIZE);
            gLocationY = rnd(MAP_SIZE);
            gBatteries = min(gBatteries,rnd(5) + 10);
            gCombatPage = COMBAT_WHOOP;
```

```
                              gGameMode = MODE_MAP;
                              printf("RANDOM JUMP to %d,%d\n",
gLocationX,gLocationY);

                              break;
                          }
```

At the end of each combat turn, you check to see whether the attacking Mingon's armor is gone. If it is, you've won this battle and can show the COMBAT_WON page:

```
                      if(gMingon[gAttacker].armour <= 0)
                      {
                          gArmour = min(100,gArmour + rnd(10));
                          gSnacks = min(20,gSnacks + rnd(3) + 1);
                          gBatteries = min(100,gBatteries + rnd(10));
                          gGameMode = MODE_MAP;
                          gCombatPage = COMBAT_WON;

                          CheckNewLocation();
// in case there are 2 or more mingons here
                      }
                      break;
```

Alert mode is extremely simple. Whenever the player taps the screen, drop straight back to map mode:

```
                  case MODE_ALERT:
                      if(gTouched == 2)
                          gGameMode = MODE_MAP;
                      break;
              }
          }
      }
```

After dealing with the button touch, simply clear gTouched so you don't worry about it until another button is tapped:

```
      gTouched = 0; // reset to 0 once handled
}
```

Ideally, you should download the full project from the Apress site to see the previous code in the context of the full game's code.

I've added comments in the code for any code tricks you might find of interest. You'll also see quite a few printf() commands that have been commented out. These are one of my old-school debug techniques that I find myself using even when I have a working debugger. Simply printing data to the console is a very easy way to visualize what data is actually going through a routine, as you can see in Figure 3-13. It also stays in the console, so you can scroll through it and see any patterns or take it away and analyze it. So, for instance, if you have a sprite that isn't moving as you expected, dumping its coordinates each frame will often help you spot exactly what's happening with them and give you a good clue as to how to fix its routine. Of course, you have to make sure that the data you are printing out is in a format that makes sense to you when you see it scrolling through the console!

In Space Hike, I needed to tune the density of Mingon ships and bases and check how spaced out everything is within the game area to make sure it worked as a game. Printing out the map grid on call (I put an invisible button in the bottom right of the

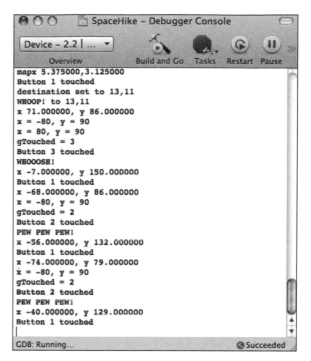

Figure 3-13. *Simply printing to the console can be a remarkably useful debugging tool. Here you're tracking button press coordinates and game flow through the combat sequence.*

screen for debugging) let me see where everything was on any given turn and see whether maybe the enemies were clustering too densely or whether there was too much empty space for the player to be able to cross practically without always running out of fuel.

Enhancing the Game

Space Hike is a pretty simple game, of course. I made it simple deliberately so it is easy to understand, but it also means that there is plenty of scope for you to add to the game and experiment with adding animation, adding different combat sequences, or simply making the game a little bigger by expanding the map area and the number of enemies and supply bases. The latter would require a bit of a rethink, of course, because not only would you have to rebalance the game, but you would have to consider things such as drawing the long-range scan, which will scale to work at a different map size but might not look so great. Making it show only the map within a 25×25 grid of the Expendable would look good but require more of a code change.

Adding sound effects would enhance the game's polish greatly. I avoided adding sound code to this version because it's a lot of nasty-looking code at first glance, and I felt that it would have gotten in the way of understanding the main features of this project, namely, the render/game play loop and the save game functions. As a base project for adding sound effects to, though, this should make it an ideal one.

Animation is a relatively simple addition. Remember, the `renderLoop` function is being called once every 30th of a second, so moving the sprites around the screen is a fairly easy task. Of course, if you want to make the Expendable move to its new location rather than just jump there, you are going to have to modify the game state code to ignore button presses while the ship is moving.

Summary

So, that's Space Hike, or at least how it turned out eventually after a few revisions. The original design document was a bit different, and just for fun, I've put it on the Apress site (`http://www.apress.com`) along with the original coder art that I knocked out to get the game going; you can compare it with Adam's finished art that you can download with the source code to build the game. You can also grab the game itself from the App Store as a free app.

I hope you have a lot of fun writing iPhone games. If you're having fun writing the game, that's a good indicator that someone's going to have fun playing it. Feel free to play with the Space Hike code and modify it as the basis for your own games. Or just use it as a learning project to see whether you can expand the game play with sound effects and maybe a bigger combat system rather than the simple "try not to use too many resources" combat in this version.

Brian Greenstone

Company: Pangea Software, Inc.

Location: Austin, Texas

Former Life As a Developer: I've developed games for the Apple II, Super Nintendo, Sony PlayStation, and Mac platforms.

Life As an iPhone Developer: I've created the iPhone games Enigmo, Cro-Mag Rally, Billy Frontier, Beer Bounce, Bugdom 2, Nanosaur 2, Otto Matic, and Antimatter.

What's in This Chapter: This chapter contains tips for getting the best performance out of an iPhone game. It provides information about optimizing code and assets so that games will run at the highest frame rates possible.

Key Technologies:

- OpenGL
- Xcode
- Objective-C

Chapter 4

Brian Greenstone's Jedi Master List for Game Optimization

i started programming video games in the early 1980s, a time when processing capabilities were incredibly limited, so game programmers like myself had to become experts in the art of code optimization. My old Apple][+ had a whopping 64KB of RAM and a blazing 1-MHz, 8-bit CPU, so, needless to say, every byte of memory and every CPU cycle counted. Cutting just one instruction out of a sprite's drawing loop would make the difference between a game being playable and not being playable; therefore, a great deal of attention was paid to every single line of assembly code written. As CPUs evolved into the multicore, multigigahertz beasts that they are today, the need to eliminate every single unnecessary cycle became a thing of the past, but the iPhone is not a multicore, multigigahertz monster, so the need to focus on low-level optimizations has once again become a critical part of the development process.

The first game that I developed for the iPhone was Enigmo (Figure 4-1). Enigmo was originally a game that I wrote for the Mac back in 2003, and although I did spend a lot of time writing fast and efficient collision code for the game, I didn't have to work too hard at it because even the low-end Macs (which ran at 400 MHz) were more than sufficient to run the game at a good rate. The CPU in the iPhone, however, is probably closer in performance to a 266-MHz iMac, and Enigmo would never run on a 266-MHz iMac. So, after getting the game running on the iPhone, I spent two more weeks doing basic optimizations to get it playable, and after that, I spent two more weeks working with Apple's engineers to find even more ways of optimizing it. In the end, I had managed to double the original frame rate of the game.

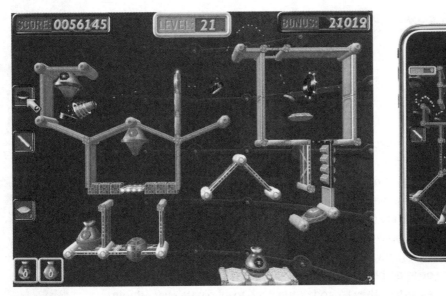

Figure 4-1. *The original Enigmo for Mac OS X (left) and Enigmo for the iPhone (right)*

In this chapter, I'll discuss many of the optimization techniques that I have used in my iPhone games. Some techniques are absolutely fundamental to writing a well-performing game, while other techniques may save a cycle here and there with the hope it will add up to an extra frame per second in the end.

Memory Matters

The iPhone and iPod touch have only 128MB of RAM, and most of that RAM is used by the iPhone OS. Therefore, apps have use only of whatever RAM remains, and that amount is generally less than 40MB. Even the 266-MHz iMac that I referred to earlier had more than 40MB of RAM, so it is safe to say that this is the number-one trouble spot for most iPhone games. It is certainly the cause of most application crashes that occur, and if you've been using an iPhone for any amount of time, then you have almost certainly realized that you have to reboot often to keep apps running smoothly. Many app descriptions in iTunes actually suggest that you reboot your device before running them. This is because rebooting the iPhone frees up any extra RAM that the OS may be using. Sometimes the built-in apps like Mail and Safari may still be running in the background even though you've "quit" them, and those apps can easily cause your available RAM to drop from 40MB to 30MB, or even less.

Obviously, you want to be very conservative about your RAM usage on the iPhone, not just because using too much RAM can cause your app to crash but because accessing memory on any computer system is slow, so you always want to access as little of it as possible. Larger textures means more memory access, and larger data types means more memory access, larger sound files, and so on. You'll see that almost every optimization technique in this chapter is somehow related to memory and bandwidth.

The iPhone will issue you a low-memory warning when it deems that you're running low. In your *AppDelegate.m* file, you should implement the following method:

```
- (void) applicationDidReceiveMemoryWarning:(UIApplication*)application
{
    printf("Memory Low!!!!\n");
}
```

This memory warning typically gets issued when you're down to about 1.5MB of free RAM. Presumably, you should free up unneeded memory when you get this warning, but real-istically it is unlikely that that is an option. If you've written your game with care, then you shouldn't have any stray assets just hanging around wasting memory in the first place, so this warning usually doesn't do much good other than to notify you that your app is prob-ably about to crash.

In my games, I use this warning during the development stages to see how my memory usage is going. If I get lots of these warnings when playing the game, then I know I need to go back in and do some additional asset reduction to free up some RAM. In some games, I track the number of times this warning gets issued, and if it happens a lot, then I may bring up a warning dialog box for the user to let them know that they should reboot their iPhone.

Parlez-vous C?

The programming language that you choose to write your game in can have a big effect on the performance of your app; you have a choice of C, C++, and Objective-C.

Straight C Is Best

Many people who are new to the iPhone get the wrong impression that everything must be written in Objective-C, but this is not true, especially for games. You need to write in Objective-C only when you need to access certain features of the iPhone OS that use the Cocoa APIs. You need it to initialize your app, handle input events, receive notification callbacks (such as the low-memory warning), and bring up any of the standard OS dialog boxes, but usually none of your actual game needs it at all. For example, in my game Bugdom 2 (Figure 4-2), there are about 500,000 lines of code, but only about 700 of them are in Objective-C.

Figure 4-2. *Bugdom 2 has about 500,000 lines of C, 0 lines of C++, and about 700 lines of Objective-C.*

If you care about performance in your games, then you should avoid Objective-C, because Objective-C has a runtime component that not only causes extra computational overhead at execution time, but it prevents certain types of compiler optimizations from taking place such as inlining and constant propagation. Don't get me wrong, Objective-C is a great object-oriented language that has plenty to offer certain types of applications, but games are definitely not one of those types.

Depending on your religious leanings, you can either choose to follow my next recommendation or ignore it completely, but I always recommend that programmers write their code in straight C, not C++. In the "old days," C++ compilers generated code with a lot of extra overhead, so its use was frowned upon by the game development community, but the compilers quickly improved, and a cycle here and a cycle there just doesn't matter on a multicore, multigigahertz CPU. Now C++ is the most common form of C used in the game industry.

That being said, straight C always generates the most optimal code of any C variety. Is it going to generate *significantly* more optimal code than C++? Probably not, but if you do care about every cycle, then program in straight C. Additionally, when you write in straight C, you can visualize exactly what CPU opcodes are going to be generated by the compiler, so you can often make your own manual optimizations to the code just by moving some lines around—things that the compiler's optimizer might not catch. When you write complex code in C++, you tend to lose the ability to visualize what opcodes are going to be generated, and you lose some flexibility when manually optimizing things. Like I said, this is something of a religious issue, so the C++ diehards out there might think I'm a heretic; however, if you're not tied down to any particular programming language, then stick with good old-fashioned C just to be safe. If you're a loyal follower of C++, then by all means use it. As long as you're not using Objective-C for anything performance related, you're doing the right thing.

Cocoa vs. Core Foundation

If you're new to the Mac and the iPhone, then you might only be aware of the Cocoa APIs for accessing the iPhone OS. The only way to access the Cocoa APIs is with Objective-C, but if you want to avoid as much of that as possible, then you should know about Core Foundation. Core Foundation is the C equivalent of Cocoa. For example, there are CFStrings, which are exactly the same thing as NSStrings except that you access the APIs with C function calls instead of Objective-C method calls. Even the data types that NSString and CFStringRef represent are the same, so you can use these chunks of data interchangeably with the Cocoa or Core Foundation APIs. The same goes for CFData/NSData, CFURL/NSURL, CFDictionary/NSDictionary, and many others.

I try to use the Core Foundation calls as often as possible to avoid Objective-C, but all the source files in my projects are still .m files. That way, I can always use Cocoa and Objective-C if I absolutely must, even though everything else in that source file is straight C.

Compiler Optimizations

You can improve your game's performance in many other ways simply by changing some compiler settings or by making some minor alterations to your code. Most of these tweaks are easy to do, and the results can be significant.

The Thumb Instruction Set

Perhaps the most important single compiler setting you can change to get an instant, free performance boost is the Compile for Thumb setting. By default, your Xcode project will have this option turned on, but if your game is floating-point intensive, as most games are, then you'll want this option turned off (see Figure 4-3).

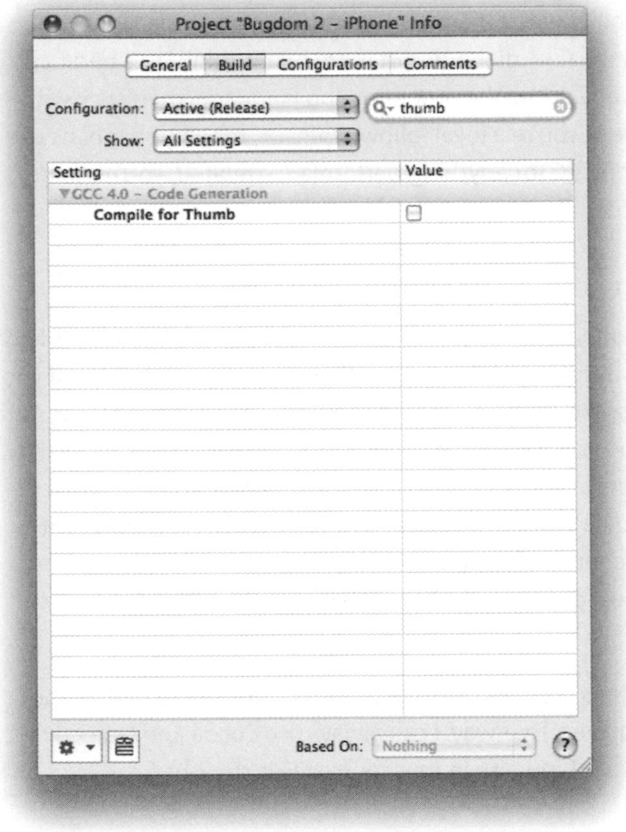

Figure 4-3. *Games that are floating-point intensive should always have Compile for Thumb turned off.*

The ARM processor in the iPhone essentially has two instruction sets: the regular 32-bit instruction set and a simpler 16-bit instruction set called Thumb. The Thumb instructions will execute faster because they are denser, meaning the compiler can cram twice as many instructions into the same amount of memory. As your code executes, millions of instructions are fetched from memory every second, and fetching them takes time. If you can cut the number of fetches in half, then you get a performance improvement. Sounds great, right? Sorry, not for most games, because the Thumb instruction set is only a benefit for integer operations, not floating-point operations. Performing floating-point instructions with

Thumb is extremely expensive, so having Compile for Thumb turned on in a piece of code that's floating-point intensive will crush your performance.

When I learned about this during the development of Enigmo, I immediately turned the Compile for Thumb option off to see what would happen. I got an instant 20 percent speedup in the game's frame rate. Enigmo is especially floating-point intensive because of the complex collision detection, so that game really benefited from this simple action.

You can turn Thumb on or off for different source files. So, if you have a source file that's mostly just integer operations or code that isn't performance oriented (like, say, your file I/O code), then you can tell Xcode to compile that source file for Thumb to reduce the amount of RAM that the code will consume. To turn on the Thumb option for specific source files, just select the file in Xcode, do a Get Info on it, and then select the Build tab in the Info dia-log boxes. Here you can add compiler flags for the file, and the flag for turning on Thumb is -mthumb (see Figure 4-4).

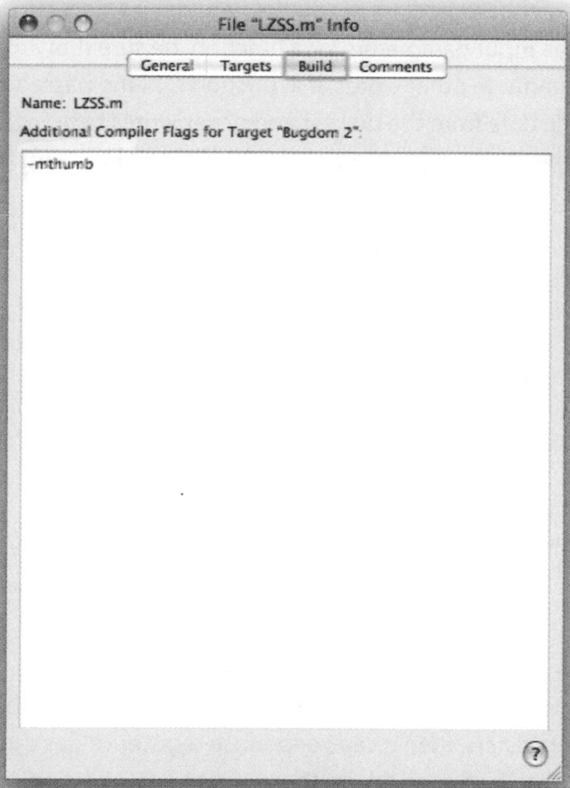

Figure 4-4. *Turning Thumb on per source file with the –mthumb compiler flag*

Compiler Optimization Level

If you were developing a game for the Mac or the PC, you would almost certainly choose the `Fastest [-03]` optimization level when compiling your code for distribution. But on the iPhone, it isn't quite that simple of a decision because of the memory constraints; therefore, you might want to choose the `Fastest, Smallest [-0s]` optimization level because this will generate code that uses less memory. Not only does that shrink your code size down and leave more RAM for your game to use, but once again, it means that the processor will not have to touch as much memory while the code executes, and that can speed things up.

The choice between –03 and –0s is unlikely to have any perceptible effect on performance, but if you know that your app is very tight on RAM, then use the –0s setting to free up some space. If RAM is not a problem in your app, then it's really a subjective call on whether you should use –03 or –0s. Try it both ways, and see whether it makes any detectable difference.

Optimizing Function Calls

Here's a little trick that is really good practice regardless of whether you get any real performance boost from it. When defining the input parameters for a function, be sure that any read-only pointers are marked as constants. In other words, if a function is being passed a pointer but that function only reads the data from the pointer and never writes to it, then let the compiler know so it can make further optimizations. For example, here's a function that would be called repeatedly in any 3D game:

```
void NormalizeVector(const Vector3D *inVec, Vector3D *result)
{
    float length = sqrt((inVec->x * inVec->x) +
                        (inVec->y * inVec->y) +
                        (inVec->z * inVec->z));

    float oneOverLength = 1.0f/length;

    result->x = inVec->x * oneOverLength;
    result->y = inVec->y * oneOverLength;
    result->z = inVec->z * oneOverLength;
}
```

This function never modifies the values pointed to by inVec, so we define it as const, thereby making it read-only. Doing this lets functions calling NormalizeVector know that if inVec has already been loaded into registers, then it can keep those register values upon return from NormalizeVector rather than having to reload them. If we had not defined inVec as const, then the calling code would have to assume that inVec may have been modified, so it would have to reload the values the next time they were needed. Consider this very simplistic example:

```
n = theVector.x * PI;
...
NormalizeVector(&theVector, &normalizedVector);
...
q = theVector.x / EPSILON;
```

In this code snippet, the value `theVector.x` will be loaded into a register to compute the value n. Later, `theVector.x` is used for another calculation, and the most optimal outcome is that `theVector.x` is still in that register. By defining `inVec` as a `const`, the compiler knows that the register containing `theVector.x` is still valid after `NormalizeVector` has been called because `NormalizeVector` could not have changed the value in `theVector.x`.

Audio Optimizations

The iPhone and the iPod touch are audio devices, and as such, you'd think that they have a lot of awesome audio hardware in them to make audio playback inexpensive, but this is not the case. The iPhone actually has very limited audio hardware, and most of the audio processing is actually done in software. As a result, audio can be very expensive in an iPhone game, but there are ways to minimize the impact.

The original Mac version of Enigmo had music as well as sound effects, but the CPU load is so high in the iPhone version that we could not afford to play any music, and even the sound effects take their toll on the frame rate. I nearly had a heart attack when I first got the audio in Enigmo working because it caused more than a 20 percent reduction in frame rate. Even after taking out the music, the sound effects alone were hitting us with about a 5 percent reduction. Some of my games have warnings in the Settings dialog boxes, letting the user know that the game will run smoother if the user turns off the music.

I don't want to bore you with all the details about how the audio channels work on the iPhone. Instead, I want to focus on the proper ways to format your audio to get the maximum possible performance from the system, so let's start with music.

Streaming Music Playback

Streaming music is typically played by using the Audio Queue API. This API can play only a single track of compressed audio at a time, so don't try to cross-fade two songs, because it won't let you. There is very little that you can do to improve performance of an audio queue in your code. Instead, the optimizations for this are centered around the format of the audio file itself. You should not stream MP3 files because these are not in an optimal format for the iPhone to work with. The preferred format is the MPEG-4 format, and the most reliable way to generate this is with QuickTime Player. All you have to do is load your source audio file into QuickTime Player and then select **Export from the File** menu. Select **Movie to MPEG-4** from the **Export** pop-up menu, and click the Options button to set the quality parameters for the song (see Figure 4-5).

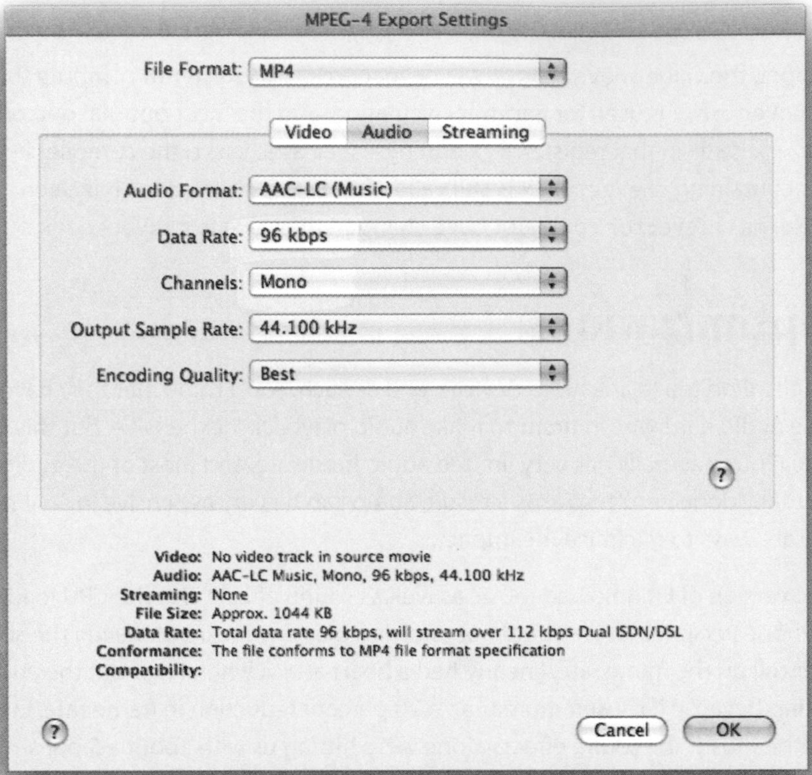

Figure 4-5. *Set your streaming music to these settings for optimal performance.*

Not all MPEG-4 files are created equal, however. You may want your music to sound the best it can by setting the export settings to Stereo with a high bit rate. Yes, that will make the music sound great if the user is wearing earphones, but it will be at a high cost to performance. My game Cro-Mag Rally plays stereo, 128 Kbps music, and the cost of playing it is around 10 percent, but I figured the game could handle that speed hit, so I kept it at that high quality. Some of my larger games, such as Nanosaur 2 and Bugdom 2, really pushed the CPU to its limits, so 10 percent was just too much, and therefore I had to cut the quality down.

To get back some of the CPU time lost to processing the high-quality music files, you simply need to reduce the data size of the MPEG-4 file. Most people will play the game on their iPhone using the built-in speakers, so there's no point in having the song be stereo. That just creates twice as much work for the sound system to do. High bit rates create more data to be loaded and processed, so reducing the bit rate will significantly reduce the CPU and memory pipeline demands on the system. For most of my newer games, I've chosen to reduce the MPEG-4 files to mono, 96 Kbps. It is almost impossible to tell any quality difference on the iPhone's internal speaker, yet this change reduces the song playback hit from 10 percent to a much more reasonable 2 to 3 percent.

Sound Effects with OpenAL

There are many ways to play sound effects on the iPhone, but for games you should be using OpenAL only. OpenAL provides the most optimized method for playing multiple channels of sound effects, and it is an efficient cross-platform API that is available on many platforms.

In OpenAL a sound effect is stored in a buffer and then played when needed. The format of the sound data in this buffer is critical because if you have 30 sound effects all going off simultaneously, then you don't want the CPU to have to do any extra work converting the hundreds of thousands of samples every second from the buffer's format to Core Audio's native format. Therefore, all sound effects should be identically formatted and in Core Audio File Format (CAFF) format. You should never have some of your sounds be 22 kHz and some 44.1 kHz. They must all be the exact same frequency, bit depth, and format, and they must be mono. Even having just one oddball effect can destroy the audio pipeline and cause serious performance issues.

The most optimal format for your CAFF files is 16-bit at 44.1 kHz since this is the native format for the device. However, these sound files can use up a lot of precious RAM very quickly, so that format may not be practical in many games. For example, Nanosaur 2 (Figure 4-6) is incredibly tight on RAM, and the game has a lot of sound effects, so there was no way I was going to get the game to work if my effects were all 16/44.1. They had to be smaller than that.

Figure 4-6. *Nanosaur 2 has way too many sound effects for them to fit at 16-bit/44.1 kHz.*

It ends up that the second most optimal format is 16-bit/22.050 kHz. What Core Audio does in this case is mix all of your effects together into a single 16/22 kHz buffer and then make a single pass to convert the data to the device's native 16/44.1 format. Even though this requires a little extra CPU processing, that lost CPU time is mostly made up by the fact that the CPU had to process only half as much source audio when it mixed the tracks in the first place. So, there really is no perceptible performance difference between 16/44.1 and 16/22. There will be a slight audio quality difference since even with the iPhone's speakers you can tell the difference between 44.1 kHz and 22 kHz, but when playing a game with explosions and gunfire going off all around you, nobody is going to notice. It is generally worth the quality loss to save memory space with the smaller files.

Luckily, Apple has provided a command-line tool, afconvert, for converting just about any audio file into a CAFF file. This tool is installed with the iPhone SDK, and to access it you run the Terminal app where you execute it the old-fashioned way: from the command line. To generate a 16-bit/44.1 kHz CAFF file, enter the following:

```
afconvert -f caff -d LEI16 {INPUT PATH} {OUTPUT PATH }
```

Or, if you want to create a 16-bit/22 kHz file, then enter the following:

```
afconvert -f caff -d LEI16@22050 {INPUT PATH } {OUTPUT PATH }
```

OpenGL Optimizations

If your game is a performance-oriented game, then you should be using OpenGL for all of your graphics needs because it gives you hardware-accelerated drawing of sprites and 3D geometry. There are many ways to get the most performance out of OpenGL, and once again, most of them are going to deal with memory and bandwidth. The variety of OpenGL on the iPhone is called OpenGL ES 1.1, and it is basically a stripped-down, streamlined version of OpenGL that is built for compactness and speed. For example, in OpenGL ES you cannot pass 4-byte integers in your triangle arrays. Instead, you are limited to 2-byte shorts, because it compacts the data, and therefore it is faster to process. Besides, the iPhone probably couldn't handle a single vertex array with more than 65,535 triangles in the first place.

Construct an Efficient OpenGL Draw Context

You can use many combinations of settings to create an OpenGL context, but some will perform better than others. First up is the issue of your render buffer's bit depth, because regardless of how much RAM is free on your iPhone, you have only 24MB of memory available for both textures and render buffers (also known as *surfaces* in OpenGL ES). This 24MB is not dedicated VRAM, but rather it is just regular RAM, so the more memory your textures and buffers use, the less memory there will be for your app. Therefore, you should be allocating a 16-bit buffer instead of one that is 32-bit. There are cases where you might see some color banding with a 16-bit buffer, but those instances are rare. Also worth noting is that if your game is processing a lot of pixel data, then having a 32-bit buffer can actually overload the system, and you'll occasionally see a black frame. In simplistic terms, this happens because the memory pipeline gets too full and the GPU can't keep up, but 16-bit buffers have half the data, so the pipeline doesn't get overloaded.

To set up a 16-bit render buffer, you use the kEAGLColorFormatRGB565 value in your drawableProperties dictionary. You should also be sure to set the eaglLayer to opaque and set kEAGLDrawablePropertyRetainedBacking to FALSE. The retained backing mode would tell OpenGL to keep a copy of the render buffer around in case you need to read something from it, but you should never do this in a performance-oriented game, so set it to FALSE to prevent an extra buffer from being created and copied:

```
CAEAGLLayer     *eaglLayer = (CAEAGLLayer*)[self layer];

eaglLayer.opaque = YES;
eaglLayer.drawableProperties = [NSDictionary dictionaryWithObjectsAndKeys:
                                [NSNumber numberWithBool:FALSE],
                                kEAGLDrawablePropertyRetainedBacking,
                                kEAGLColorFormatRGB565,
                                kEAGLDrawablePropertyColorFormat, nil];
```

If you are making a 3D game, then you will also need to allocate a z-buffer (depth buffer), but if you are developing a 2D sprite-based game, then odds are you don't need one, so you should not allocate one. An unnecessary z-buffer only uses up more RAM and potentially more pipeline bandwidth.

For the best performance, your OpenGL context should be full-screen, 320×480, and have no other views or windows overlaying it. That means no iPhone status bar and no UIViews or controls of any sort. You should never apply any Core Animation transforms to your CAEAGLLayer object either. Doing that will cause your OpenGL view to become a nested subview of the animation layer, which means your game's frame rate will come to a screeching halt.

Some developers get confused about how to make their game play in landscape orientation without using an animation transform to rotate the view. The solution to this problem is incredibly easy—just rotate the OpenGL projection matrix by 90 degrees:

```
glMatrixMode(GL_PROJECTION);
glLoadIdentity();
glRotatef(-90, 0,0,1);                  // rotate for landscape orientation
```

That's all you need to do to tell OpenGL to draw the scene in landscape mode. However, as far as the iPhone is concerned, you're still in portrait mode, so you will need to remember to swap any x/y values that the iPhone gives you such as touch coordinates and accelerometer vectors.

Avoid State Changes

OpenGL is a giant state machine. You turn things on and off and set states to one thing or another such as glEnable(GL_BLEND), glDisable(GL_BLEND), glColor4f(1,1,1,1), and so on. These calls are all state changes, and state changes are expensive because they can stall the pipeline even if you're only setting a redundant state. In other words, if you already have fog turned on via glEnable(GL_FOG) and then you enable it again with another call to glEnable(GL_FOG), this will cause a state change even though fog was already enabled. To avoid redundant or unnecessary state changes, you need to cache the state values yourself and update the state only if the state has actually changed. You will want to replace all the OpenGL calls that cause a state change with calls to your own state change functions that perform these state tests. Here is an example of how you might want to handle state changes for GL_TEXTURE_2D:

```
Boolean    gMyState_Texture2D = false;  // init to the OpenGL default
                                         // state

void MyEnable_Texture2D(void)
{
        /* only set state if texture currently is NOT enabled */

    if (!gMyState_Texture2D)
    {
        glEnable(GL_TEXTURE_2D);   // change the state
        gMyState_Texture2D = true; // cache the current state so we
                                   // don't do this again if not needed
    }
}
void MyDisable_Texture2D(void)
{
        /* only set state if texture currently IS enabled */

    if (gMyState_Texture2D)
    {
        glDisable(GL_TEXTURE_2D);   // change the state
        gMyState_Texture2D = false; // cache the state
    }
}
```

These two functions should be the only place in all your code that you ever see glEnable(GL_TEXTURE_2D) or glDisable(GL_TEXTURE_2D). Whenever you need to set the texture state elsewhere, you will instead call MyEnable_Texture2D or MyDisable_Texture2D. You may even want to make these macros instead of functions to eliminate the cost of the function branching. You should do this for every state change in your code, even for color changes:

```
GLfloat     gMyState_CurrentColor[4];    // rgba color

Void MyColor4f(GLfloat r, GLfloat g, GLfloat b, GLfloat, a)
{
    if ((r != gMyState_CurrentColor[0]) ||  // did the color change?
        (g != gMyState_CurrentColor[1]) ||
        (b != gMyState_CurrentColor[2]) ||
        (a != gMyState_CurrentColor[3]))
    {
        glColor4f(r, g, b, a);                 // set new color

            // cache the color so we don't do this again if not needed

        gMyState_CurrentColor[0] = r;
        gMyState_CurrentColor[1] = g;
        gMyState_CurrentColor[2] = b;
        gMyState_CurrentColor[3] = a;
    }
}
```

Similarly, you should be careful about calling glGetError because that too can cause a pipeline stall and affect your performance. Build your project such that calls to glGetError get issued only in debug builds, but for optimized builds you should take them out to get the maximum performance.

When rendering a scene, do your best to draw all state-similar objects at the same time to avoid state changes. If you have enemies in your game that all use the same texture, then try to draw all of them one after the other so that the texture state will not need to be changed. Or, if you have lots of objects that share a particular lighting scheme, then draw those back-to-back as well.

Reducing Texture Sizes

All of the Mac games that I have ported over to the iPhone (Enigmo, Cro-Mag Rally, Nano-saur 2, Bugdom 2, and Billy Frontier) have one thing in common: none of them would run on the iPhone without serious texture size reduction. All of the sprites and 3D model textures got shrunken down to a fraction of their original size. On the Mac, these textures needed to be high resolution because they were being displayed on large monitors with lots of resolution. Even things like letters for the game fonts needed to be 64×64 on the Mac, but the iPhone's small, high-resolution screen makes it possible to get away with much less.

Almost every texture in those games was cut in half, and this actually cut the memory usage to one fourth. So, 256×256 textures got cut to 128×128, 64×64's were cut to 32×32, and in many cases we were able to reduce textures to a quarter of their original dimensions without any noticeable quality difference when viewed in the game on the iPhone (see Figure 4-7). In cases where the texture doesn't need an alpha channel, you can often get away with reducing the texture to 16-bit instead of 32-bit. That cuts the memory usage in half. This massive effort to reduce texture sizes is the primary reason why the iPhone version of Bugdom 2 is only 86MB, whereas the Mac version is 187MB.

Figure 4-7. On the left is a sky texture from Nanosaur 2 for the Mac, and on the right is the same texture for the iPhone.

The reduction in texture size not only saves space, but it will also improve the performance of your game. In Cro-Mag Rally, the frame rate improved about 10 percent after I reduced in size a number of the key textures that were being used repeatedly. The fewer pixels the GPU has to deal with, the faster things go. I keep saying it over and over, but touching memory is bad, so always do your best to limit the number of bytes that get touched.

Using Compressed Textures

In addition to simply shrinking your textures down, the iPhone also supports PowerVR Texture Compression (PVRTC). PVRTC textures are lossy, compressed textures that give you an 8:1 or 16:1 compression ratio depending on which format you choose—4-bit or 2-bit, respectively— but it works only on square, power-of-two textures, not rectangular or non-power-of-two textures. This huge reduction can obviously have a beneficial impact on your memory usage and performance, and most of the time it is hard to tell the difference when using the 4-bit compression. The 2-bit compression often results in poor-quality textures, but not always, so it is worth experimenting to see what works best for each texture in your game.

The iPhone OS does not provide any built-in way to generate PVRTC textures on the fly. Instead, you need to precompress them on the Mac using another great command-line tool that Apple provides called `texturetool`. To run `texturetool`, you launch the Console application and then enter the `texturetool` command that is located at `/Developer/Platforms/iPhoneOS.platform/Developer/usr/bin/texturetool`. You can even output a preview image to see what the compressed texture will look like when it is rendered in OpenGL. So, to see how this is done, let's take a texture and compress it using the 4-bit format. We start with the original texture shown in Figure 4-8.

Then we compress it with this command:

```
bin user$ texturetool -e PVRTC --channel-weighting-linear
--bits-per-pixel-4 -o Output.pvrtc -p Preview.tif Source.tiff
```

In this command string we are telling `texturetool` to output a PVRTC file using linear weighting and 4-bits per pixel. Here, the output file that our game would use is called `Output.pvrtc`, the preview file is `Preview.tif`, and the source image that we're compressing is `Source.tiff`. The source files can be just about any image format that the Mac knows about, but you should probably stick with PNG, TIFF, or JPEG. The resulting compressed image looks like Figure 4-9.

It is virtually impossible to tell the difference between the original and the compressed texture. A trained eye can tell when looking closely at the files, but in a game they would appear identical.

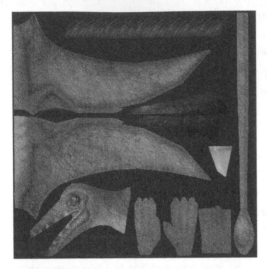

Figure 4-8. *An uncompressed texture from Nanosaur 2*

Figure 4-9. *The compressed texture is almost identical to the original—but at one-eighth the size.*

Loading this texture into OpenGL is very similar to loading a regular uncompressed texture, but instead of calling glTexImage2D, call glCompessedTexImage2D. Assuming you've already loaded the PVRTC texture into memory and the pointer data points to it, then this is how you would load it into OpenGL:

```
GLenum     format = GL_COMPRESSED_RGBA_PVRTC_4BPPV1_IMG; // 4-bit
GLsizei    widthAndHeight = 128;            // 128x128 square texture
Glsizei    sizeOfData     = 8192;           // size of the PVRTC data
GLuint     textureName;

glGenTextures(1, &textureName);             // generate a new texture
glBindTexture(GL_TEXTURE_2D, textureName); // make it the current
                                            // texture

        /* load the PVRTC data into the texture */

glCompressedTexImage2D(GL_TEXTURE_2D,
                  0,
                  format,
                  widthAndHeight, widthAndHeight,
                  0, sizeOfData, data);
```

Geometry Data Reduction

One of the first things that we noticed when we got our games running on the iPhone was how good they looked on the device. The iPhone's small, high-resolution screen makes old, low-resolution polygon models and textures look pretty darn nice. This visual effect allowed the artists to do some pretty severe polygon reduction and even entire object reduction in the scenes. For example, in Nanosaur 2, the terrain is so densely populated with trees that on the tiny iPhone screen most of that detail was simply lost, so we actually removed more than 50 percent of the trees, bushes, rocks, and other items from the levels, yet it is hard to tell any difference, and the game still looks amazing. Eliminating all of that unnecessary geometry is what allowed a game that originally needed a 700 MHz G4 iMac to run on an iPhone with far less horsepower.

Obviously, just cutting back on the detail of your 3D models and the quantity of them will make the largest difference in performance, but there are other things that you should be doing to speed things up, and guess what . . . it has to do with memory again. Every time you submit a piece of geometry for drawing, the triangles indices, vertex and UV coordinates, normals, and so on, all get sent through the pipeline to the GPU for processing. The more data you send, the longer it will take. So, you want to compact your vertex arrays as much as possible to get the best possible performance.

OpenGL ES was designed for mobile platforms, so it forces you to do some data reduction whether you want to or not. In OpenGL ES, the data type GL_INT isn't even defined in the gl.h header file because this version of OpenGL does not let you pass integers as triangle array indices. The assumption here is that you'll never have a single piece of geometry with more than 65,535 vertices in it (a very reasonable assumption to make on any mobile device), so there's no reason to use 4-byte integers for the triangle indices. Passing 2-byte GL_UNSIGNED_SHORT indices uses only half as much memory and needs half as much pipeline bandwidth to process:

```
glDrawElements(GL_TRIANGLES, numTriangles*3,GL_UNSIGNED_
SHORT,&triangleData);
```

You can still send 32-bit float values in other vertex arrays (colors, UVs, and normals), but very often you can get away with using bytes instead, which will reduce the data size by 75 percent. Vertex color arrays are a good use of this because there's really no need to represent a vertex color component with an expensive floating-point value. You can't visually tell the difference between a floating-point RGBA color and a byte-based RGBA color:

```
glColorPointer(4, GL_UNSIGNED_BYTE, 0, colorArray);
```

If you're drawing sprites, then odds are your UV values are all 0 or 1, so there's no need to represent those values as floating point either. You can represent them as bytes:

```
glTexCoordPointer(2, GL_UNSIGNED_BYTE, 0, uvArray);
```

Limit the Quantity of Draw Calls

There is a significant amount of overhead in every call you make to `glDrawElements`, so you always want to draw as much geometry as possible in each call. In sprite-based games, you'll be drawing lots of four-vertex polygons, which is often unavoidable, but there are cases where with a little effort you can group multiple sprites into a single draw command. One example of this is the particle effect engine that I use in most of my games. Antimatter is a game that I wrote that has thousands of particle sprites flying around the screen, and if each one of those particles were drawn as an individual quad, the game would probably run at one frame per second. So, what I do in my code is queue up all the individual sprites and form large vertex arrays for them that get submitted as one piece of geometry. If I have 600 red sparks on the screen, I build one vertex array with 1,200 triangles in it and submit it once. This is very efficient (see Figure 4-10).

You can even optimize things like the sprites in your status bar by using what's called a **texture atlas** (see Figure 4-11). A texture atlas is a single texture that contains image data for multiple objects. If a texture can be shared among different sprites in a scene, then those sprites can be merged into a single piece of geometry that gets submitted just once to OpenGL instead of once for each sprite.

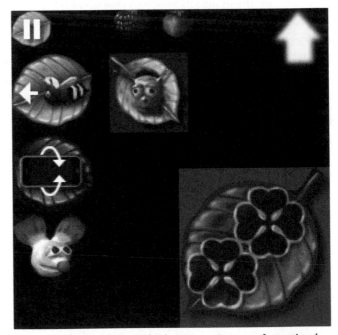

Figure 4-10. *The game Antimatter groups each particle sprite into large vertex array meshes for optimal performance.*

Figure 4-11. *Combine multiple textures into one for optimal performance.*

Performance Tools

Apple provides two very useful tools for analyzing the performance of iPhone applications: Instruments and Shark. The Instruments tool is useful for tracking your memory usage and watching other system allocations such as Objective-C objects or OpenGL resources. Shark, on the other hand, is used to find performance bottlenecks in your code and to see where the CPU is spending most of its time all the way down to the opcode level.

Using Instruments

Instruments can track many different things going on in your app, and I find tracking memory usage most useful. With Instruments you can see a real-time display of the free and used memory, so it helps you figure out not only how tight you are on RAM but also where the trouble spots occur in the game.

To use Instruments, you can start it directly from Xcode with the **Start With Performance Tool** item in the **Run** menu, but I recommend that you do it manually by launching Instruments from the Developer/Applications folder because this gives you a better chance to configure it before sampling data. When Instruments launches, it will ask you to select a template, so select Blank. Now, to set it up for tracking memory usage, look in the Library window, locate the Memory Monitor instrument (Figure 4-12), and drag it into the main Instruments window.

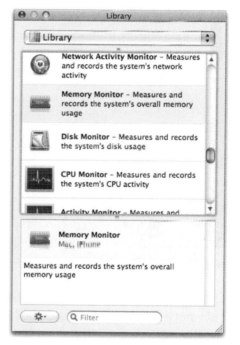

Figure 4-12. *You can select from dozens of different instruments to monitor.*

Next, you need to tell Instruments which app to process, which you do in the **Default Target** pop-up menu. You can tell it either to attach to an existing process (if your game is already running) or to launch one of the apps that is installed on the device (see Figure 4-13).

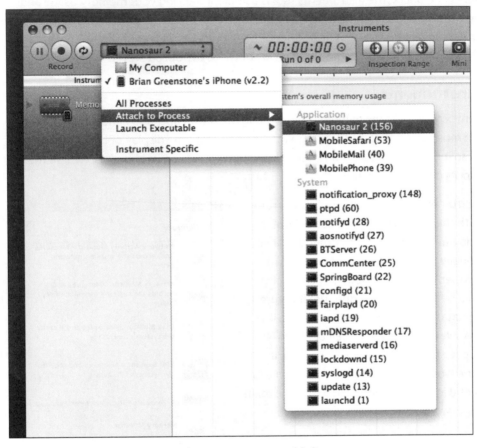

Figure 4-13. *Select your app from the process or executable list.*

Click the Record button to start sampling data. You'll see a graph indicating memory usage, but what is more useful is to click the Diagram View button at the bottom of the window and then click the # column to have it display the most recent samples at the top of the list. This way, you can easily see the exact state of your memory usage and how it is changing (Figure 4-14).

The most important column here is the Physical Memory Free column because this tells you exactly how much RAM is free on the device. As a general rule, anything over 4MB is safe, anything between 2MB and 4MB is getting dangerous, and anything less than 2MB is critically low. The iPhone OS typically starts issuing the applicationDidReceiveMemoryWarning notifications once you reach about 1.5MB. If you get below 1MB, your app is likely to crash at any moment.

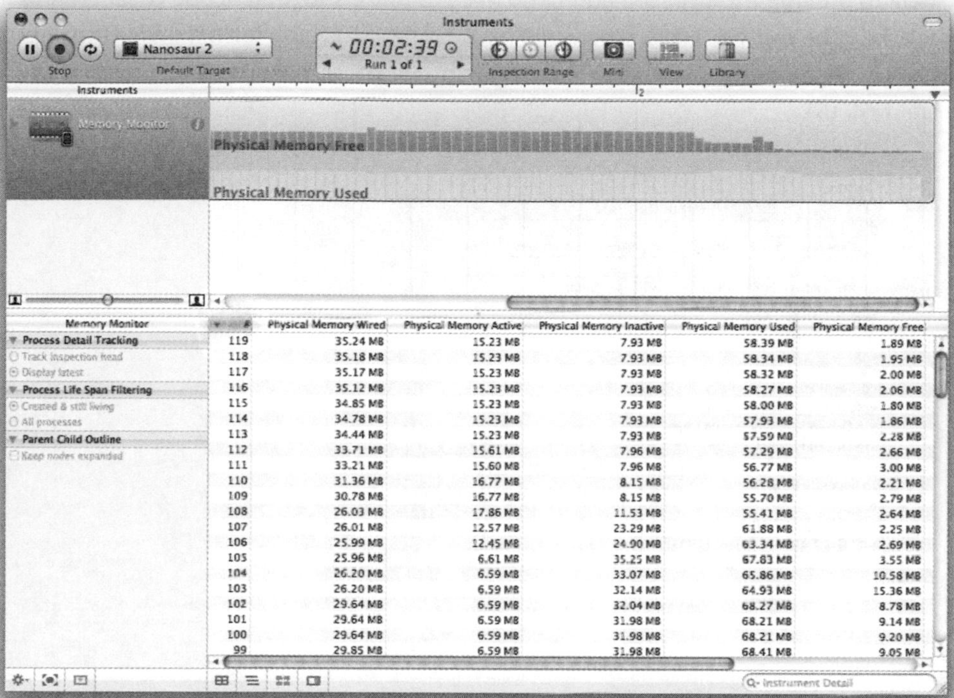

Figure 4-14. *You can monitor the real-time memory usage.*

You can also use this to quickly detect large memory leaks. To do this, see how much memory is free on your game's menu screen, observe how low it gets when you play a level, and then end the game and return to the menu screen. If you freed up all of the level's data, then the Physical Memory Free value should return to its initial value, but if you see a 10MB discrepancy, then it's safe to say you're leaking something somewhere.

Using Shark

Most experienced programmers have enough skill to know what parts of their code are causing bottlenecks, but it is still a good idea to run your code through Shark every now and then as a sanity check just to see whether any of your critical loops can be improved. The Shark application is located in the Developer/Applications/Performance Tools folder.

NOTE

Shark is a very finicky program when it comes to connecting to the iPhone. You should always unplug and reboot your iPhone before attempting to use it with Shark.

For Shark to provide useful information, you need to make sure that Xcode is generating symbols for your app. Normally, you would have symbol stripping turned on for the deployment build of your game, but to use Shark properly, you need to turn all symbol stripping off (see Figure 4-15).

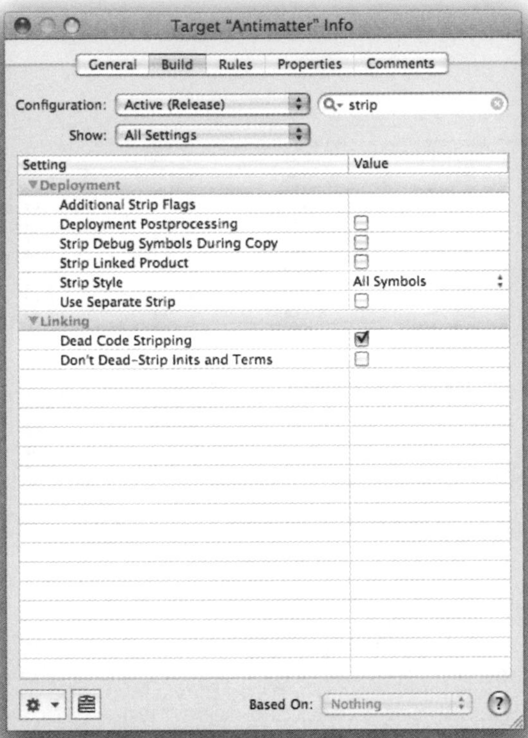

Figure 4-15. *Be sure symbol stripping is turned off.*

When you launch Shark, you will see a window that lists all connected iPhones and iPod touches (see Figure 4-16), but if not, then make sure you have selected **Network/iPhone Profiling** in the **Sampling** menu. When your device appears in the list, click the Use check box to activate the device for sampling. You will sometimes have to wait several seconds after clicking the check box before anything happens.

NOTE

On occasion, Shark will give you the timeout error "The computer you selected has not responded to network traffic," and it is very hard to make this go away. Rebooting the Mac and/or iPhone may or may not help. The only known reliable cure is to simply wait a few hours and try again.

Now launch your game on the iPhone, and once it is running, select it in Shark's Target pop-up menu. This way, Shark will collect sample data only for your app and nothing else.

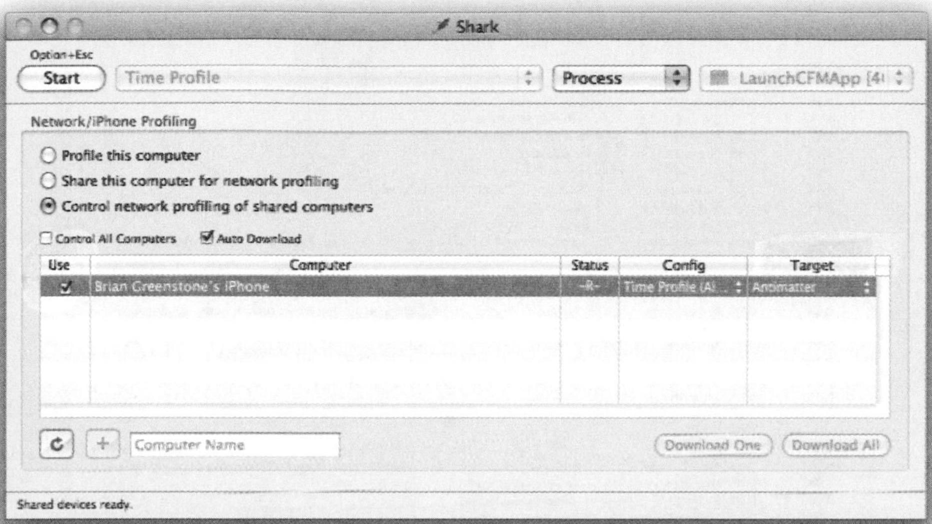

Figure 4-16. *Select the Use box, and then select your target.*

Before starting the sampling, it is a good idea to play the game to the point that you are interested in profiling. In other words, skip over any title sequences, menu screens, and such, and get into the game where you really care about performance. Once the game is where you want it to be, click the Start button in Shark to begin collecting performance data. During this time, your app may stutter quite a bit, but that's normal. Let this run for as long as you can because the more samples that are collected, the more accurate the performance analysis will be.

Once you are satisfied that you have collected enough data, then click the Stop button and be prepared to wait. Shark will say, "Shared devices processing samples." Do not quit your app during this. Doing so will usually cause Shark to lock up, so just be patient and wait for the message to change to "Analyzing samples."

NOTE

If the "Shared devices processing samples" message doesn't go away after a minute, then Shark has probably locked up again, so you'll need to quit and try again.

Upon completion of the analyzing process, you will be presented with a Time Profile window (see Figure 4-17).

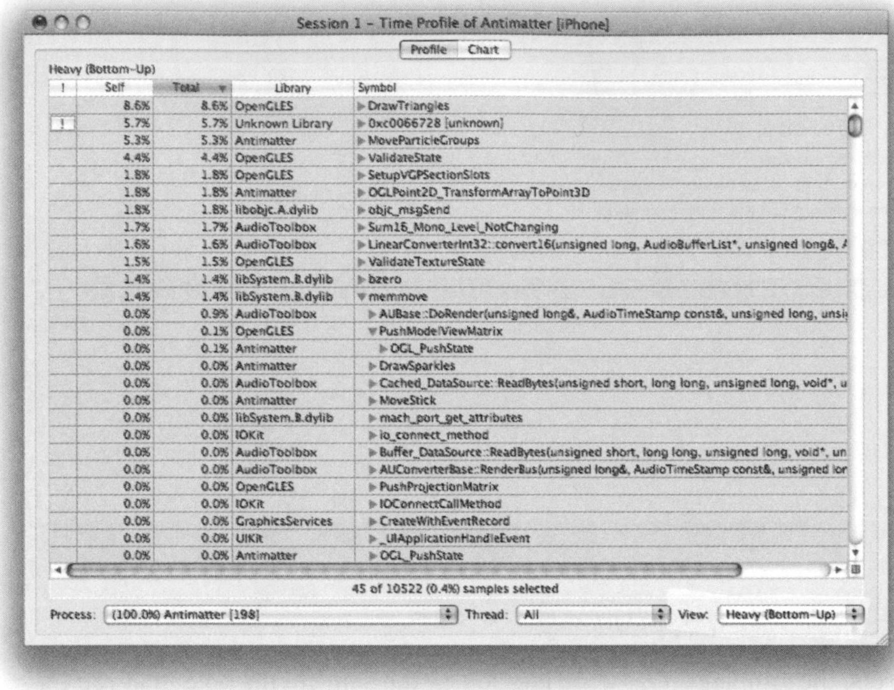

Figure 4-17. *The Time Profile window generated by Shark*

In the **View** pop-up menu at the bottom of the Time Profile window, select **Heavy (Bottom-Up)** to have it sort the data with the most CPU-intensive functions at the top. In this case, I've profiled my game Antimatter, and you can see that the single most expensive function is DrawTriangles, which is actually a function inside the OpenGL ES library, as noted in the Library column. The first function that appears for Antimatter itself is one called MoveParticleGroups, so this tells me that MoveParticleGroups is the single most expensive function in my code, and it is using 5.3 percent of the CPU. This makes sense because Antimatter is basically a particle effects game, and that's most of what's going on.

Take a closer look at any function by double-clicking it in the Time Profile window. This is where Shark's real magic comes in because here you can view your original code alongside the actual ARM assembly instructions that were generated by the compiler. It displays a per-line breakdown of how much time was spent on each instruction (Figure 4-18).

Here you can select a line of source code on the left, and Shark will show the matching assembly on the right. You should be careful about paying too much attention to the per-opcode time percentages because these may vary wildly each time you profile the application. However, the longer you let Shark capture sample data, the more accurate these values will be.

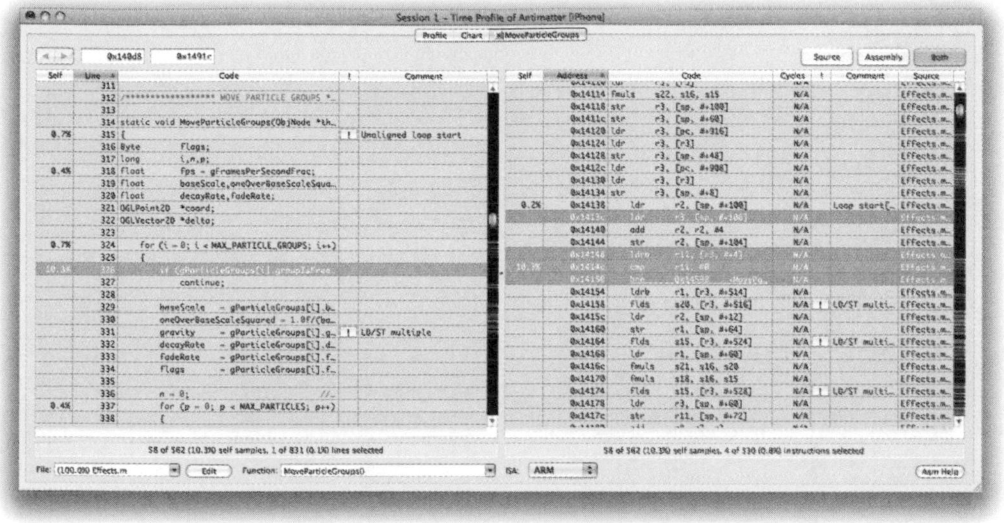

Figure 4-18. *Shark's analysis of the MoveParticleGroups function*

At this point, you really need to rely on your programming skills to determine where you can improve performance, and being able to read the assembly code will help you a lot. You really don't need to be an ARM assembly master because the ARM opcodes look pretty much like opcodes in any other architecture, so it's very easy to read. Just look for lines of source code that seem to be generating lots of load and store commands, and then think about whether there is any way that you could rewrite the function so that it won't need to do so many. Also, keep an eye out for unnecessary branches since branching is expensive and can stall the execution pipeline.

Summary

What you have learned in this chapter will help you squeeze out a few more frames per second in your game. A faster, smoother game is always a better experience for the player, so spend the time trying to eliminate every cycle of CPU power that you can. Very often you will spend a lot of time working on an optimization that yields no noticeable results, but it is the sum of all your optimizations that will make a difference.

There are additional resources on Apple's iPhone Developer web site about optimization strategies, and one of the most useful things you can do for yourself is to attend Apple's annual Worldwide Developer's Conference. At WWDC you have direct access to Apple engineers who can look at your code, offer suggestions, and work with you on finding ways to speed it up.

Olivier Hennessy and Clayton Kane

Company: PosiMotion LLC

Location: Ormond Beach, Florida

Former Lives As Developers: As a mechanical engineer and industrial designer, I (Olivier) have designed and engineered high-end architectural audio components, as well as iPod and iPhone docking stations. The software platforms I've worked on include SolidWorks, Solid Edge, Photoshop, and several other 2D/3D design software packages.

As a systems engineer, I (Clayton) have researched and developed innovative products in the GPS and pedestrian navigation category for the private sector, as well as the US Department of Defense and Department of Homeland Security.

Lives As iPhone Developers: As iPhone developers, we believe that variety is the spice of life, and our PosiMotion games clearly reflect this. All of our apps are listed at http://www.posimotion.com/index. php?argv=apps.

What's in This Chapter: This chapter covers the steps for building a successful game, from preproduction to implementation. You will read about how important design, execution, and detail are for developing a well-polished iPhone game. You will also get some tips on creating artificial intelligence and using the iPhone's special features to make your games fun to play.

Note: Special thanks to Steven Mattera, Lisa Hoffman, Miklos Kamondi, Patrick Cossette, and Joshua Kitchener.

Key Technologies:

- Accelerometer
- Core Location framework
- Core Animation framework
- Game engines

Chapter 5

Starting with a Game Design Document: A Methodology for Success

*a*t PosiMotion, it has been our mission to develop games that cover a broad spectrum of genres. Our goal is to harness and simultaneously challenge the capabilities of mobile technology. The iPhone is arguably the most revolutionary mobile platform currently available. This is due to the amazing features integrated into one very aesthetically pleasing portable device. The iPhone SDK makes life even better by providing developer-level access to most of the platform's key features via a few lines of code or special frameworks. Our favorites include the accelerometer, multitouch interface, OpenGL ES support, Core Animation framework, and Core Location framework. When we design a game, we leverage as many of these features as possible in order to create the most engaging and satisfying end user experience.

This chapter discusses the preproduction and production phases of the game development process as they are executed at PosiMotion. Preproduction phases include creating the game vision (a.k.a. concept development) and creating the game design document. The production phase is all about turning the vision into reality (a.k.a. the implementation). Of course, testing and deployment are also necessary stages in the game development process, but they are not covered in this chapter.

The Game Vision

Game developers are, in essence, a bridge between the human imagination and the implementation. We accumulate ideas that spring from our imaginations and organize them into a viable interactive medium—the game, which we hope people will want to play.

We call the initial phase of game development the Blue Sky phase. In this phase, there are no limits and no rules; we are free to allow the concept of a game, or the game vision, to take shape. This is the time to let your imagination soar. The Blue Sky phase is the one and only time during the life of your project when you get to let go and be free with your dreams. Indulge yourself.

Focus on the purpose of your game and the targeted end user. Imagine the features and options. Lay out the potential control systems. Interview experts on subjects related to your game, to get ideas on how to enhance the realism of game play. Make a rough sketch of the elements of your game, such as characters, weapons, levels, and so on. Try to breathe life into your design, remembering that there will be a human on the other end of your final product.

Once you have completed the Blue Sky phase, it's time to take the ideal, the dream, the imagined, and introduce it to the sometimes harsh and cruel real world. If what you have put together at this stage has merit and is technically feasible, your concept will survive. Make no mistake about it, the end result will almost never be identical to the original concept. Sometimes, it may be less than what you had imagined, due to the ever-present and never-ceasing forces of time and budget that chip away at the ideal. However, more often than not, your initial concept will metamorphose into a powerful source of inspiration and collaborative effort for all involved in the project.

In the end, it is all about the people who will be using the product. The audience must be captivated, but at the same time, delivered an easy-to-use, well-polished title. The aesthetics of the game are important, but the functionality is equally critical. The app must perform flawlessly, or your judges will call you out. From rough sketch to final product, the end users must always be kept in mind. They are the ones who decide whether your app will fall into obscurity or you actually have a marketable title.

TIP

Chances are if you are a game developer, you are also a big fan of playing video games. This means that you are your best touchstone for judging and learning which aspects of games and applications work well, and which areas have room for improvement. As a game developer, you will never stop learning and growing. Play everything you can get your hands on. Try to analyze all applications and entertainment titles on the market. *The more gaming experience and understanding of the market you have, the better your game will be.*

After you've created the game concept, or the game vision, the next step in the preproduction phase of game development is producing the game design document.

The Game Design Document

The game design document defines the game concept, as well as the functional and technical specifics of the game. This document will become the Holy Grail by which all game production will flow.

At PosiMotion, our game design documents for iPhone-specific games generally have the following structure:

- Title
- Game summary
- Game detail
- Game setting
- Game system/engine
- Game play: controls and user interface
- Level map
- Aesthetic design
- Title and information screens
- Sound effects

Here, we'll give you a brief description of each section to get you started in the right direction. Add to, use, and abuse this as you see fit. At times, it's simply better to start with something than from nothing.

Title

The name of your game goes here. This can be just a working title for now, to be finalized at a later time.

Game Summary

Describe your game in a short paragraph. Imagine that you are creating the paragraph for the App Store description. Write a description that will help to sell your game to the user market.

Game Detail

Here, you should describe the story of the game. From a high-level perspective, define the characters, tasks, and so on that the players will encounter as they progress through the game. Pump this up to three paragraphs.

You may wonder why you should rewrite what you've already briefly conveyed in the game summary paragraph. Keep in mind that you will be working with some people who are not gamers. They may not fully comprehend your ideas for the game without more explanation.

Consider the game detail section as the game idea pitch. You have a willing audience who wants to hear about your game idea. They may be able to help make your idea a reality, but their time is precious and limited. What you write here will make or break your dream.

We all start somewhere, so the current reality may be that your core team is small. But if your dreams are big enough, your team will grow, and so will the number of people supporting the game production. There may be lawyers, accountants, funders, corporate executives, and sales and marketing personnel. These are people who will need only the high-level concept of the game design in order to do their jobs, so this is as far as they will likely need to read into the game design document.

Game Setting

Describe the setting of your game here. This section should include location, type of surroundings, music style, and a few examples of important elements that represent the setting's ambience.

Game System/Engine

As you set about developing your iPhone game, the game system, or game engine, will consume the bulk of your efforts. Go into every detail. Consider sections such as rules, combat systems, scoring, power-ups, firepower, health system, character creation, quests, location descriptions, and so on. Everything you can think of goes in this section of your game design document, and in as much detail as possible.

As different as games may seem from one another, they actually share many attributes, and typically involve functions like moving objects around, raising events, and triggering actions for each raised event. Game engines are designed to handle much of this common functionality. And, unless you are determined to build a game engine for the iPhone from scratch, which can take years to do correctly, you will use a premade game engine for your game development.

Premade game engines already have the basic game play implementation requirements for a broad base of game play genres, Many premade engines specialize in certain genres, such as first-person shooters or racing games.

Almost all game engines include functions to help you work with matrices. A *matrix* is basically an array of numbers that, together, describe an object's position and orientation in space. Once you become comfortable working with matrix functions, you will realize how powerful they are in controlling the objects in your game.

What should you look for when choosing a game engine? Different engines offer different levels of control to the programmer. A simple game engine will be relatively easy to work with, but a complex engine will let you do much more, once you have scaled the high learning curve. You need to decide how much time you are willing to invest, and how much flexibility your game requires.

NOTE

An important consideration when using a game engine is the license. There's no such thing as a free lunch, and someone had to work hard to produce that wonderful function library you get to use. Most often, game engines allow you to purchase a license with which you can distribute copies of your game. Open source game engines often include a license that allows you to distribute unlimited copies of your game for free, but some allow you to sell your game, and require nothing more than mention in the game credits. If legalese isn't your thing, you can get help from people on newsgroups or Yahoo! Answers, who are happy to answer questions.

So what game engines are available now for making great iPhone games? We've listed the major ones here, and there will likely be more by the time you read this.

Torque: This popular 3D engine from GarageGames has been ported to the iPhone. Torque makes it easy to produce first-person-shooter games, although that's certainly not all it can do. Programmers write high-level scripts to define characters and attributes, and the engine takes care of the rendering. Torque is available from `http://www.garagegames.com/`.

cocos2d: This is an iPhone port of a popular 2D game engine. cocos2d includes many functions for impressive screen effects, such as page turning and cinematic wipes. cocos2D is available from `http://cocos2d.org/`.

Unity: This is a full-featured 3D game engine with support for a wide array of features, including physics, terrain, and audio. It also includes a powerful world editor for setting up your scenes. Used for desktop and console games for years, Unity was recently ported to the iPhone. At PosiMotion, we are currently working with the Unity iPhone SDK to develop a martial arts game. This game engine is available from `http://unity3d.com/`.

SIO2 Interactive: This engine is extremely well crafted, with tutorials and an active support forum to match. SIO2 provides a 3D development solution right out of the box. Although the library is new, it already includes some amazing particle effects, physics, support for OpenAL sound, and more. The developer has placed paramount importance on the speed of the rendering engine and strictly controls the code base for quality assurance. SIO2 is available from `http://sio2interactive.com/HOME/HOME.html`.

NOTE

Without question, one of SIO2's biggest attractions is the Blender Exporter. With this tool, you can export a 3D mesh, or even an entire scene, from Blender into an OpenGL ES context. This makes SIO2 an indispensable part of our toolchain. In fact, SIO2 is the only OpenGL ES-compatible model exporter.

Oolong: This is the most complex of the current iPhone development frameworks, and is most suited for software engineers or people with similar experience. Oolong is available from `http://code.google.com/p/oolongengine/`.

Game Play: Controls and User Interface

In this section, elaborate on the mechanics of how the players actually play the game—how they control or interact with the game. Break game play down into subsections that detail the user controls and the user interface elements that relate to user actions.

Working with the iPhone is incredibly exciting for several reasons. Among them is the fact that the touchscreen is a relatively new way of interacting with technology. Up until now, game players expected to use a peripheral controller for console systems or the phone keypad for mobile entertainment.

With the arrival of the iPhone, all the rules can be thrown out the window. This is wonderfully fascinating, because we have the opportunity to create new interface systems, set standards, and make history that other designers will imitate for years to come. And let's not forget the exceedingly cool accelerometer function! This adds an entirely new dimension to game play interface, limited only by our imaginations.

"What about the other buttons on the iPhone?" you ask. Ha!—forget about them. Strike the thought from your mind this instant. This is a big no-no according to the rules put forth by Apple regarding game development for the iPhone.

Level Map

Once you have figured out the game play, you can move on to describing the various levels (or worlds or rooms) that will be incorporated in your game. This is where you provide a map of the physical layout of the game, detailing different levels and how they are ordered or connected.

Storyboarding is an effective way to conceptualize and paint a picture of the game levels, as well as the overall game vision. It is vital that the graphic design and development teams work together to achieve the desired concept. Storyboarding provides a necessary starting point for setting a foundation for what is yet to come. This process begins with the original concept being drafted on paper as simple sketches. As Figure 5-1 illustrates, at PosiMotion, we create hand sketches for our games before jumping on the computer and creating more elaborate digital designs, or mock-ups.

Figure 5-1. *A rough sketch of PosiMotion's soon-to-be-released martial arts game*

TIP

While doing rough sketches on paper, a debit card or credit card makes a good outline for the screen on an iPhone or iPod touch.

Remember to design your game in a way that supports adapting it for more features in later versions. Take your time. Quality in these early stages of development will lead to quality down the line.

After you have drawn your storyboard and settled on a design, the next step is taking those drawings and making the necessary graphics, 3D models, and/or worlds. To do this, you can use your favorite image editing and 3D modeling software. We use Adobe Photoshop and Adobe Illustrator for our image editing, and a mixture of Autodesk 3ds Max and Blender for our 3D modeling.

TIP

Never stop with the first mock-up or design. Make at least three to four designs for your game, and then choose from those designs. Also get end-user opinions. Take your designs outside the office and ask people which they prefer.

Aesthetic Design

Let's face it—the world revolves greatly around appearances. For the same reason Jessica Alba gives guys goose bumps, a game needs to look good to get any attention in this industry. A game with phenomenal play value and no aesthetic design will not do as well as a simple game that is beautiful. It is this beauty that captures your gamers' attention and makes them want to play the game. The aesthetic also supports the replay value of the game. In other words, if they like what they see, they will come back for more.

The theme, colors, and animations are major contributing factors to a successful, well-rounded game. Let's look at each of these:

Theme: To begin the journey into aesthetics, you need to decide on a visual style, along with surrounding and supporting elements. If it's a ninja game, a Japanese dojo setting would make sense, perhaps with samurai swords, throwing stars, and black belts as elements. These elements can be used as selection items in the menu (for example, tap the throwing star icon to start the game) or simply be in the background to support the setting. The setting and surrounding elements immerse the player deeper into the game.

Colors: A color scheme is extremely important to maintain consistency throughout the game. Color schemes can include finishes, such as brushed aluminum or pinewood. Keep the colors continuous and relevant to the theme. A defined color scheme will ensure a consistent identity in the game, which greatly contributes to the gamer's experience.

Animations: To really polish a game, animations are a must. Everything in the game needs to be entertaining from the moment the end user turns on the game, not just during the actually game play. The intro screen, instruction screen, and especially the menus should all breathe elements that support the game play and its aesthetic. Simple page-to-page transition animations add life to the game. From simple button-press jiggles to changes between screens, animations that are relatively simple to implement can have a colossal impact on the end user's experience.

All of these elements create the identity of the game. A successful identity will support a memorable experience for the gamers. If the game is memorable, they will remember to come back and play it again. They will then trust you as a game provider and be more apt to buy your next title. A consistent identity will maintain a level of quality that end users will be able to expect every time they play one of your games.

Title and Information Screens

Splash screens are the very first screens the player will see after touching the icon to start the application. These usually show the names of the publisher, the studio, and/or the developing parties. Use your logo or create a splash animation that will convey your entity or brand to the end user.

What choices will you allow your user at the start of the application? A Start Game option is certainly one of them. Then there are credits, settings, sounds, and difficulty level, if applicable. This is where you walk your game design document reader through the choices the end user will have displayed on the main menu screen.

It's a good idea to tell the player the rules of the game. Include these instructions in the game as well as in the App Store description of your game.

Sound Effects

Nothing will breathe abundant life into your graphics and animations like sound. Sound sells the game play and communicates with unspoken eloquence the meaning behind many actions. Whether it is the sound a laser gun makes each time it fires or the short audio cue that lets your player know the correct timing for completing a combat action, sound effects can make or break game play.

In your game design document, list every sound effect required for your game in advance, so that you can collect or create the sounds more efficiently.

From Vision to Reality

The next phase for the development team is taking the design of what the application will look like and implementing those concepts in artwork and in code. Generally, the brains behind game and interface design differ from those coding the game.

Sometimes, a team member may come to you with an idea that can be easily implemented via adding a couple simple lines of code. Other times, you will be asked to code something frustratingly complex that achieves very little. In that case, you'll want to work out a compromise that fits with your schedule and budget.

The designer is not the only one who may overestimate what's possible. As you gain more experience in game programming, the limits of your abilities can become somewhat fuzzy at times. If this happens—and it will—the solution is simple: try it! If the idea doesn't work, or is becoming too troublesome or too time-consuming, then just revert to a simpler model, and no harm is done.

If you find that an idea is difficult or impractical to implement, it may be possible to substitute a very similar feature that's easier to create. Replacing a fancy feature with something slightly less elegant is sometimes the way to go. However, you don't want to stray too far from the original design. If your substitution feature puts a completely new twist on the purpose or function of the application, it probably isn't a good idea.

Applications are quickly judged by appearance, and applications that lack good design often fall behind. The quality of the interface has a large impact on user reviews. However, design isn't everything, and functionality shouldn't be sacrificed to achieve it. If a new design feature causes your application to lag, it's probably a good idea to simplify, or completely remove, that feature. On the other hand, if the new feature runs smoothly and looks nice, people will love it and leave good reviews.

Tips for Creating Realistic Artificial Intelligence

Many games don't require any form of artificial intelligence (AI) to operate effectively. However, such games usually are not nearly as interesting or challenging as those that mimic playing against a human opponent. AI can be very simple or very complex, depending on the game, but in either case, the AI algorithms and methods can be formed the same way.

The key point to keep in mind when creating an AI is that the finished result should be effective and unpredictable, just as any human opponent would be. Accomplishing this goal requires a few steps.

The first step, which is perhaps the most important one, is to play the game without the AI, either versus yourself or a friend. Take note of every thought that runs through your mind pertaining to your next move.

After jotting down some notes outlining how your own thoughts work when strategically planning each move in the game, it's time to start turning those into methods and processes that can be translated into code and implemented in your AI. When doing this, keep these pointers in mind:

- Offense usually transcends defense.

- When there is more than one equally logical option, choose randomly.

- If you're searching for something in a grid, search in a random checkerboard pattern, as this is more efficient than searching the entire grid in a linear pattern.

- Everything is a variable. (Every decision is based on something that can change, which is based on something that can change.) So try not to hard-code *anything*.

After you've structured your AI, it's time to start testing it. Take note of any "stupid" moves it makes, find out why it made them, and tweak your algorithms so it doesn't happen again. This could take some time. If you have trouble, just go back to the game and take more notes about how you think when playing it.

When you think you have finished your AI, let someone else try it out. A fresh eye can catch things you didn't notice.

Once you have done all that, you should be just about finished. The only thing left to do is test the AI over and over again, ensuring it doesn't fail or crash in certain scenarios.

TIP

Many people think that an AI is only as smart as its creator. Although it's true that the AI thinks just like you would, consider that it does so in a mere fraction of a second. Therefore, the AI might end up making the game too difficult for some players. To make your game more enjoyable, you can add difficulty settings (which change how far ahead the AI "thinks" into the game). You could also intentionally tell your AI to make certain moves that will give the human opponent an edge (or perhaps, even a chance).

Challenges of Designing for the iPhone

When designing games for the iPhone, the biggest challenge that awaits you relates to the physical design of the device itself. The screen size is small and supports graphic elements that can span only a maximum of 320 by 480 pixels. This small space leaves little room for heads-up displays or menus during game play.

One way to conserve screen space is to show only what's necessary. If a particular button or control doesn't need to be accessed often, you can slide the button into view only when it's needed. For example, the instructions for Bikini Hunt are hidden but easily accessible, as shown in Figure 5-2.

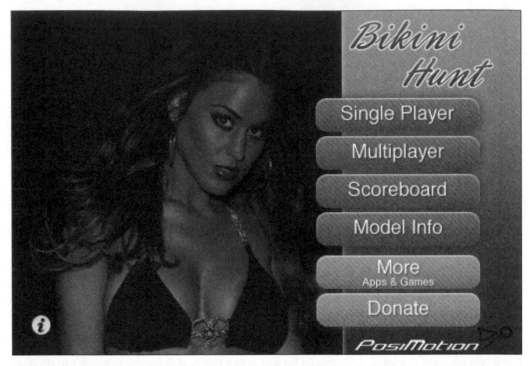

Figure 5-2. *In PosiMotion's Bikini Hunt image-matching game, the icon in the lower-left corner brings up the instructions page, yet takes up little screen real estate.*

Although the physical screen size is limited and care must be used when implementing on-screen controls, the multitouch interface has opened new and exciting user interface design opportunities. This is no ordinary touchscreen like on the Nintendo DS. This is a completely revolutionary touchscreen that supports and can track multiple touches simultaneously. This user interface breakthrough expands the creativity in touchscreen gaming and has already manifested a paradigm shift in the way designers approach an iPhone game.

The ability of the iPhone touchscreen to detect swipes and pinches gives us new ways of differentiating and responding to user input. For example, instead of using buttons to zoom in and out of a game level, you can allow the user to zoom in and out using a pinch motion. Users can also take a look around a particular level just by swiping their finger across the screen to control the direction the camera will pan.

The limited screen real estate has also inspired us to select novel control schemes when designing a game. For example, you can use the built-in accelerometer to tilt or steer characters or other game objects, instead of putting controls on the screen.

NOTE

Despite a popular misconception, an accelerometer is not a compass; it will not tell you which way is north or south. Rather, the accelerometer is a little device in the iPhone that measures gravitational forces at certain axes. The iPhone's accelerometer is a thee-axis accelerometer, which means it can read the gravitational forces on the x, y, and z axes (or pitch, yaw, and roll).

Apache Lander, a game our company created in 2008, is a classic-style game designed primarily around input from the accelerometer. By mapping the user's movement of the accelerometer to corresponding rudder and thrust controls, we were able to provide a new way for a user to interact with a traditional game concept. The object of Apache Lander is simply to guide a helicopter safely to a landing pad; however, this is made much more interesting when you need to manipulate the new accelerometer-based control scheme. If the user tilts the device in an excessive fashion, she is sure to tumble to her demise and subsequently receive the dreaded "Apache Down" message, signifying failure. On the other hand, excellent hand-eye coordination and mastery over the sensitive accelerometer-based control system can result in high scores, making it fun to compete with friends.

The accelerometer is also great for detecting shakes or movements. We use this capability in our games to trigger an action or to reveal a hidden surprise. For example, Shake N' Break is a popular jigsaw puzzle game that presents the user with an image in a picture frame behind a piece of shimmering glass. When the user "shakes" the device, the glass "breaks"— the underlying image divides into pieces that randomly scatter about the screen. The user is then invited to reform the original image by reordering the scattered pieces. This game also allows users to select photos from their camera or photo library, which creates a more personalized feel within the game.

The Location Service, a.k.a. the Core Location framework, is a major feature that is typically overlooked by many game developers. The Assisted GPS (A-GPS) in the iPhone 3G can be used in many creative ways. For example, you can use it to control a user's motion during game play or to identify other users who are playing the same game nearby. Both uses make for a unique and fun game experience.

Game Development Tips

This section provides tips that we've picked up while developing games for PosiMotion that can help you create better and more exciting games that remain competitive.

Solitaire Top 3

Solitaire is the most widely played computer game in the world. Add a touchscreen to the mix, and it is even more fun. Some of you may recognize this game from the jailbroken realm. Well, that's because it originally came from the jailbroken realm. If there is a game that you love and play that already exists, don't be afraid to contact the developer. Working in conjunction with others can lead to some amazing results.

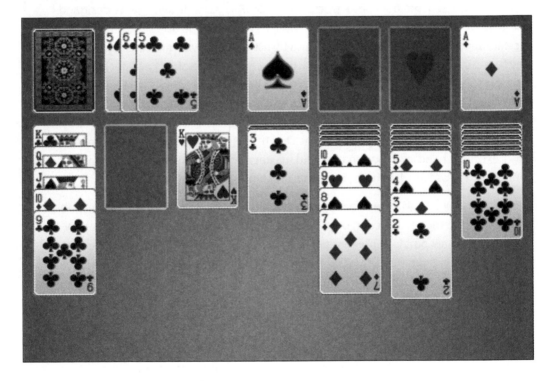

Backgammon

Backgammon is another classic game. Some of the greatest features of this game are in the small details. The option to show your available moves helps ease new players into the game, while the ability to turn this feature off appeals to more advanced players. And implementing the accelerometer so you can shake the phone to roll the dice takes the fun to the next level.

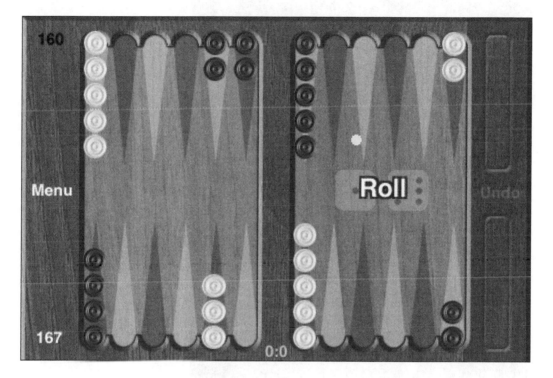

Pool

Pool proves that 3D graphics aren't necessary to make a great game. Clean and detailed 2D graphics, combined with a great physics engine and realistic sound effects, have kept this game competitive against its 3D rivals. With the addition of network multiplayer capabilities, you can challenge a friend, which adds to the fun.

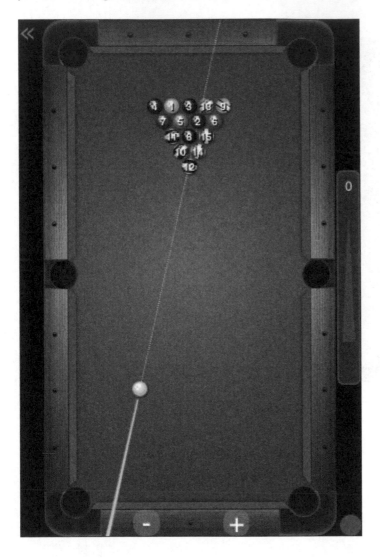

Kaleidoscope

The Kaleidoscope game brings a tube filled with mirrors, prisms, and beads to your iPhone or iPod touch. To make this game as interesting as possible, we implemented every input method we could think of. The accelerometer and touchscreen increase the fun factor by allowing you to manipulate your image in many different ways, while stored pictures and the camera increase playability.

Shake N' Break

Shake N' Break lets you take your favorite pictures and break them to pieces so you can put them back together. Again, the physical action of smashing the picture provides an additional level of fun, while use of your own pictures adds to the replay factor. However, the most important feature of this game comes from the multiple difficulty settings.

Bikini Hunt

With Bikini Hunt, we took a game concept that you can find in most any bar and brought it to the iPhone. Some of the aspects of the game that make it stand out (other than models in bikinis) are things that most will take for granted. The interface was given a clean, modern look by limiting the palette to shades of blue and gray, and rounding off most of the edges. However, the most innovative concept was in how we alert the user that features are limited due to lack of Internet connectivity. Instead of a using a bothersome pop-up, we merely change the color of a button and drop a notice down from behind it. This method informs the user of the change and adds to the aesthetics.

YoYo

The YoYo game showcases the versatility and possibilities of the iPhone and iPod touch platform. Use of a 3D yo-yo allows us to easily and continuously add new tricks and features by changing a few lines of code. This is far better than needing to produce a multitude of new 2D animations with each change.

Apache Lander

Last, but certainly not least, is Apache Lander. This is our simplest and most challenging game. It is also one of the most popular games on the entire App Store. You won't find any fancy graphics here, nor settings or special features. All you need to do is land the Apache using the accelerometer controls. Interestingly enough, it is the extreme difficulty of this game that keeps people playing. This goes to show that, despite everything you have just read, all that really matters is that the games you create are fun. This game alone has achieved over a million downloads and counting.

Summary

iPhone game development is still in its early years, There is plenty of room to learn and grow and experiment with genres and interfaces. This is reminiscent of the early years when one of our team members was creating video games for the Super Nintendo Entertainment System (SNES) and the first PlayStation. Back then, teams were small, production time was short, and there was an untapped flow of new game ideas.

Now console-based game development has evolved into huge teams closer in number to the military strength of a private army. Production times are jokingly measured by the number of team members' children who will be born during the three- to five-year project schedule. New game ideas are hoarded over like golden treasure chests, by menacing megalomaniacal corporate dragons who guard licenses and IP addresses with equally fierce firepower.

Am I saying that this is the future of iPhone game development? No, or at least, I hope not. The true future of iPhone game development is up to you, dear reader. As I've said, this is a very exciting time to be creating games for the iPhone. There is plenty of room for more game developers and game designers, and programmers are in great demand. I sincerely wish you, the reader, the best in your new adventure into iPhone game development. Now go make history.

Michael Kasprzak

Company: *Sykhronics Entertainment*

Location: *London, Ontario, Canada*

Former Life As a Developer: *I've been developing games professionally since 1999, and independently most of my life. I've worked on more than a dozen titles for various game systems, including Game Boy Color, Game Boy Advance, cell phones, Nintendo DS, and PlayStation. I founded Sykhronics Entertainment in late 2005. Previously, I worked at Big Blue Bubble, Digital Illusions, and Sandbox Studios.*

Life As an iPhone Developer: *I created Smiles, a family-oriented puzzle game, and a personal iPhone Development Toolset, which is a custom cross-platform API that lets me work on Windows, Linux, and Mac machines.*

What's in This Chapter: *Using the development of Smiles as an example, this chapter covers creating iPhone games that are cross-platform and portable. It demonstrates the concepts with a tilt-and-touch physics example.*

Key Technologies:

- *Portable game code*
- *Game loops*
- *Event-driven operating system cooperation*
- *Unix time*
- *Frame skipping*

Chapter 6

Multiplatform Game Development: iPhone Games for Linux and Windows

*t*his chapter is about creating portable game code. I'll introduce the approach I used personally in the development of my iPhone game Smiles, which we'll look at first. Next, we'll dive into the subject of portability—what it means and how to get started. Then we'll dig in to the specific issues and considerations for working portably on the iPhone, including the iPhone operating system, system time, and how to support frame skipping in a portable way. I'll end the chapter with a practical example of a portable application. For this occasion, I cooked up a simple physics demo you can play on your iPhone, or download and compile for your PC.

The Development of Smiles: A Collection of Puzzle Games

Smiles is a collection of puzzle games for the iPhone, as shown in Figure 6-1. At its heart, Smiles is a matching game. It features a unique swapping game mechanism that, to the best of my knowledge, is not found in any similar game.

Figure 6-1. *Title screen of Smiles for the iPhone*

I discovered the game mechanism while prototyping a number of game concepts for my debut iPhone title. The original prototype was a patience (solitaire) game I named Pattern Trade, shown in Figure 6-2. This became the basis for the Zen game mode in Smiles.

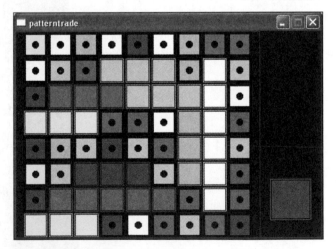

Figure 6-2. *The Pattern Trade prototype, which later became the Zen game in Smiles*

Of the several game concepts and prototypes I was considering, Smiles seemed to be short-est project with the clearest end goal. Pattern Trade was a solid working concept, but since I hadn't released a game in a few years, I wanted my first self-published title to be more of a big deal. I began with the idea of a minimum of two distinct game modes. As shown in Figure 6-3, I started with Zen, the patience game, and the action puzzler Drop. Drop is based on the same game mechanism used in Zen, but is much flashier. Artistically, the game is tied together with a cheerful visual style and three distinct themes, as shown in Figure 6-4.

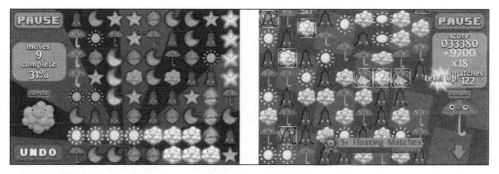

Figure 6-3. *The Zen (left) and Drop (right) games from Smiles*

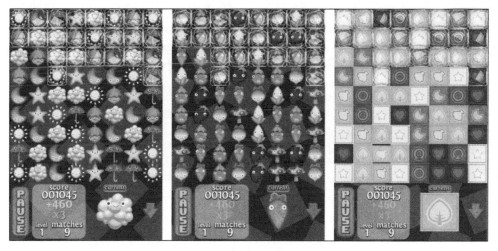

Figure 6-4. *Multiple themes in Smiles: Weather (left), Vegetables (middle), and Blocks (right)*

I'm not a classically trained artist by any stretch of the definition, but I do draw characters. Over the years, I've worked with dozens of brands on numerous games, many kid-related, and I've also been known to dabble in my own design. "Smiles" was the name and motif I came up with to give the game its identity: family-friendly, cheerful, easy to remember, and not just a bunch of diamonds and blocks (although I did include a block theme).

To make Smiles stand out, I didn't stop at just two games. The final product included 14 different game modes. Many are different difficulties, and some are actually variations (Long Play and Avalanche, for example). The games had to look complete, so they feature particle effects, numerous uses of physics, sound effects, high scores, statistics, achievements, and bucket-loads of polish. Figure 6-5 shows the statistics and achievements screens. The project took four months to complete from start to finish, full-time, with only one person on the project (me).

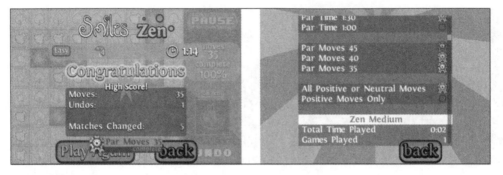

Figure 6-5. *Statistics and achievements in Smiles*

Smiles was an opportunity to bring together a number of game design ideas. I wanted it to be a puzzle game that does "broadly accessible" right, for casual to seasoned players—a game to be played at the user's own pace and worth playing by a broad audience. I also wanted Smiles to bring the experience of a well-made console game to the iPhone.

Smiles has fared extremely well in eyes of players and press alike, scoring many five-star ratings and numerous accolades. Notably, it was a finalist for Best Game in the 2009 Independent Games Festival (IGF) Mobile contest.

But for everything Smiles does, cheerful harmless attire and all, it still has a dark little secret. Smiles was developed *almost entirely* on Windows, as shown in Figure 6-6. My tools of choice are MinGW and MSYS, a GCC port and Unix environment for Windows. To learn more about both, visit http://www.mingw.org. I do virtually all of my programming in the UltraEdit text editor (http://www.ultraedit.com/).

Mac fanatics, before you torch this book for my heresy, you really should hear me out. Think of me as a Linux developer who found a comfortable way to work in Windows. As it turns out, most console software development kits just happen to be entirely Windows-based, featuring Linux/Unix tools like GCC. In fact, that's one of the things that make the iPhone attractive to console developers. Xcode also uses GCC. It's hidden behind the scenes, but it's there.

After that, it should be less surprising to learn that Smiles was also *partially* developed on Linux. Figure 6-7 shows the text editor Geany (http://www.geany.org/) running on Xfce.

Figure 6-6. *Smiles, the iPhone game, running on Windows*

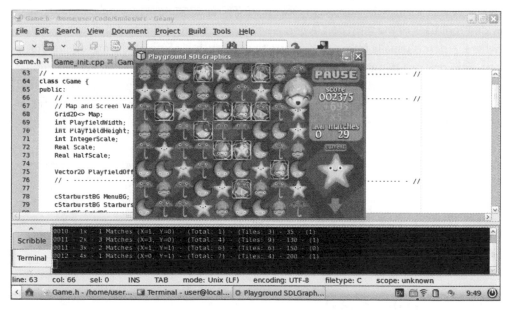

Figure 6-7. *Smiles also runs on Linux.*

My primary laptop during Smiles development was a lightweight Linux netbook. I would have loved a MacBook Air, but $300 compared to $1,800 was a good argument for the Linux system.

I should make it clear that Smiles was *not* developed without a Mac. I have a Mac mini I turn to whenever I need to test on an iPhone. But by following some guidelines, I was able to develop and run the game on three platforms simultaneously: Windows, Linux, and iPhone.

I could go on and on about Smiles (and I do on my blog), but here seems a good place to move on to the subject of this chapter: portability.

What Are Cross-Platform and Portability?

Developing something *cross-platform* means that it runs on multiple platforms: Windows, Linux, Mac, iPhone, and so on.

Portable refers to code. Just as a suitcase is portable enough to pick up and take somewhere, portable code can be picked up from one platform and taken to another.

While the two terms certainly don't mean the same thing, they address the same goal. You share code across platforms. Code that runs across platforms is portable.

As you delve further into the subject of cross-platform development, you may also run into a few different uses of the term *port*. A *port* is what you call an application that originated elsewhere. A *port* is usually from one platform to another, but some platforms require that a port be from one programming language to another (for example, from C to Java). *Porting* is the process of creating a port of something (converting or adapting the code). In discussion, *port* is sometimes used as a verb meaning the same thing as *porting* (as in, "I will port this code"). *Ported* means the porting is done.

NOTE

Porting code from one programming language to another creates a dependency on the original code. Any changes or fixes made to the original code must be made to the ported code manually. Since it can be tricky to maintain separate code bases per language, in practice, language-to-language ports usually occur only after an application is considered final.

Why Write Portable Code?

The obvious reason to write portable code is to reach more users. The iPhone may have a user base of several million, but if your game runs on the Mac, a Windows PC, and mobile devices, millions more potential customers are available to you.

Each platform is different, with varying screen sizes, input capabilities, and so on. On the plus side, there's much common ground to be found on the various platforms. A mouse can simulate a touchscreen; a multi-touchscreen can be used as a single-touchscreen. And at the very least, a large chunk of game code can be shared among platforms. Why rewrite the game from scratch?

Ultimately, my game Smiles was designed and released for the iPhone and iPod touch only. That's not to say you won't eventually see it elsewhere, but this demonstrates yet another advantage to developing cross-platform: potentially lower costs.

If you're an established PC or mobile developer, or just a couple students working out of an apartment, buying MacBooks or iMacs for everyone might be too costly. For about the same price as a low-end MacBook, two people could share a Mac mini and purchase an iPod touch each. You can continue to work on existing Windows or Linux machines, hopping on to the Mac mini to test.

Video games are part of the entertainment and media industries and, like other media, the game industry is one of trends. We move around and change platforms every few years, providing new games for the latest and greatest systems. If you take game making seriously, you'll want to be as flexible as possible. Embracing portability will help you stay on top of the latest developments in gaming.

Why Not Write Portable Code?

I won't kid you—the cost-saving advantages of working portably come at a price. It's more work. You can't use the convenient font and printing code, 2D vector primitives, menus, and graphics loading provided by Apple. You need to stay platform-agnostic, and that means OpenGL, OpenGL ES (OpenGL for Embedded Systems), or software rendering. Pixels and polygons are your tools.

But with more work comes more flexibility. You gain the ability to fully style every element of your game. Button graphics and menus can take on a flat or a full 3D look. You can go above and beyond the styles and fonts provided by Apple, and create completely seamless visual experiences.

However, to work portably, you need to start from virtually nothing. For some people, that can be a scary proposition. That's not to say you can't draw vectors, print text, and so on. It just means you may need to write that code yourself. You can pick up and evaluate several open source and liberal license projects along the way. For example, compression is some- thing done extremely well and made freely available (zlib, bzip2, and LZMA). But for the ultimate flexibility, you may need to "reinvent the wheel" by writing some fundamental code yourself.

Portability from the Ground Up

To keep game code portable, it should *not* be written in Objective-C. The iPhone operating system does require you to work with Objective-C (at least to get started), but game code should not be written in it. The code should be written in either C or C++.

C and C++ are the de facto standard programming languages today. This isn't to belittle Objective-C as a language—it's just not available on every platform. Modern compilers combined with low-level experience can do wonders. You can virtually work low level by learning the assembly opcodes that are generated by C and C++ code. An understanding of assembly language goes a long way toward getting the best performance, so you rarely need to break out the *moves*, *loads*, and *stores* yourself anymore.

I work in C++ myself, but to keep things more accessible, I've used C for the examples in this chapter. I'll leave the task of converting them to C++ as an exercise for those who are interested.

That covers the language. The other thing you need for games is graphics.

One option would be to write a software renderer and use graphics hardware to quickly copy it to the screen, but I'll be using OpenGL ES. OpenGL ES is a subset of the OpenGL standard. In a way, it's a bit like the "best of" OpenGL. Some features that were previously OpenGL extensions were promoted to full features; others that didn't offer much and took up space were removed.

OpenGL is actually a fairly old standard, with origins in the early 1990s. Today, OpenGL or OpenGL ES is available on virtually every platform supporting 3D graphics hardware. The few exceptions often feature extremely similar APIs of their own.

I won't talk much about OpenGL ES in this chapter, although the examples use it. Instead, the focus will be more on the lower-level fundamentals of programming a game.

Let's start with possibly the most fundamental aspect of game programming: the game loop.

The Classic Game Loop

I thought about saying something profound here, like how the game loop is some sort of ancient super-secret methodology that has been passed down through the ages. But as shown in Listing 6-1, it's really just a plain old loop.

Listing 6-1. *A Classic Game Loop Written in C*

```
while ( GameIsRunning() ) {
    /* Do Game */
    ...
}
```

The game loop is such a simple idea, I wouldn't be surprised if it was "invented" hundreds, if not thousands, of times throughout the history of game making. If you would like an academic take, the game loop is a classic game design pattern for real-time games.

In Listing 6-1, the code found between the braces is called the *body* of the game loop, or a *frame* of the game loop. It's no coincidence that the term *frame* is used here. It's the same idea as a frame in a movie or animation. From the top to the bottom of that block of code, things are moved and drawn. This is a frame of a game.

On modern game consoles and operating systems, you might not be able to create a `while` loop type of game loop (like the one shown in Listing 6-1). You may need to deal with things like a message system that polls and triggering events, watchdog timers, threads running in the background, or separate multiprocessor cores performing work in parallel. Though a `while` loop won't work for the game loop on every platform, the idea of a frame will. It still continues to be a game loop, but the looping part may be handled in some system-specific way.

A Practical Game Loop

To demonstrate a game loop in action, let's create a project. Starting with the OpenGL ES template found in Xcode, I'll walk through some changes you can make that will be first steps toward working portably.

The OpenGL ES template uses a regularly triggering timer that calls a function. By default, it's set up to call 60 times per second. This timer will be used to call the frame code, thus creating the loop. The iPhone doesn't require you to create a game loop this way, but this approach is good on battery power (in the case of the iPhone). Alternatively, for better performance, you may want to look into creating a thread.

After you've created the project, navigate to the project folder in Finder. Create a folder named `Source`.

All your game-specific code will go in `Source`. The Objective-C code will live in its default folder, `Classes`. This way, the game code and system code are separate. Objective-C code does us little good on other platforms, so why let it get in the way?

Inside your `Source` folder, create the files *game.h* and *game.c* containing the game code shown in Listings 6-2 and 6-3, respectively.

Listing 6-2. *The game.h File*

```
#ifndef __GAME_H__
#define __GAME_H__

void GameLoopFrame();

#endif /* __GAME_H__ */
```

Listing 6-3. *The game.c File*

```
#include "game.h"

void GameLoopFrame() {
    /* Move game elements */
    /* Draw game elements */
}
```

Be sure to add the files to Xcode, if you haven't already.

Next, let's make changes to the parts generated by the OpenGL ES template. Open the *EAGLView.h* file in the Classes folder, and include the header file at the top, as shown in Listing 6-4.

Listing 6-4. *Top of the EAGLView.h File*

```
#import <UIKit/UIKit.h>
#import <OpenGLES/EAGL.h>
#import <OpenGLES/ES1/gl.h>
#import <OpenGLES/ES1/glext.h>

#include "../Source/game.h"
```

Next, open *EAGLView.m* in the Classes folder and find the drawView function. While the name drawView was accurate for the template application, I suggest renaming it to updateView, to reflect what it actually does. For simplicity, I'll continue to refer to it as drawView.

Remove everything from the drawView function except the context and bind calls, inserting a call to GameLoopFrame.

TIP

Instead of outright deleting everything in drawView, you may want to move the OpenGL ES code to the GameLoopFrame function in *game.c*. Be sure you're including the OpenGL ES headers at the top of the file.

When you finish, the function should look like Listing 6-5.

Listing 6-5. *The Cleaned-Up drawView Function in EAGLView.m*

```
- (void)drawView {
    [EAGLContext setCurrentContext:context];
    glBindFramebufferOES(GL_FRAMEBUFFER_OES, viewFramebuffer);
```

```
    GameLoopFrame();

    glBindRenderbufferOES(GL_RENDERBUFFER_OES, viewRenderbuffer);
    [context presentRenderbuffer:GL_RENDERBUFFER_OES]
}
```

TIP

To call C++ code instead of C code from here, rename the file from *EAGLView.m* to *EAGLView.mm*. The extension *.mm* tells Xcode (GCC) to compile the code as Objective-C++. It's recommended that if you've renamed one *.m* file to *.mm*, you rename them all (*EAGLView.m* and *MyProjectAppDelegate.m* in the `Classes` folder, and *main.m*). And for consistency, you should save your *.c* files as *.cpp* files.

Now you have a program that isolates the game code from the Objective-C code. It doesn't do anything, but it's a good place to start.

Frames and Refresh Rates

In games, frames are both a block of code and a measurement of time. Frames are usually spoken of in terms of frames per second (fps). You might be familiar with 60 fps (NTSC video), 50 fps (PAL video), or 24 fps (film and movies). Depending on the context, those numbers are either called the *frame rate* or the *refresh rate*.

Needless to say, 60 fps was adopted by many modern display technologies, including LCDs. The iPhone's screen refreshes at 60 fps (refresh rate), so for the best results, your game should, too (frame rate).

In the OpenGL ES template, Apple provides code that runs at 60 fps. The default sample doesn't do much, which is why it has no trouble keeping up. However, your game may start taking more than a 1/60 second to finish drawing. When that happens, your game will slow down. You can always optimize your graphics code to avoid this, but eventually you may hit a wall. When that happens, it might be time for frame skipping. I'll get to a frame skipping implementation later in this chapter, but first, you need to do a few things to prepare for it.

Work and Draw Frame Code

The first step to supporting frame skipping is breaking up your frame code. Specifically, you need to isolate moving and drawing.

To do this, get rid of the GameLoopFrame function, and then create two new functions in its place: Work and Draw, as shown in Listings 6-6 and 6-7.

Listing 6-6. *The New game.h File*

```
#ifndef __GAME_H__
#define __GAME_H__

void Work();
void Draw();

#endif /* __GAME_H__ */
```

Listing 6-7. *The New game.c File*

```
#include "game.h"

void Work() {
    /* Move game elements */
}

void Draw() {
    /* Draw game elements */
}
```

Next, update drawView to reflect the change, as shown in Listing 6-8.

Listing 6-8. *The Updated drawView Function in EAGLView.m*

```
- (void)drawView {
    Work();

    [EAGLContext setCurrentContext:context];
    glBindFramebufferOES(GL_FRAMEBUFFER_OES, viewFramebuffer);

    Draw();

    glBindRenderbufferOES(GL_RENDERBUFFER_OES, viewRenderbuffer);
    [context presentRenderbuffer:GL_RENDERBUFFER_OES]
}
```

In the Work function, you move, step, tick, or do the work of a frame. In Draw, you render or draw the frame. I prefer the term *work* rather than *move* here, since you're not always moving things in games, but you are always doing something (that is, working).

By splitting the game loop into two parts, you've created a foundation for frame skipping. Nothing else needs to be changed in *game.c* and *game.h*, but you must be sure to place all your code that draws in Draw, and everything else in Work.

Cooperating with an Event-Driven Operating System

Like most operating systems, the iPhone operating system is event-driven. This means that, at any time, your application could receive a message. While you're drawing, performing complex calculations, or idling, you need to be ready. As a rule, this message becomes the system's top priority and is handled immediately. The system automatically calls your event handler(s), and it's your job to do something about it: handle the message or ignore it. Messages can be any number of things, from touches, to battery warnings, to application shutdown notices.

Game loops tend not to lend themselves well to getting messages at any time. In practice, they don't have to, but it means you need to work with messages in a different way.

With that in mind, you're almost ready start tracking touches. But first, you need to make a small preparation.

Preparing to Track Touches

To simplify upcoming code, you can use a type to represent a position or a point, as shown in Listing 6-9. Apple does provide a type for us (CGPoint), but as I said earlier, you can't rely on anything Apple-specific when writing portable code.

Listing 6-9. *A Simple 2D Vector Type*

```
typedef struct {
    float x, y;
} Vector2D;
```

Without going into vector math, let's just say points and positions are vectors, but not the other way around. For that reason, you're starting with a vector right now, instead of changing it later.

Tracking Touches

To play nice with a constant barrage of system events, you'll need to write event handlers. But instead of doing anything extravagant with the results, you'll simply store them. Take note of anything that happens (that you care about)—touches, releases, and moves.

Add the variables and event handler functions shown in Listing 6-10 above the drawView function.

Listing 6-10. *Objective-C Event Handlers That Track Touches in EAGLView.m*

```objc
Vector2D ActiveTouchPos;
int ActiveTouchValue;

- (void)touchesBegan:(NSSet *)touches withEvent:(UIEvent *)event {
    int CurrentTouch = 0;
    for (UITouch *touch in touches) {
        CGPoint touchPoint = [touch locationInView:self];

        /* First touch only */
        if ( CurrentTouch == 0 ) {
            ActiveTouchPos.x = touchPoint.x;
            ActiveTouchPos.y = touchPoint.y;

            ActiveTouchValue = 1;
        }

        CurrentTouch++;
    }
}

- (void)touchesMoved:(NSSet *)touches withEvent:(UIEvent *)event {
    int CurrentTouch = 0;
    for (UITouch *touch in touches) {
        CGPoint touchPoint = [touch locationInView:self];

        /* First touch only */
        if ( CurrentTouch == 0 ) {
            ActiveTouchPos.x = touchPoint.x;
            ActiveTouchPos.y = touchPoint.y;
        }

        CurrentTouch++;
    }
}

- (void)touchesEnded:(NSSet *)touches withEvent:(UIEvent *)event {
    int CurrentTouch = 0;
    for (UITouch *touch in touches) {
        CGPoint touchPoint = [touch locationInView:self];

        /* First touch only */
        if ( CurrentTouch == 0 ) {
            ActiveTouchPos.x = touchPoint.x;
            ActiveTouchPos.y = touchPoint.y;
```

```
            ActiveTouchValue = 0;
        }

        CurrentTouch++;
    }
}
```

The event handler functions in Listing 6-10 track only the first touch. You're more than wel-
come to track more by creating arrays, but I chose not to do that in this example.

Being event handlers, the touch information stored in Listing 6-10 can change at any time.
Accessing the information inside the Work or Draw function isn't safe, as the event handlers
can change it at any time during a frame. To be safe, take a snapshot of the touch information.

Immediately after the code in Listing 6-10 and before drawView, add the code shown in Listing 6-11.

Listing 6-11. *Code for Taking a Snapshot of Active Touch Information, in EAGLView.m*

```
Vector2D TouchPos;
int TouchValue;

void Update_Input() {
    /* Copy the Active Touches */
    TouchPos.x = ActiveTouchPos.x;
    TouchPos.y = ActiveTouchPos.y;

    TouchValue = ActiveTouchValue;
}
```

The Update_Input function in Listing 6-11 looks at the touch information variables and
makes a copy. The copy is the version you're allowed to use inside your Work and Draw functions, since they will change only when Update_Input is called. With the simple change to
drawView shown in Listing 6-12, you can now guarantee this.

Listing 6-12. *drawView Modified to Use Update_Input, in EAGLView.m*

```
- (void)drawView {
    Update_Input();
    Work();

    [EAGLContext setCurrentContext:context];
    glBindFramebufferOES(GL_FRAMEBUFFER_OES, viewFramebuffer);

    Draw();
```

```
    glBindRenderbufferOES(GL_RENDERBUFFER_OES, viewRenderbuffer);
    [context presentRenderbuffer:GL_RENDERBUFFER_OES]
}
```

Now would be a good time to make your touch-tracking variables available to the game code. The easy way is to make the changes to *game.h* shown in Listing 6-13.

Listing 6-13. *Updated game.h with Access to the Touch Tracking*

```
#ifndef __GAME_H__
#define __GAME_H__

typedef struct {
    float x, y;
} Vector2D;

extern Vector2D TouchPos;
extern int TouchValue;

void Work();
void Draw();

#endif /* __GAME_H__ */
```

Note that I didn't include `Update_Input` here. I could have, but it's not necessary. The actual `Update_Input` function relies heavily on variables found only inside *EAGLView.m*. And it's also called there, so it doesn't need to be seen outside.

Simulating Touch and Release Events in a Game Loop

Next, some improvements to the `Update_Input` function. Right now, it only lets you know when the finger is down. You may also want to know when the user has recently touched the screen or released it. You can do this without changing your event handlers. Listing 6-14 shows how.

Listing 6-14. *Update_Input in EAGLView.m with Old Value Tracking*

```
Vector2D TouchPos;
int TouchOldValue;
int TouchValue;

void Update_Input() {
    /* Copy the Active Touches */
    TouchPos.x = ActiveTouchPos.x;
    TouchPos.y = ActiveTouchPos.y;

    TouchOldValue = TouchValue;
    TouchValue = ActiveTouchValue;
}
```

By tracking the old value and the current value and comparing the two, you can learn many things. Listing 6-15 includes a few functions you can call *instead* of sharing the variable.

Listing 6-15. *Several Functions to Use for Testing Specific Combinations of TouchValue and TouchOldValue*

```
int TouchChanged() {
    return (TouchValue ^ TouchOldValue);
}

int TouchIsDown() {
    return (TouchValue ^ TouchOldValue) & TouchValue;
}

int TouchIsUp() {
    return (TouchValue ^ TouchOldValue) & TouchOldValue;
}

int Touching() {
    return TouchValue;
}
```

You may have noticed that I'm doing something clever here. Because I treat a touch as TouchValue becoming 1, I can use bit operations to learn about it. I use the XOR (^) bit operation to detect change. Whenever TouchValue and TouchOldValue are different, the XOR will result in 1. I can then use an AND (&) bit operation to test what type of change it was. Finally, I rely on the C Boolean logic that any value *not zero* is true, so I can write easy-to-read code like that shown in Listing 6-16 in *game.c*.

Listing 6-16. *Example Usage of the TouchIsDown Function*

```
if ( TouchIsDown() ) {
    /* Finger has (this frame) touched the screen */
    ...
}
```

These functions could live outside *EAGLView.m*, since they rely entirely on the snapshots of data. But to keep the example simpler, I'll leave them there. A modified *game.h* in Listing 6-17 hides the TouchValue variable behind functions.

Listing 6-17. *Sharing Functions Instead of TouchValue Inside game.h*

```
#ifndef __GAME_H__
#define __GAME_H__

typedef struct {
    float x, y;
} Vector2D;
```

```
extern Vector2D TouchPos;
int TouchChanged();
int TouchIsDown();
int TouchIsUp();
int Touching();

void Work();
void Draw();

#endif /* __GAME_H__ */
```

TIP

When writing user interface code, touch down and touch up events are especially useful. If you remember which user interface element was touched (down event), you can test for the same element when released (up event). If they are the same, you activate the action. This is how you make a button that users can touch, while giving them the option of dragging their finger off the button to not activate it. Most standard buttons on Mac OS X and Windows systems work this way.

Frame Skipping

Frame skipping is a visual compromise. It's the idea that if the previous frame took too long, you can skip drawing until you've caught up. This relies on the fact that most work done during a frame is less intensive than actually drawing. As a rule of thumb, you should be able to perform two or more frames of work when not drawing. Frame skipping code can handle the occasional heavy frame of work, but for best results, it should be avoided if possible.

There are two common types of frame skipping:

Fixed frame-rate skipping: This is as easy as it sounds. In a game that normally runs at 60 fps, you can run at half the frame rate by changing the timer to tick at 30 fps, and by calling your Work code twice per frame. That's all there is to it. In practice, fixed frame-rate is usually not what you want.

Floating or dynamic frame-rate frame skipping: This is the most common kind. It's more complicated, but it is the one you want. To do it, you need to check system time to learn about the actual time that has passed.

Rather than hit you with all the code for floating frame skipping at once, I'll show you the code in steps, as follows:

- Prepare drawView to make multiple Work function calls in a single frame.

- Build a library of system time operations.

- Use the library to implement frame skipping.

To see how frame skipping works in drawView, take a look at Listing 6-18.

Listing 6-18. *Modified drawView in EAGLView.m, Roughly Showing How a Frame Skipping Loop Appears*

```
- (void)drawView {
    int WorkFrames = 1;

    while ( WorkFrames-- ) {
        Update_Input();
        Work();
    }
    [EAGLContext setCurrentContext:context];
    glBindFramebufferOES(GL_FRAMEBUFFER_OES, viewFramebuffer);

    Draw();

    glBindRenderbufferOES(GL_RENDERBUFFER_OES, viewRenderbuffer);
    [context presentRenderbuffer:GL_RENDERBUFFER_OES]
}
```

This hard-codes WorkFrames to be 1. Eventually, you'll have a real function that says how many frames have passed, and you'll be looping for every frame of work you need to do.

Again, I'm doing something clever here. WorkFrames-- will decrease the value of WorkFrames *after* the test in the while loop. As before, I rely on the C Boolean logic that any value *not zero* is true. As a result of WorkFrames being 1, you end up looping exactly once.

Next, you need to look to the system time to find out how much time has actually passed.

Creating a Unix System Time Library

The Mac OS X and iPhone operating systems are BSD (Unix) derivatives. Because of this, you need to rely on the Unix way of checking time passed. This same code will work on Linux, but it's done differently on Windows.

A moment in Unix time is represented by a timeval, a high-precision type that stores time. It is capable of representing billions of seconds and is precise down to a millionth of a second. Since what we care about is 1/60 second, it's far more precision than we need.

The timeval structure is normally defined as shown in Listing 6-19.

Listing 6-19. *A Standard Unix timeval Structure*

```
struct timeval {
    int tv_sec;    /* Seconds */
    int tv_usec;   /* Microseconds */
};
```

You don't need to define `timeval` yourself, but you do need to work with this type. As a rule, microseconds will never go over a million. But as soon as you start playing with the type, it becomes your responsibility to make sure you don't break that rule.

A common place to start with a `timeval` type is with the function `gettimeofday`. As the name suggests, using it as shown in Listing 6-20 will tell you what time it is right now, microseconds and all.

Listing 6-20. *Common Use of timeval, with gettimeofday*

```
timeval tv;
gettimeofday( &tv, 0 );
```

NOTE

> Unix time has an amusing history and future. It doesn't count from year zero, but instead counts from midnight January 1, 1970. If you do the math, you'll note we have another "Y2K" coming. On January 18, 2038, times relying on Unix time will start to numerically overflow. The *hope* is that by the time it becomes a problem, we'll all be running 64-bit operating systems on 64-bit CPUs.

The library of functions shipped with `timeval` can tell you a lot of things. Unfortunately, there aren't enough operations for frame skipping. So this is where you write your own functions.

Create two new files under `source`: *UnixTime.h* and *UnixTime.c*. This will be a library for working with Unix time. Start with the header file *UnixTime.h*, as shown in Listing 6-21.

Listing 6-21. *The UnixTime.h File*

```
#ifndef __UNIXTIME_H__
#define __UNIXTIME_H__

#include <sys/time.h>

typedef struct timeval TIMEVALUE;

TIMEVALUE GetTimeNow();
TIMEVALUE AddTime( TIMEVALUE a, TIMEVALUE b );
TIMEVALUE SubtractTime( TIMEVALUE a, TIMEVALUE b );

void SetFramesPerSecond( const int Ticks );
int GetFrames( TIMEVALUE* tv );
void AddFrame( TIMEVALUE* tv );
void ResetTime();

#endif /* __UNIXTIME_H__ */
```

This file includes seven brand-new functions and a `typedef`. Notice that I'm *not* using the `timeval` type, but instead a new type `TIMEVALUE`. There are two reasons for this:

- `timeval` is defined in C as a structure (struct). In the C programming language, you must prefix *all* instances of a structure with the `struct` keyword, as in `struct timeval GetTimeNow();`. The clean way around this is by using the `typedef` keyword. From then on, you can use the name of a type without any mention of the `struct` or `typedef` keywords. This makes future code easier to read and write.

- An important issue to be aware of when writing portable code is naming conflicts. A common practice when using the `typedef` keyword is to give the new type a name that is the same but in all uppercase. The problem here is that on Windows, the name `TIMEVAL` has some other use. However, the name `TIMEVALUE` is unused on Linux, Windows, and Mac/iPhone systems.

TIP

The C++ namespace feature can come in handy when dealing with naming conflicts. Names in global scope can be referenced with the `::` operator (for example, `::timeval`). In addition, names can be reused in custom namespaces (such as `MyLibrary::timeval`).

The implementation in the *UnixTime.c* file is shown in Listing 6-22.

Listing 6-22. *Includes and Variables in UnixTime.c*

```
#include "UnixTime.h"

int FrameRateConstant;
TIMEVALUE OneFrameConstant;
```

Listing 6-22 contains two global variables. `FrameRateConstant` holds the desired frames per second, which is usually set to 60. `OneFrameConstant` is a `timeval` value representing the length of a frame in microseconds. You need this for converting a `timeval` value into frames.

Now let's create the functions. Listing 6-23 shows a function for getting the current time, `GetTimeNow`.

Listing 6-23. *Function to Return the Current Time in UnixTime.c*

```
TIMEVALUE GetTimeNow() {
    TIMEVALUE tv;
    gettimeofday( &tv, 0 );
    return tv;
}
```

Notice that I didn't go with the obvious name GetTime. The reason is *yet another* naming conflict, but this time with a function. The name GetCurrentTime is also taken, so I had to be a little creative.

CAUTION

Be warned, some C libraries rely on macros (#define). You may need to undefine (#undef) a macro or symbol prior to use, so it doesn't break your code. Alternatively, you may be able to get around a naming conflict with the #undef keyword. Use this with caution though, as some macros may rely on symbols to work.

Next up is a pair of functions for adding or subtracting timeval values, shown in Listing 6-24.

Listing 6-24. *Functions for Adding or Subtracting timeval Values in UnixTime.c*

```
TIMEVALUE AddTime( TIMEVALUE a, TIMEVALUE b ) {
    TIMEVALUE tv;
    tv.tv_usec = a.tv_usec + b.tv_usec;
    tv.tv_sec = ta.v_sec + b.tv_sec + (tv.tv_usec / 1000000);
    tv.tv_usec %= 1000000;
    return tv;
}

TIMEVALUE SubtractTime( TIMEVALUE a, TIMEVALUE b ) {
    TIMEVALUE tv;
    tv.tv_usec = a.tv_usec - b.tv_usec;
    tv.tv_sec = a.tv_sec - b.tv_sec + (tv.tv_usec / 1000000);
    tv.tv_usec %= 1000000;
    return tv;
}
```

The bulk of the work you see in Listing 6-24 is to keep the "no value over a million" microseconds rule (tv_usec) in check.

The function GetFrames, shown in Listing 6-25, converts a timeval value into frames. This is the code to detect when you've taken more than a frame's worth of time.

Listing 6-25. *Function to Convert timeval to Frames in UnixTime.c*

```
int GetFrames( TIMEVALUE* tv ) {
    return (tv->tv_sec * FrameRateConstant) +
        (tv->tv_usec / OneFrameConstant.tv_usec);
}
```

The function AddFrame, shown in Listing 6-26, is used to add a single frame of time to a timeval value.

Listing 6-26. *Function for Adding a Frame's Worth of Time to a timeval in UnixTime.c*

```
void AddFrame( TIMEVALUE* tv ) {
    *tv = AddTime( *tv, OneFrameConstant );
}
```

The AddFrame function is used inside the looping work part to minimize numerical error (you'll see why this important in the next section).

Finally, the helper function SetFramesPerSecond, shown in Listing 6-27, is for setting the frame rate.

Listing 6-27. *A Helper Function for Setting the Frames per Second in UnixTime.c*

```
void SetFramesPerSecond( const int Ticks ) {
    FrameRateConstant = Ticks;
    OneFrameConstant.tv_sec = 0;
    OneFrameConstant.tv_usec = (1000000 / Ticks);
}
```

Be sure to add both files (*UnixTime.c* and *UnixTime.h*) to Xcode if you haven't already done so.

TIP

> The nice thing about frame skipping once it's working is that you can think of everything in a game as frames (whole units, as opposed to fractions of time). For example, by counting the number of frames, you can know how much game time and real time have passed. Dividing by your frame rate tells you how many seconds you've been playing. Counting while a game is not paused gives you a "play time" statistic.

So now you have your first piece of library code. You can use this same code on iPhone, Mac, and Linux platforms.

On Windows, you get system time with a different call (timeGetTime). Windows time is measured in thousandths of a second; Unix time is more precise, measuring in millionths of a second. timeGetTime counts from the moment the application was started. Unless you handle this correctly, the clock in an application can overflow in about 25 days (50 days if unsigned). It's not usually a problem for games, but a multiplayer server dying every few weeks wouldn't be a good thing.

Using the UnixTime Library for Frame Skipping

Now that you have some utility functions for dealing with timeval values, it's time to implement frame skipping in your OpenGL ES template application.

First, include the utility library at the top of *EAGLView.h*, as shown in Listing 6-28.

Listing 6-28. *Adding Unix Time Support to EAGLView.h*

```
#import <UIKit/UIKit.h>
#import <OpenGLES/EAGL.h>
#import <OpenGLES/ES1/gl.h>
#import <OpenGLES/ES1/glext.h>

#include "../source/UnixTime.h"
#include "../source/game.h"
```

Next, open *EAGLView.m* and find `initWithCoder`. As shown in Listing 6-29, declare a `timeval` variable for tracking the most recent work time completed, and initialize it.

Listing 6-29. *Adding a Unix Time and Initializing It in EAGLView.m*

```
TIMEVALUE WorkTime;

- (id)initWithCoder:(NSCoder*)coder {
    if ((self = [super initWithCoder:coder])) {
        // Get the layer
        CAEAGLLayer *eaglLayer = (CAEAGLLayer *)self.layer;

        eaglLayer.opaque = YES;
        eaglLayer.drawableProperties =
            [NSDictionary dictionaryWithObjectsAndKeys:
                [NSNumber numberWithBool:NO],
                kEAGLDrawablePropertyRetainedBacking,
                kEAGLColorFormatRGBA8,
                kEAGLDrawablePropertyColorFormat,
                nil];

        context =
        [[EAGLContext alloc] initWithAPI:kEAGLRenderingAPIOpenGLES1];

        if (!context || ![EAGLContext setCurrentContext:context]) {
            [self release];
            return nil;
        }

        animationInterval = 1.0 / 60.0;
        SetFramesPerSecond( 60 );
        WorkTime = GetTime();
    }
    return self;
}
```

Finally, scroll down to drawView and implement frame skipping, as shown in Listing 6-30.

Listing 6-30. *drawView with Frame Skipping in EAGLView.m*

```
- (void)drawView {
    TIMEVALUE TimeDiff = SubtractTime( GetTimeNow(), WorkTime );
    int WorkFrames = GetFrames( &TimeDiff );

    while ( WorkFrames-- ) {
        Update_Input();
        Work();
        AddFrame( &WorkTime );
    }

    [EAGLContext setCurrentContext:context];
    glBindFramebufferOES(GL_FRAMEBUFFER_OES, viewFramebuffer);

    Draw();

    glBindRenderbufferOES(GL_RENDERBUFFER_OES, viewRenderbuffer);
    [context presentRenderbuffer:GL_RENDERBUFFER_OES]
}
```

At the top of Listing 6-30, you take the difference between the working time (WorkTime) and the system time. You then figure out how many frames that is. Loop that many times, each iteration adding a frame's worth of time to WorkTime.

Notice you're adding whole frames to WorkTime, instead of just assuming you're caught up. The problem with assuming you're caught up is that you're never exactly a frame or two over, but rather fractions of frames. However, the work you have completed is *exactly* a frame or more, not fractions of a frame.

WorkTime is the working time snapshot. It's how much actual time you've finished of real work. You detect when the actual time becomes a frame or more than WorkTime, and catch up. That is frame skipping.

Tilt and Touch Physics Sample

So far in this chapter, I've covered a number of technical nuances related to game loops, frame skipping, style, and portability. I've tried my best to explain what everything is and where you would use it, but sometimes it's nice to look at a real-world example. So, for the rest of the chapter, you'll be doing exactly that.

The sample application I've prepared is a simple physics simulation with multiple objects interacting, and support for iPhone tilting and touching. It's far more interesting in action, but Figure 6-8 should give you an idea.

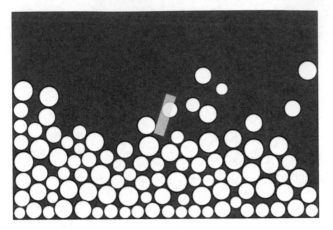

Figure 6-8. *The physics simulation sample application*

The sample application features everything I've talked about in this chapter, and a few surprises. You can consider this a practical example of a game-loop-style iPhone game in action. The full source is available from this book's details page on the Apress web site (`http://www.apress.com`).

The Game Code for the Physics Simulation Sample

Let's look at the game code, starting with the header file in Listing 6-31.

Listing 6-31. *The game.h File*

```
#ifndef __GAME_H__
#define __GAME_H__

typedef struct {
    float x, y;
} Vector2D;

extern Vector2D TouchPos;
extern Vector2D Orientation;

int TouchChanged();
int TouchIsDown();
int TouchIsUp();
int Touching();

void Game_Initialize();
void Game_Exit();
```

```
void Game_Work();
void Game_Draw();

#endif // __GAME_H__ //
```

This should look familiar, but there are a number of changes from what I showed you earlier, including these:

- In addition to a touch position (TouchPos), there's now an Orientation vector. This vector tells you which way the iPhone is oriented. When tall, Orientation.y is greater than Orientation.x; when wide, Orientation.x is greater than Orientation.y. The implementation of the accelerometer reading is extremely bare bones. It doesn't attempt to filter or smooth the values. It simply plugs the x and y values right into the vector.

- The Work and Draw functions now have a Game_ prefix.

- There are two new functions: Game_Initialize and Game_Exit.

The *game.c* file is a lot more complicated than the earlier example. To better explain what's being done, I'll step through the file *out of order*. Listing 6-32 begins with the four functions mentioned in the header file (Listing 6-31).

Listing 6-32. *The Game_ Functions, Near the Bottom of game.c*

```
void Game_Initialize() {
    InitGraphics();
    LoadBallGraphic();

    InitBallPhysics();
    SelectedBall = -1;
}

void Game_Exit() {
    FreeBallGraphic();
}

void Game_Work() {
    DoInput();
    StepBallPhysics();
}

void Game_Draw() {
    ClearBackground();

    DrawBalls();

    DrawArrow();
}
```

These functions work as follows:

- Game_Initialize calls a function to initialize the graphics system (InitGraphics), loads a ball graphic (LoadBallGraphic), initializes the physics simulation (InitBallPhysics), and finally notes that currently no ball is selected.

- Game_Exit simply frees the ball graphic (FreeBallGraphics).

- Game_Work handles the inputs (DoInput) and steps the ball physics (StepBallPhysics).

- Game_Draw starts by clearing the background (ClearBackground), draws the balls (DrawBalls), and draws a graphic on top to identify the tilt direction (DrawArrow).

Next, let's look at the physics simulation. To start, Listing 6-33 shows some of the types and variables used.

Listing 6-33. *game.c from the Top*

```
typedef struct {
    Vector2D Pos, Old;
    float Radius;
} tBall;

#define BALL_X 10
#define BALL_Y 10
#define BALL_MAX (BALL_X * BALL_Y)

tBall Ball[BALL_MAX];

int SelectedBall;
Vector2D SelectedOffset;

Vector2D GravityVector;
```

The Vector2D type from earlier is here, in addition to a new type, tBall. The physics simulation moves several balls around, and tBall is a type for representing a ball. Balls have a current position, old position, and radius. And since one or two balls wouldn't be much fun, the game will have a hundred of them.

Next, Listing 6-34 shows the creation process.

Listing 6-34. *game.c Continued: The Ball Creation Process*

```
void InitBallPhysics() {
    int x, y;
    int Offset = 0;

    // Populate Balls list //
    for ( y = 0; y < BALL_Y; y++ ) {
```

```
        for ( x = 0; x < BALL_X; x++ ) {
            int idx = x + (y * BALL_X);

            Ball[idx].Pos.x = ((x-(BALL_X>>1)) * 32) + 16 + Offset - 4;
            Ball[idx].Pos.y = ((y-(BALL_Y>>1)) * 32) + 16;

            Ball[idx].Old.x = Ball[idx].Pos.x;
            Ball[idx].Old.y = Ball[idx].Pos.y;

            Ball[idx].Radius = 10 + Offset;

            Offset++;
            Offset &= 7;
        }
    }
}
```

This creates several balls of varying sizes slightly offset from each other. The reason for the offsetting is so it's less perfect to start. If you removed that, and fixed the angle to be straight down, the balls would actually stack on top of each other like a snowman. This is not really a bug—just weird.

Now let's look at the meat of the application. Listing 6-35 shows the ball physics.

Listing 6-35. *game.c Continued: The Ball Physics*

```
void StepBallPhysics() {
    int idx, idx2;

    // Move Balls (Verlet physics simulation) //
    for ( idx = 0; idx < BALL_MAX; idx++ ) {
        float Velocity_x = Ball[idx].Pos.x - Ball[idx].Old.x;
        float Velocity_y = Ball[idx].Pos.y - Ball[idx].Old.y;

        Ball[idx].Old.x = Ball[idx].Pos.x;
        Ball[idx].Old.y = Ball[idx].Pos.y;

        Ball[idx].Pos.x += Velocity_x * 0.99f + GravityVector.x;
        Ball[idx].Pos.y += Velocity_y * 0.99f + GravityVector.y;
    }

    // Solve collisions between balls //
    for ( idx = 0; idx < BALL_MAX; idx++ ) {
        for ( idx2 = idx+1; idx2 < BALL_MAX; idx2++ ) {
            float Line_x = Ball[idx2].Pos.x - Ball[idx].Pos.x;
            float Line_y = Ball[idx2].Pos.y - Ball[idx].Pos.y;
```

```
            float Magnitude =
                sqrt( (Line_x * Line_x) + (Line_y * Line_y) );

            if ( Magnitude <= 0.0f )
                continue;

            Line_x /= Magnitude;
            Line_y /= Magnitude;

            float RadiusSum = Ball[idx2].Radius + Ball[idx].Radius;

            float Diff = Magnitude - RadiusSum;

            if ( Diff < 0.0f ) {
                Ball[idx].Pos.x += Diff * Line_x * 0.5f;
                Ball[idx].Pos.y += Diff * Line_y * 0.5f;

                Ball[idx2].Pos.x -= Diff * Line_x * 0.5f;
                Ball[idx2].Pos.y -= Diff * Line_y * 0.5f;
            }
        }
    }

    // Constrain Balls to Walls //
    for ( idx = 0; idx < BALL_MAX; idx++ ) {
        if ( Ball[idx].Pos.x - Ball[idx].Radius < -160.0f )
            Ball[idx].Pos.x = -160.0f + Ball[idx].Radius;

        if ( Ball[idx].Pos.y - Ball[idx].Radius < -240.0f )
            Ball[idx].Pos.y = -240.0f + Ball[idx].Radius;

        if ( Ball[idx].Pos.x + Ball[idx].Radius > 160.0f )
            Ball[idx].Pos.x = 160.0f - Ball[idx].Radius;

        if ( Ball[idx].Pos.y + Ball[idx].Radius > 240.0f )
            Ball[idx].Pos.y = 240.0f - Ball[idx].Radius;
    }
}
```

NOTE

I was hoping this code would be shorter, but I forgot how many lines doing this in C adds. You could simplify this code with a well-written C++ vector math class (not the same thing as an STL vector), including various operators to eliminate the duplicate lines, and functions to calculate magnitude and clip coordinates.

The code in Listing 6-35 is the complete physics simulation—once set up, it will handle everything. It's also a *simplified* physics simulation. It doesn't support mass or torque, and the friction is a cheat (the 0.99f scalar). But that doesn't matter, because it looks cool.

Listing 6-35 implements a *Verlet integrator* (the move part), with a relaxation-based solver. A proper stiff relaxation-based solver would iterate both solves several times, but doing it once makes it more bouncy (and I like bouncy). You can learn more about Verlet physics in the "Advanced Character Physics" article, written by Thomas Jakobsen, at http://www.teknikus.dk/tj/gdc2001.htm.

Now that you have an idea what's actually being done, take a look at Listing 6-36, which shows the DoInput function.

Listing 6-36. *game.c Continued: The DoInput Function*

```
void DoInput() {
    // Tilting //
    GravityVector.x = 0.1f * Orientation.x;
    GravityVector.y = 0.1f * Orientation.y;

    // Grabbing //
    if ( TouchIsDown() ) {
        int idx;

        for ( idx = 0; idx < BALL_MAX; idx++ ) {
            float Line_x = TouchPos.x - Ball[idx].Pos.x;
            float Line_y = TouchPos.y - Ball[idx].Pos.y;

            float MagnitudeSquared = (Line_x * Line_x) + (Line_y * Line_y);

            if ( (Ball[idx].Radius * Ball[idx].Radius) > MagnitudeSquared )
            {
                SelectedBall = idx;

                SelectedOffset.x = Ball[idx].Pos.x - TouchPos.x;
                SelectedOffset.y = Ball[idx].Pos.y - TouchPos.y;

                break;
            }
        }
    }
    if ( TouchIsUp() ) {
        SelectedBall = -1;
    }

    if ( SelectedBall != -1 ) {
        Ball[SelectedBall].Pos.x +=
            ((TouchPos.x + SelectedOffset.x) -
```

```
            Ball[SelectedBall].Pos.x) * 0.15f;
        Ball[SelectedBall].Pos.y +=
            ((TouchPos.y + SelectedOffset.y) -
            Ball[SelectedBall].Pos.y) * 0.15f;
    }
}
```

This code contains a number of things related to Verlet physics. Here, you see TouchIsDown
and TouchIsUp, which were introduced in the earlier example. This code says that in the
frame where I put a finger down, find me the first ball I'm touching and select it. When I
release the finger, deselect it. And as long as I have a selected ball, move it with the finger.

Listing 6-37 shows the final *game.c* function, DrawBalls.

Listing 6-37. *game.c Continued: The DrawBalls Function*

```
void DrawBalls() {
    int idx;

    for ( idx = 0; idx < BALL_MAX; idx++ ) {
        DrawBall( Ball[idx].Pos.x, Ball[idx].Pos.y, Ball[idx].Radius );
    }
}
```

This contains a simple loop for all balls, and a call to a function that draws a ball graphic.

That sums up the contents of *game.c*, and the look at the game loop sample.

Further Portability Considerations

Finally, I'll present one extension to the portability idea. As part of the sample project, let's
take a look at a file Graphics.h, as shown in Listing 6-38.

Listing 6-38. *The Graphics.h File*

```
#ifndef __GRAPHICS_H__
#define __GRAPHICS_H__

void InitGraphics();
void ExitGraphics();

void LoadBallGraphic();
void FreeBallGraphic();
void DrawBall( float x, float y, float Radius );

void ClearBackground();
void DrawArrow();

#endif // __GRAPHICS_H__ //
```

This is a header file for graphics initialization and drawing functions used inside the game loop sample. You'll note that these calls make no mention of OpenGL. There are no OpenGL calls, types, or includes to be found anywhere in this file. Being completely devoid of an OpenGL mention isn't a requirement, but a tip for making game code even more portable.

Most of what you do with libraries like OpenGL are large batch operations—load a graphic, draw a 3D model, and so on. Here's a thought: you could build yourself an optimal library of calls that can be ported to completely unrelated graphics APIs (DirectX, for example).

Another file, ESGraphics.c, contains OpenGL ES implementations of the functions shown in Listing 6-38, completely self-contained. I won't show that file here, since it is rather long, but it's available with the rest of this book's downloadable code.

Another long file, BallGraphic.c, is a raw, uncompressed graphic that was converted to a C array. This embeds the data directly in your code, without the need to load it from a file. I did this using a custom tool that reads a binary file and writes a text file formatted exactly like a standard .c file. Practically speaking, you wouldn't normally do this with image files, as they are often quite large, but it's something to consider if you have many small data files. Rather than loading them from disk, you might prefer to have them compiled right in.

GCC's linker (the program that combines compiled source files and makes an executable) is especially useful here. When something is defined as one type, it can be made visible to the rest of the program as a different type via a trick with the extern keyword. Listing 6-39 shows an example of how you would define the data (*DataFile.c*), and Listing 6-40 shows how you would make it accessible by including a header file (*DataFile.h*).

Listing 6-39. *The DataFile.c File*

```
extern char MyData[];
char MyData[] = {
    /* Comma separated data goes here */
    0, 1, 2, 3
};
```

Listing 6-40. *The DataFile.h File*

```
#ifndef __MYDATA_H__
#define __MYDATA_H__

#include "MyCustomType.h"

extern MyCustomType MyData[];

#endif // __MYDATA_H__
```

There are no includes in the *DataFile.c* file (Listing 6-39). Including *DataFile.h* here would create a symbol conflict, as there would be two conflicting symbols with the same name (MyData). To the linker, it's just a name. Also, you must be sure to make the type visible via the extern keyword inside the *.c* file, as some compilers will optimize the symbol away if you don't use this keyword.

I've included a portable version of the physics simulation example along with the other downloadable code available from the Apress web site. The file *GLGraphics.c* is used on Windows and Linux systems, instead of *ESGraphics.c*. In addition, the file *SDLMain.c* is used in place of your Objective-C code. The portable example uses the Simple DirectMedia Layer (SDL) graphics library as a host for OpenGL. You can learn more about SDL at http://www.libsdl.org.

Summary

This chapter covered many topics related to the idea of portability, including the following:

- The pros and cons of working portably
- Fundamental considerations for portability
- Game loops, frames, and refresh rates
- Working in C (or C++) on the iPhone instead of Objective-C
- Cooperating with an event-driven operating system in a portable way
- Unix time
- Frame skipping

Working portably has some very real and practical advantages. This chapter covered the fundamentals for writing iPhone game code that compiles and runs on different platforms. I recommend taking a look at the sample code and investigating working with the SDL graphics library and OpenGL further. Both have much to offer for portability.

Working portably is just the first step in porting a game to new and exciting platforms. Understanding the issues of portability from the beginning will save you time in the long run. Each platform has its differences and standards to consider when building a product, but your code doesn't have to be the bottleneck that slows down development.

Mike Lee

Company: *United Lemur*

Location: *Silicon Valley, USA*

Former Life As a Developer: **Since leaving my home in Hawaii, I've somehow been lucky enough to work with some amazing teams: Alaska Airlines, Tapulous, United Lemur, and of course, Delicious Monster. At the latter, I lived in Wil Shipley's basement while he, Lucas Newman, and I worked on Delicious Library 2, which won the Apple Design Award for best Leopard application in 2007.**

Life As an iPhone Developer: **When Apple introduced the iPhone SDK, I left Delicious Monster and Seattle and moved to Silicon Valley to cofound an iPhone startup called Tapulous. As chief architect, I led the engineering and design team that created many of the Apple App Store's early titles, including its most popular game, Tap Tap Revenge.**

After leaving Tapulous, I founded United Lemur, an altruistic company dedicated to raising money and awareness for the lemurs and people of Madagascar. United Lemur produced the puzzle game Puzzllotto. I and several members of United Lemur also contributed to the official Obama '08 campaign app.

What's in This Chapter: **Squeezing the state of the art from the finite silicon of a phone-sized computer is not easy. Along the way, I've learned from some of the best developers in the business. I've also made my share of mistakes and learned from those, too. Using Shark, Xcode, and some clever engineering, I'll show you how to optimize game performance.**

Key Technologies:

- **Core Graphics**
- **Core Animation**
- **Xcode build settings**
- **Shark**

Chapter 7

Code Optimization with Mike Lee, the "World's Toughest Programmer"

*i*f you're in the habit of making video games, you're eventually going to need to figure out how to set something on fire. Like any good problem, burning pixels has multiple solutions. This makes it an excellent example for learning the black art of optimization.

Of course, *optimal* is a relative term. You can optimize in many ways, and the laws of physics and algorithmic complexity still apply. Engineering hours are expensive, so this chapter iterates over the problem a few times, examining each solution in terms of three requirements:

- *Suitability* is the degree to which a solution solves the problem. It stands to reason that a solution must be correct, but correctness is typically not absolute. Perfection can be very expensive, so compromise is the order of the day.

- *Performance* is how expensive a solution is to run. How much CPU time, memory space, and battery power will this code convert into useless heat? Even here, perfection is expensive, and compromise is inevitable.

- *Value* is how expensive a solution is to design. Usually, when engineers say something is expensive, they mean it will not perform well. The real-world scarcity of engineering hours converts that into hard currency. Expensive code can be optimized, but that requires expensive engineers.

Iteration 1: Particle Effects

Let's begin by considering how similar problems have been solved in the past. I came across the problem of burning pixels while part of the team building Delicious Library 2, a Mac application for organizing media collections. Deleting books in the library causes them to burst into flames, as shown in Figure 7-1. We used a particle generator implemented with Apple's Core Animation technology. It looked good enough to win an Apple Design Award, so it seems like a good start.

Figure 7-1. *Core Animation particle effects in Delicious Library 2*

Unfortunately, I got a D in trigonometry, so even simple Newtonian particle physics are beyond me. Luckily, smart people wrote this stuff down a long time ago, and C looks enough like math that you can write a particle engine in an afternoon without knowing a damn thing about the physics. But should you?

If you're looking for a good time, by all means, create a particle engine. I was, and I did, and it was a blast. You'll get a vivid demonstration of a solution that's perfectly suitable, but too computationally expensive to be feasible.

Apple would have you believe that, in terms of system resources, particle effects are cheap. When Core Animation debuted, we benchmarked it at 60,000 particles. That's just us, on then-current hardware. With the new crop of programmable GPUs and the insane parallelization efforts of the upcoming Mac OS X 10.6 (Snow Leopard), particle effects are definitely an attractive option—on a Mac. On an iPhone, there's no way.

Pangea Software won an Apple Design Award for the game Enigmo. It looks like the generator is getting maybe 100 particles. Having subjected my own iPhone battery to this game, it's clear that's probably about as optimized as an iPhone particle engine is going to get.

As I said, it doesn't take long to make a particle generator, and the effects can look pretty nice, but they are also really expensive, as shown in Figure 7-2. Unless the app has nothing to do but animate fire, you probably don't want to spend all your resources just yet.

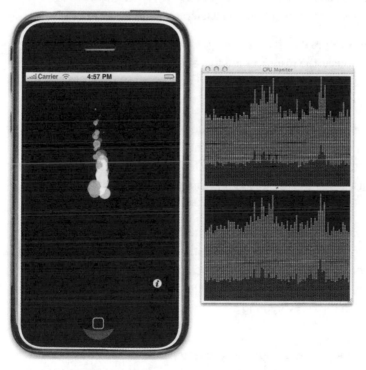

Figure 7-2. *Particle effects burn the iPhone battery beautifully.*

When the tried-and-true method is not an option, it often helps to step back and look at the big picture.

The Big Picture

Three things limit your ability to fix bugs and add features. The first is your ability to make sense of the code. The second is your ability to find those bugs and implement those features. The machine's ability to process your instructions is a distant third.

That said, machines have finite resources, and every feature uses some of them. Consider the finite traction on a car tire. Each of the car's basic features—braking, accelerating, and steering—uses some of that traction. Applying too much brake in a corner can overuse that traction and send the car skidding off course. So it is with a computer.

The more memory and processor time your new feature uses, the less memory and processor time will be available to your next feature. If the needs of all the features running at a given time are more than the machine has available, bad things happen. You might drop frames in audio, video, or animation, or the system might protect itself by crashing your application.

On the iPhone, you have the additional worry that every clock cycle you use is draining the battery that much faster. Obviously, the resources are there to be used, but remember that those resources belong to the user. If you waste users' resources, they may well decide to give their business, and their money, to your competitor.

The big picture is what makes performance such a hard problem. The questions of what needs to be faster and how much faster it needs to be do not have absolute answers. A feature that sucks up half the CPU by itself is bad, but having five features sucking up a quarter of the CPU each is worse. This scenario is not uncommon; in fact, it occurs during every application launch.

Every line of code you run before accepting the user's input is making the user wait. You could blow your entire development cycle trying to make that code faster, but it will never be fast enough. It's much more effective to remove as much code as possible from that space. The idea is to load only the visible user interface (UI), start the event loop, and then load the data necessary to fill in the UI. Everything else should be loaded lazily; that is, only as needed.

Laziness won't make the individual lines of code execute faster, but neither will it make them larger or harder to understand. What laziness will do is make your application faster. As an engineer, you may appreciate elegant algorithms and clever code, but to the user, none of that matters. Perceived performance is the only kind that matters.

The saying goes that an ounce of mathematics is worth a pound of engineering. I maintain a clever engineer can fake a lot of math. A rather primitive method for making fire fakes all the expensive math that goes into a particle engine. I can't take credit for inventing the method—that honor goes to some anonymous, clever third-grader—but I have given it a name: Smoke and Mirrors.

Iteration 2: Smoke and Mirrors

The idea behind the Smoke and Mirrors technique is simple. Take a picture of smoke, and animate it in an infinite, treadmill-like loop. For each fire, mask off a nice smoke plume. Put a translucent fire-colored overlay over the bottom, and the "smoke" animating in the background gives a nice simulation of a particle emitter without any of the math.

When I was a kid, we used butcher paper and paper towel tubes. Nowadays, I prefer Photoshop, which I used to create two images:

- A smoke image that can be tiled (I'm no artist, but the Render Clouds filter does a good job)

- A plume-shaped image that will be used to mask the smoke image into separate fires

On the Mac, Core Animation provides a mask property on the CALayer class that makes masking easy, but that property is not available for the iPhone. Alpha masks can still be done using the 2D drawing API, which is referred to as Core Graphics or Quartz 2D. Adding animation is a simple matter of creating an NSTimer instance to call the view's drawRect: method every 1/30 second, assuming you're looking for the standard frame rate of 30 frames per second.

When drawRect: is called, a bit of fancy math will convert the time to the smoke's position, which can then be masked and drawn. It looks pretty good in a screenshot, as seen in Figure 7-3. It's about as fast as the screenshot, too. Instead of 30 frames a second, the iPhone barely puts out 2.

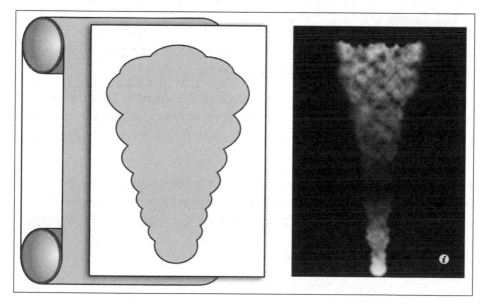

Figure 7-3. *Smoke and Mirrors in theory and practice*

When it comes to drawing on an iPhone, there are two rules of thumb:

- Alpha compositing is very expensive.

- Core Animation is more efficient than custom drawing code.

This first attempt violates both rules, and the resulting code is unacceptably slow.

Hope is not lost. You can move the animation back into Core Animation, while keeping the mask in Core Graphics. If it takes almost half a second to apply an alpha mask, that's 15 times slower than you need to draw the smoke layer. On the other hand, the background never changes.

By cutting holes in the background, rather than masking the smoke, you can reduce the number of masking operations and leave the details of compositing the frame to Core Animation, as shown in Listing 7-1.

Listing 7-1. *Cutting Holes in the Background Using an Alpha Mask*

```
UIGraphicsBeginImageContext(self.bounds.size);
CGContextRef context = UIGraphicsGetCurrentContext();
UIImage *mask = [UIImage imageNamed:@"plume.png"];
CGContextClipToMask(context, background.frame, mask.CGImage);
[[UIImage imageNamed:@"BoardBackground.png"] drawAtPoint:CGPointZero
    blendMode:kCGBlendModeNormal alpha:1.0];

[self setBackgroundImage:UIGraphicsGetImageFromCurrentImageContext()];
UIGraphicsEndImageContext();
```

Experiments confirm that this is reasonably fast. The half-second masking operation makes changing the fires lag, but the actual effect performs well.

But wait—this means that the smoke, which should be in the foreground, must now animate behind the background. It turns out that this doesn't necessarily matter. This is 2D drawing, so as long as you're careful not to give any contradictory depth cues, the fact that the smoke is technically behind the background is irrelevant.

Computers can often behave in ways that are not obvious to the people programming them. This is a particular problem in optimization. Humans are bad at knowing what makes computers slow, leading to ham-fisted attempts at optimization that at best do nothing and at worst make things slower.

Premature Optimization

There are two opinions about optimization, which seem to be at odds. The voice of experience suggests that you should optimize code the way they vote in Chicago: early and often. On the other hand, the eminent computer scientist Donald Knuth once wrote, "We should forget about small efficiencies, say about 97 percent of the time: premature optimization is the root of all evil."

To clear up this apparent contradiction, it helps to consider the different types of optimizations and the efficiencies they address.

Build Efficiency

Just as there are multiple ways to write the same program, there are multiple ways for a compiler to translate your code into machine language. Since it's already hardware-dependent, the compiler can take advantage of specific optimizations without adding those dependencies to your application code.

The advantage of build-time optimization is that it's essentially free. The build settings in Apple's Xcode development environment include a number of optimizations, the most obvious of which is the compiler optimizations level, shown in Figure 7-4. The settings range from no optimization (-O0) to full optimization (-O3). There's also an option to optimize for memory usage (-Os), which turns out to be the best option in most cases.

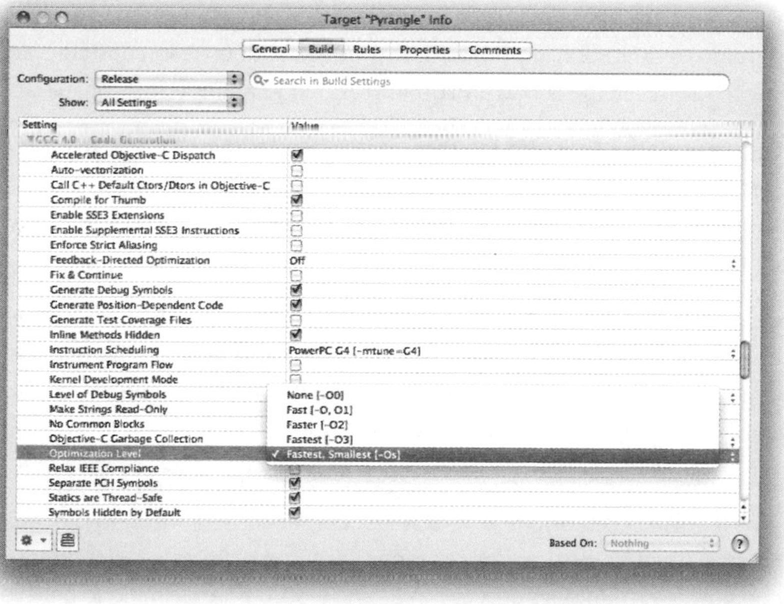

Figure 7-4. *Setting the optimization level in Xcode's target inspector*

Using compiler optimizations does have a couple of small disadvantages:

- It completely destroys your ability to step through code in the debugger. Instead of executing your instructions in order, the optimized code seems to jump all over the place.

- It increases build time. This isn't as much of an issue for iPhone applications, since the build system is usually much, much faster than the target hardware. For larger applications, this can become an issue. Adding a minute to compile time doesn't seem like a big deal, but it adds up. Build 60 times a day, which is hardly unreasonable, and you're wasting an hour.

These problems can be ameliorated by using smarter builds. Use different build configurations to disable optimization during debugging, which will keep builds fast and execution orders predictable. Caching build products also improves build times. Avoid building from clean whenever possible to prevent longer build times.

Build-time optimization can have tricky interactions with your own optimization efforts. An application built at two different optimization levels is two different applications. Optimizing the wrong one can lead to misleading results. Release builds also tend to do things aside from optimization, like stripping the debugging symbols necessary to find bottlenecks in your code.

The solution is to create a separate build configuration for optimizations. This can be done by opening the Project Info panel in Xcode, selecting the Configurations tab, and duplicating the Debug configuration, naming the new configuration Optimize, as shown in Figure 7-5. Edit the new configuration, turning optimization on. This adds symbols, but doesn't fix code stepping, so you may need to switch between the debug and optimize configurations to get the full story.

Compiler optimization has safety issues, though these are relatively minor. Because it pushes your code harder, this optimization may uncover bugs and crashers. Overly clever code that relies on undefined language quirks is particularly prone to breakage. If at all possible, it's better to fix the bugs than to disable optimization.

Compiler settings and other build-time optimizations are never premature. They are, however, still subject to another rule of optimization: never assume. Every application is different, and different combinations of compiler flags will yield different results. Never assume any configuration is best without having hard data to back up that conclusion.

For example, building an application for the iPhone using the Compile for Thumb setting generally produces smaller, faster code. Thumb is a subset of instructions for the ARM processor that fit in 16 bits, versus the usual 32. However, applications with a lot of floating-point operations might actually be slower in Thumb. It's best to run timing tests before claiming to believe in either option. As the saying goes, "In God we trust. All others bring data." Nowhere is this more true than code-level optimizations based on perceptions of performance. These are nearly always premature.

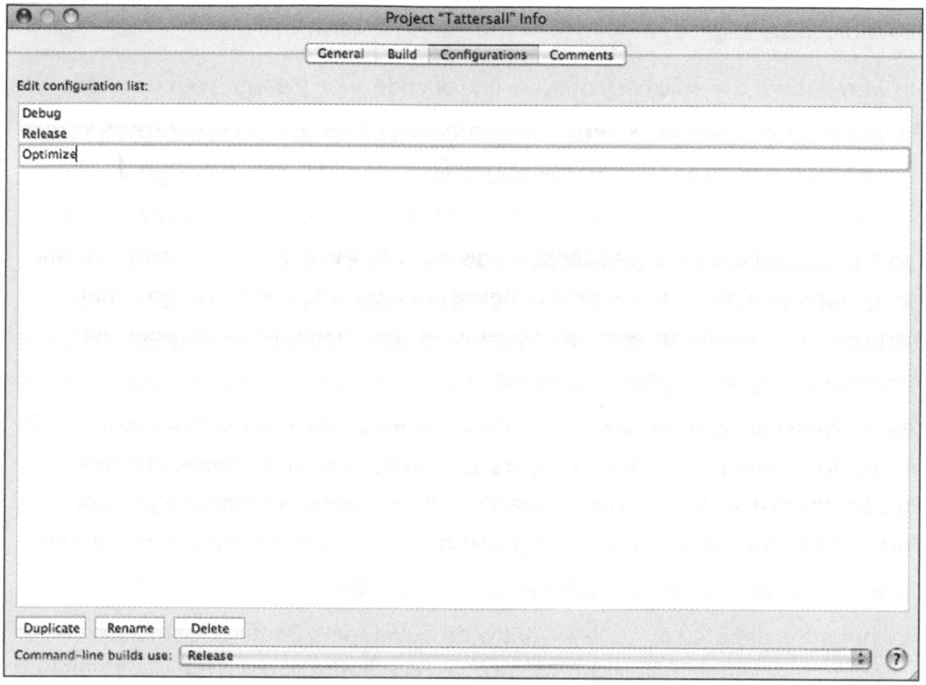

Figure 7-5. *Creating an Optimize configuration in Xcode's Project Info pane*

Code Efficiency

Every block of code takes a different amount of time to execute. Just like products in a supermarket, the individual methods of an API have their own cost. These small differences add up, but the supermarket strategy of comparing prices when selecting each item will not work for code. Unlike a shopping cart, which might contain a few dozen items, an application can contain hundreds of thousands of lines of code. Hand-picking each one would take far too long.

Just as the cost of items will vary from store to store, the cost of a method will vary from platform to platform. Making code-level decisions based on architectural quirks is like recommending a brand because one store has it on sale. It's also just as prone to obsolescence.

For example, in Objective-C, it used to be much more expensive to enter a `try` block than to throw an exception. You might make coding decisions based on that knowledge, but that's a risky proposition. Implementation details are not guaranteed, so code that relies on them is prone to breakage. In the 64-bit version of Objective-C, throwing exceptions is now much more expensive than entering a `try` block.

Worse, it's likely such optimizations make no difference to your application's performance. An application is only as fast as its slowest part, and even trivial applications contain a mind-boggling web of parts. Shaving off picoseconds at random is like spitting in the ocean. You're much more likely to get in trouble than you are to hit a fish.

Rather than worry about the efficiency of every line of code, worry about your own efficiency. Adding code complexity to an application without making it faster is a waste of time. It's much more efficient to write 100 percent of your code to be readable, logical, and terse, then go back and speed up the 3 percent that's actually slow.

The code you do not write is a gift that keeps on giving. It doesn't cause bugs or get in the way of adding features. It doesn't take time to figure out later, and it requires no maintenance. Unwritten code is never broken by an operating system update, nor does it ever become obsolete.

The best way to keep your code base fast, small, and future-proof is to use the vendor-provided frameworks. This code is written by platform experts who are better engineers than you or I. Let them deal with hardware-specific optimizations. Not only do you not need to worry about your code breaking, but you'll also get future performance upgrades for free.

When Core Animation debuted at Apple's Worldwide Developers Conference in 2006, it obsoleted thousands of lines of painstaking animation code in the nascent Delicious Library 2. Although our code was arguably better than what Apple had demonstrated, our boss, Wil Shipley, knew better than to let hubris lead us down the road of "rolling our own." We ripped out our code and spent the next year helping Apple nail down bugs in the new framework by filing reports with Apple's Bug Reporter (also known as RadarWeb).

Our work paid off the next year, as shown in Figure 7-6. Delicious Library 2 won the Apple Design Award for Best Leopard Application. Apple demoed our app on the same stage where Steve Jobs had delivered the keynote speech days before. The application loaded, looking much like the shipping version, with its iconic woodgrain shelves. Then the sample library materialized in a gorgeous fade-in animation, and the entire room literally gasped. The funny thing is that we gasped, too. We had never seen anything like it before either, because *we didn't do that*. All we did was use the Core Animation framework. The sexy fade-in that so impressed our peers was a gift from Apple.

Figure 7-6. *The Delicious Monster team, from left: Lucas Newman, Wil Shipley, and Mike Lee*

Algorithmic Efficiency

While individual lines of codes almost always don't matter, the order those lines appear in almost always does. The efficiency of the algorithm the code implements has a significant effect on its performance.

Before I broke the bad habit of code-level optimization, I wrote a naïve array comparison based on the assumption that sorting the arrays before comparing them would take longer. I could have tested that assumption by writing it both ways and timing them, but it's much more efficient to familiarize yourself with the efficiency of basic algorithms.

Sorted arrays can be compared in $O(n \log n)$, while my unsorted solution was $O(n^2)$. This means that if the arrays each contained 10,000 items, the naïve algorithm would require 100,000,000 operations, while the sorted algorithm would require 133,000 operations. With one million items, the better algorithm will perform eighty million operations, while the naïve algorithm will cause your computer to burst into flames on its way to one quadrillion operations.

To put that in perspective, at one billion operations per second, that's 80 milliseconds versus about 17 minutes—for the same amount of work. On the other hand, if the arrays would only ever have 100 items each, the difference would be a mere 7 microseconds. That isn't really worth the extra code.

Algorithmic optimizations are platform-independent and generally a good idea, but the rules still apply. You should keep an eye out for signs of potentially expensive algorithms, like nested loops, but don't spend too much time optimizing algorithms you don't know are slow.

Many optimizations make trade-offs between different types of efficiency, particularly time versus space. Caching is a perfect example of this, saving the time of calculating something by using the space to keep it in memory. At a certain point, space efficiency becomes its own problem. Memory pressure is a major source of crashes on the iPhone.

This pattern holds true orders of magnitude down the performance scale. Packaging files with your application is much faster than having to download them over a network. But if your application bundle is too large, your initial download time becomes unreasonable.

If your application is being distributed through the App Store and it exceeds a certain size limit, it can be downloaded only over broadband and the faster 3G cellular network. Customers on first-generation iPhones or outside 3G range are stuck on the slower EDGE network, and they will be unable to buy your application directly from their phones. You would do well to heed this limit. As an example, the audio files packaged with Tapulous's Tap Tap Revenge game were carefully optimized for size to keep the total bundle under the then-current 10MB limit.

The size limitation may be spelled out in the fine print, but finding most pain points requires some hunting. Apple provides a companion tool to Xcode to help, named for nature's most ruthless hunter: Shark.

Iteration 3: Shark Attack Time

The black art of optimization cannot be accomplished solely by man or machine. It takes the cool logic of Shark to know why an application is slow, but it takes the human gift of intuition to know what to do about the problem. Every case is unique and frequently surprising. Optimizing the fire effects is no exception.

Running Shark on iPhone applications is a bit tricky. There's no sense trying to optimize in the simulator. In general, you want your optimization environment to be as close to your deployment environment as possible, which means turning compiler optimizations on and copying the binary to the device. This makes optimization build times quite a bit longer than those in the normal development work flow.

Rather than launching the app in Shark from Xcode, follow these steps:

1. In Xcode, set your configuration to Optimize and Device.

2. Build and run on a tethered iPhone.

3. Launch Shark from `/Developer/Applications/Performance Tools/`.

4. In Shark, enable remote profiling by selecting **Network/iPhone Profiling** from the **Sampling** menu. This will add the Network/iPhone Profiling pane to Shark's main window, as shown in Figure 7-7.

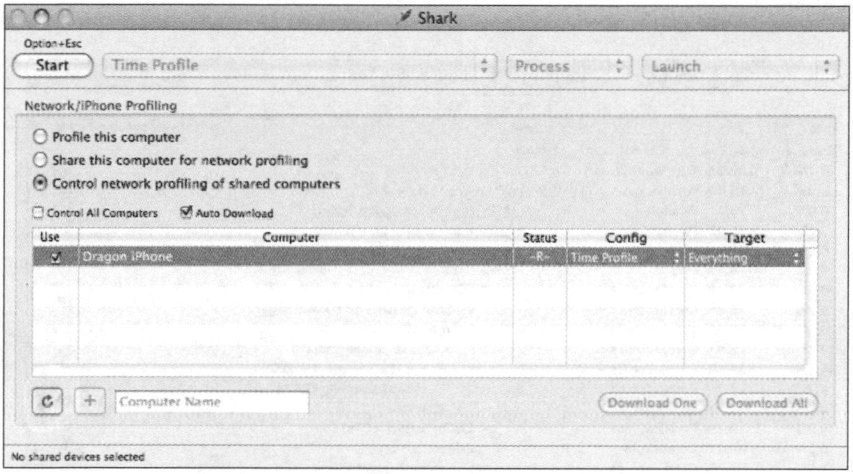

Figure 7-7. *Using Shark to remotely sample on an iPhone*

5. From the Network/iPhone Profiling pane, select "Control network profiling of shared computers." If your device is not listed, click the Refresh button (the button with a semicircular arrow in the lower-left corner).

6. Select the application name from the Target column.

7. Set the type of profile you want in the Config column.

8. Click the Start button.

Shark relies on the remote device for a lot of processing, so try to keep your samples as small as possible. Once you click the Stop button, even the smallest sample can take a minute or two to process and load into Shark.

Shark works by polling the application to see what it's doing. The more time the program spends doing a task, the more often that task will come up during polling. Shark describes the time spent per task as a relative percentage.

Interpreting Shark's results is a book in and of itself. Luckily that book has been written. Shark's documentation is excellent, and it's included in Xcode's built-in documentation system. While you're there, read up on Shark's Windowed Time Facility mode, which is a great way to keep your iPhone samples from getting too large.

In this case, Shark made very clear where all the snappy had gone. I was spending most of the graphics time drawing the images to make my mask, as shown in Figure 7-8. The first rule of Quartz 2D on the iPhone strikes again: alpha compositing is expensive. There's not a lot you can do about that—it costs what it costs. Although you may be tempted to grab the reins from the drawing API and see if you can do a better job, in these situations, it's good to keep a level head.

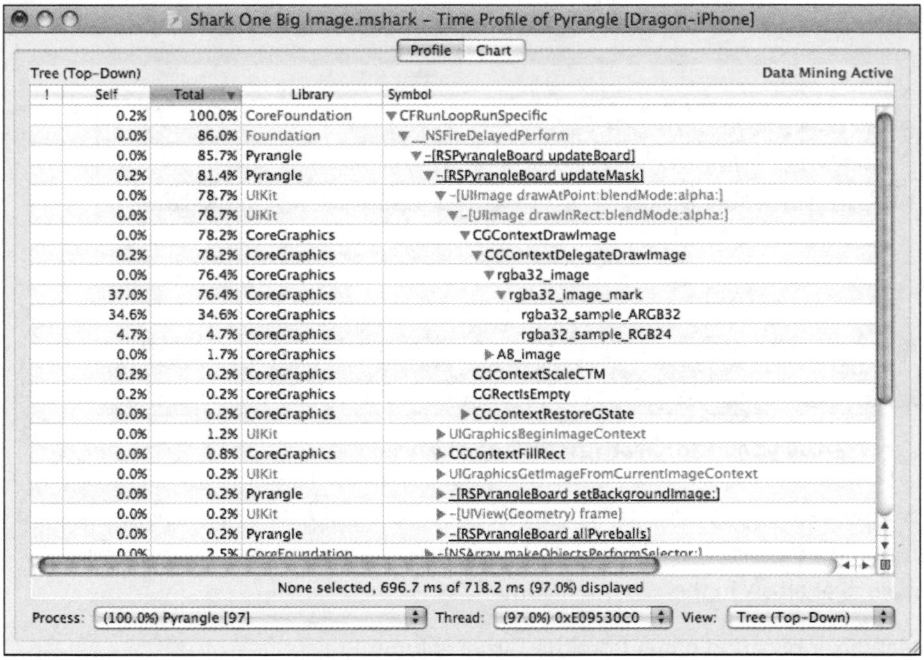

Figure 7-8. *Shark identifies the line of code that's hogging all the processing time.*

Level-Headed Performance

Many high-level frameworks are built on a lower-level framework, at least conceptually. The difference between these frameworks is the difference between dollars and cents, or if you will, bills and coins. Coins can represent odd, specific amounts, like 99 cents, but are impractical for larger transactions. Most of the time, you stick with paper money and use a little coinage to fill in the gaps. So it is with high-level and low-level frameworks. Most of the time, it's better to stay high level, because things are faster, easier, and require less code. When necessary, and with Shark's blessing, you can use the lower-level frameworks to fill in the gaps.

Two graphics APIs are available for the iPhone: Quartz and the Open Graphics Language for Embedded Systems (OpenGL ES). Most applications use the native Quartz framework, which on iPhone includes the Quartz 2D drawing library, also called Core Graphics, as well as the 2.5D layer-based Core Animation library. Quartz is what makes Mac OS X applications all swooshy and lickable, with little or no graphics code.

Quartz is optimized to perform operations common to most applications efficiently, and with minimal programming effort. Quartz is based on the Portable Document Format (PDF), which makes programming graphics like laying out a page. This abstraction works well for most applications, but is cumbersome for others. Games are the obvious example. Developers who need 3D graphics, intense performance optimization, or portable code turn to OpenGL ES.

OpenGL ES is a lightweight implementation of the OpenGL interface specification. Instead of using publishing metaphors, OpenGL uses the metaphors of graphics hardware. Programming in vertexes, triangles, and texels is more flexible, but more complicated. It's like telling the operating system to just turn over the graphics hardware to you for a while.

OpenGL is a software abstraction, a hardware-agnostic hardware language. Like C, OpenGL allows you to address the hardware on its own terms, without resorting to device-specific assembly language. This means that, with careful programming, you can get the hardware to do exactly what you want, and nothing else.

OpenGL does not have better performance than Quartz. Using OpenGL thinking that performance will be free is a mistake. What it has is better *potential* performance. Actually getting there will require a lot of optimization work. OpenGL is harder to write, harder to debug, and harder to maintain, so OpenGL programmers are particularly expensive.

My rule of thumb is to use Quartz to at least get to a playable demo. If performance dictates moving to OpenGL, then you can parallelize that work with play testing.

To give a real-world example, Tap Tap Revenge 2 looks a lot better than the original Tap Tap Revenge because the graphics were finally ported to OpenGL. On the other hand, if we had used OpenGL from the beginning, we might not have finished the game in time for the launch of the App Store.

Programming to a lower-level API than necessary is a distressingly common example of premature optimization. Many people see something damning in Shark and give up too soon. Do not underestimate the difference in time and complexity between frameworks. A little bit of clever experimentation is often justified.

Iteration 4: Increasingly Clever Optimizations

In my quest for fire, I got a week into porting the graphics to OpenGL. When I saw that a change that would be trivial in Quartz was going to undo most of my work, I realized I had been too hasty choosing OpenGL. It would have taken no more than a day to try optimizing my Quartz code. Better to waste a day than a week.

I reconsidered my assessment of what Shark had to say. I assumed that there was no getting around the fact that drawing an image with alpha compositing is going to be slow. Sometimes a week of dealing with OpenGL is just the thing to see the problem from a different angle.

To the GPU, an image is just an array of numbers describing the color of each pixel. When images overlap, the GPU just draws the one on top, but alpha compositing requires performing math on each and every pixel. The only way to speed that up would be to reduce the number of pixels being blended.

The mask image is only 220 pixels wide, but I padded it to screen width, 320 pixels, for convenience. If Knuth is right, any convenience has a 3 percent chance of being too slow. It's inconvenient having to go back and redo that work, but you need to do it only once. Every convenience that makes reading code easier will be repaid many times over.

In this case, the 100 pixels of padding doesn't seem like a big deal, but at 480 pixels high, that padding adds 48,000 unnecessary blend operations each time I draw the image. Eliminating this padding brought drawing the image down from 78.7 percent of each run loop to 53.8 percent, as shown in Figure 7-9.

That's a definite improvement, but I'm still spending half the run loop drawing the same image. If I can't draw it faster, maybe I can draw it fewer times, as I'll demonstrate in the next section.

Don't be surprised if an optimization actually makes things slower. Figuring out why, aside from being instructional, can often uncover subtle bugs in the original code. Getting there requires finding a metric to give Shark's results meaning—in this case, the number of times the slow method gets called. You can get this metric in a number of ways. Apple's Instruments tool could do it, as could the Dtrace profiling technology on which that tool is built. Setting breakpoints in the debugger that count, log, and continue would also work. In a pinch, a couple of static integers and NSLog will work. Be careful with logging, though, as too many calls to NSLog will become their own performance problem.

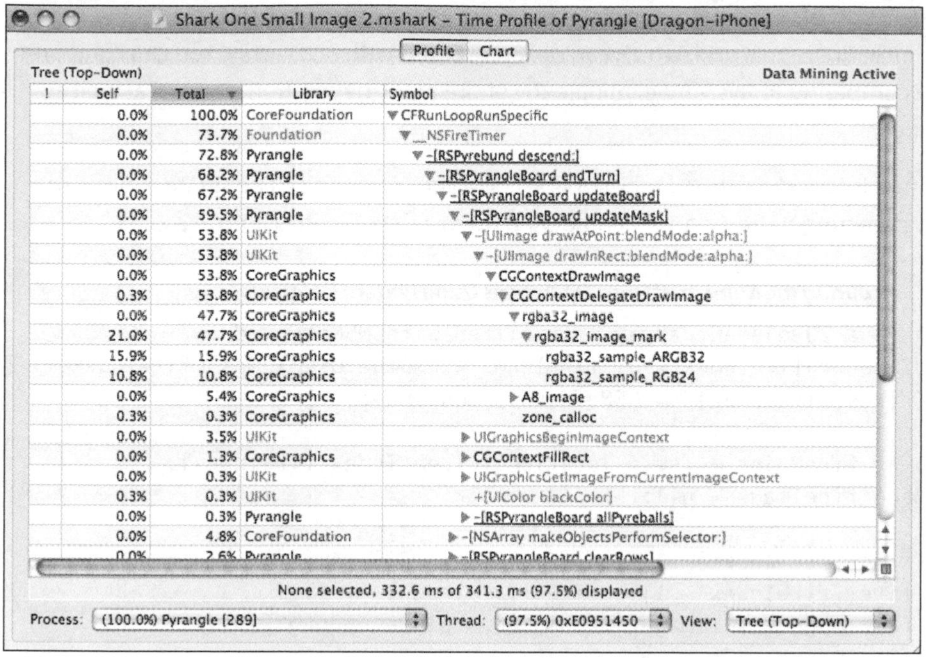

Figure 7-9. *A second Shark run shows how effective an optimization was.*

Application-Specific Optimization

The underlying principle of finite resources explains why low-level implementations are often faster than their high-level counterparts. High-level frameworks must be reusable in a number of situations, which means they must be flexible. This flexibility draws from the same resource pool as everything else.

Custom code eschews flexibility in favor of performance. That same lack of flexibility is why custom code is more prone to break. Normally, robustness is more important than performance, but when performance really matters, it's time to get specific.

Custom drawing code is common because drawing is one of the most expensive operations you can perform. Almost any amount of math is justified to avoid unnecessary drawing. This particular implementation detail is unlikely to change anytime soon, so this is a good time to leverage application-specific knowledge.

The first step is to identify redundant frames, where you're redrawing the same thing. In this case, the fires adhere to a grid, which can be represented with a 2D array. You can compare frames by comparing arrays, and eliminate the entire mask-generation process, as well as the drawing.

The next step is to reduce the number of draw operations needed to generate a mask. You do this by detecting patterns and prerendering them, as shown in Listing 7-2.

Listing 7-2. *Reducing the Number of Draw Operations Using Pattern Detection*

```
// fires is a 20-element array initialized with NSNotFound
for (NSUInteger fireIndex = 0; fireIndex < kNumberOfColumns; fireIndex++) {
    if (fires[fireIndex] == NSNotFound) continue;

    CGPoint firePoint = [self locationOfFireAtIndex:fireIndex];
    UIImage fireImage = nil;

    if (fires[fireIndex] == fires[fireIndex + 2] &&
        fires[fireIndex + 1] - fires[fireIndex] == 2) {
        fireImage = [UIImage imageNamed:@"plume-up.png"];
        fireIndex += 2;
    } else if (fires[fireIndex] == fires[fireIndex + 2] &&
        fires[fireIndex] - fires[fireIndex + 1] == 2) {
        fireImage = [UIImage imageNamed:@"plume-down.png"];
        fireIndex += 2;
    } else fireImage = [UIImage imageNamed:@"plume-one.png"];

    [fireImage drawAtPoint:firePoint blendMode:kCGBlendModeDestinationOut
        alpha:0.7];
}
```

You could write some clever code to automatically detect new patterns, create new masks, and archive and retrieve them as necessary. I just made a few images with common patterns and added them to the bundle. They add 88KB to the size of the bundle and reduce the number of draws per update by two-thirds. The whole process is illustrated in Figure 7-10.

There's no sense setting a pixel more than once per frame. You can avoid this by calculating which images will be covered by another image, as shown in Listing 7-3. In this case, only the highest fire per column is visible. Instead of using an actual 2D array, fires is a simple array containing the highest row per column containing fire.

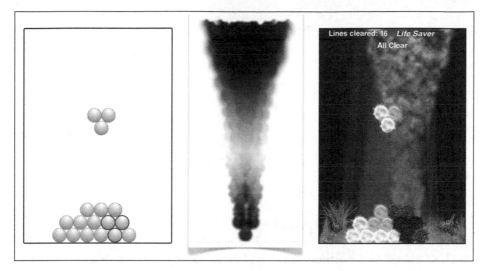

Figure 7-10. *Using pattern matching and multiple-plume masks*

Listing 7-3. *A Simple Method for Finding the Highest Fire in Each Row*

```
NSArray *allPieces = self.allPieces;
for (RSPiece *piece in allPieces)
    if (piece.kind == RSPieceFireKind)
        fires[piece.coordinates.column] = piece.coordinates.row;
```

With any luck, you can achieve acceptable performance before the optimizations get too esoteric. Let's indulge in one more: interframe compression, shown in Listing 7-4. Normally, you begin the update by filing the frame, resetting the canvas. However, if the update is adding fires, there's no sense erasing the existing fires just to draw them again.

Listing 7-4. *Eliminating Redundant Draw Operations Between Frames*

```
// oldFires and newFires are 20-element arrays initialized with NSNotFound
static BOOL clearContext = YES;

memcpy(newFires, fires, sizeof(fires));
for (NSUInteger fireIndex = 0; fireIndex < 20; fireIndex++) {
    if (newFires[fireIndex] == oldFires[fireIndex]) {
        newFires[fireIndex] = NSNotFound; // Prevents redraw
        continue;
    }

    if (oldFires[fireIndex] == NSNotFound) {
        oldFires[fireIndex] = newFires[fireIndex]; // Records new draw
        continue;
```

```
        }
        memcpy(newFires, fires, sizeof(fires));
        clearContext = YES;
        break;
}

static UIImage *mask = nil;
if (clearContext) {
        [[UIColor blackColor] setFill];
        CGContextFillRect(context, self.bounds);
        clearContext = NO;
} else [mask drawAtPoint:CGPointZero];

memcpy(fires, newFires, sizeof(fires));
```

All this code is a lot of work for the processor, but not as much work as drawing. All told, these optimizations bring drawing down to 33.4 percent of the run loop, as shown in Figure 7-11. These optimizations improve as the number of fires increases. In-frame compression can draw three fires with one operation, but adding three fires with interframe compression now requires just one additional operation instead of six.

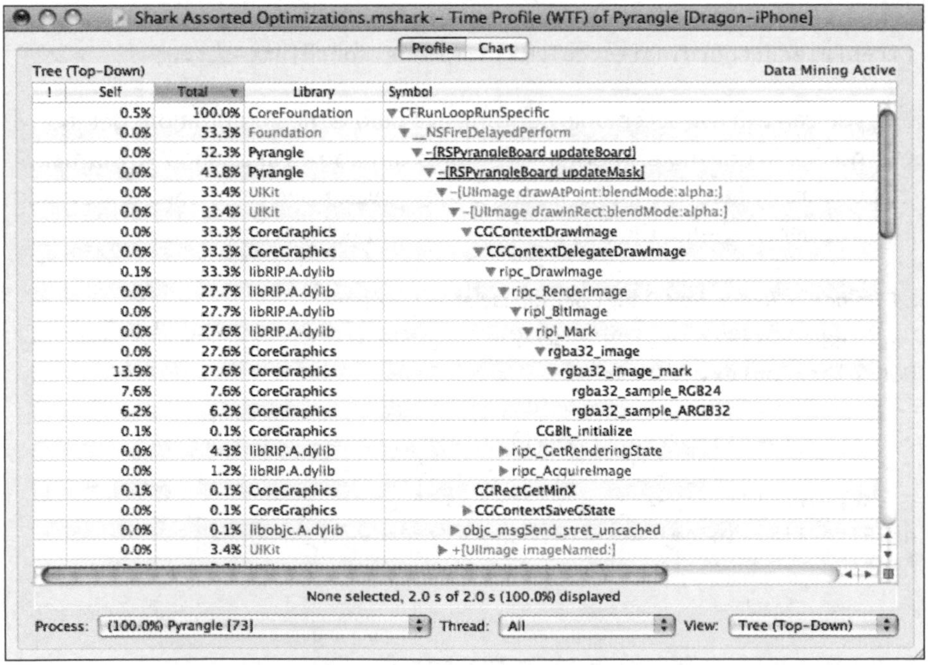

Figure 7-11. *These simple optimizations have significantly improved drawing performance.*

Summary

Engineers are terrible with endings. The complexity of modern software and the realities of shipping deadlines mean most applications are never really finished. There's always another bug to fix, another feature to add, and another clever optimization to pursue.

What I hope comes through in all of this is not the specific details of one optimization, but the single, unifying pattern behind every iteration. Whether your next project has four iterations or forty, regardless of whether you're on the iPhone or another platform, your best optimization strategy is always the same.

Code for readability and ease of implementation first, then optimize the things that are actually slow. Never assume you know what is slow or why. Use experiments to test your intuition, always returning to hard data like Shark profiles and performance metrics.

Good hunting!

Richard Zito and Matthew Aitken

Company: Swipe Interactive

Location: UK

Former Lives As Developers: Prior to working with the iPhone, our industry experience was largely in web design, development, and hosting. This meant that we worked with a wide range of platforms, with strengths primarily in LAMP-based systems and languages. In terms of gaming, we developed several web-based puzzle games, as well as some Flash/ActionScript games.

Lives As iPhone Developers: Having cofounded Swipe Interactive, we now work to develop high-end applications for the iPhone, concentrating primarily on the inherent networked multiplayer capabilities of the iPhone as a gaming platform. We currently have two games in the App Store, with many more applications in the pipeline.

- Quick Draw (Word Games category)
- Pole2Pole (Trivia Games category)

What's in This Chapter: This chapter shows you the best ways to take advantage of the iPhone's inherent interconnectivity. It covers communicating with servers and using Bonjour to manage services on a Wi-Fi network. To demonstrate, we'll walk through developing a multi-player tic-tac-toe game that's playable over any Wi-Fi network.

Key Technologies:

- Bonjour networking
- Socket programming
- HTTP requests

Quick Draw (Word Games category)

Pole2Pole (Trivia Games category)

Chapter 8

Networked Games: Choosing the Right Option

hen I first started to look at developing applications on the iPhone platform, it became clear to me that very few developers were taking advantage of the unique fact that every device is connected to every other device via the Internet. To me, this inherent connectivity meant one thing: multiplayer gaming. Moreover, the very nature of mobile devices means that they lend themselves perfectly to casual games, those appealing to users of any gaming experience that can repeatedly be picked up, played for a short time, and then put down again until next time. Under these principles, I cofounded Swipe Interactive and came to develop and release two multiplayer-based iPhone games, with many more in the pipeline.

The first of these games, and Swipe Interactive's first iPhone release, was Quick Draw—a game in which players try to identify a word based on another player's sketch of it and compete for points based on how quickly they can get it right. I learned a lot from Quick Draw and proceeded with the second application, called Pole2Pole, which is a game based upon the concept of competing against other online players in pinpointing a location on a map as accurately as possible. In Pole2Pole, we also introduced the ability to play over the local network and made use of the iPhone's gestures to zoom around the screen.

Figure 8-1 shows a screenshot of Pole2Pole in action.

By the time you finish reading this chapter, you will have learned how to use the iPhone's networking capabilities, which form the basis of the games Swipe Interactive has developed so far, to develop your own multiplayer games. I will guide you through relatively simple tasks such as getting the iPhone to communicate asynchronously with servers to send and receive data, as well as more complex applications such as how to use the Apple Bonjour services to communicate directly from one device to another.

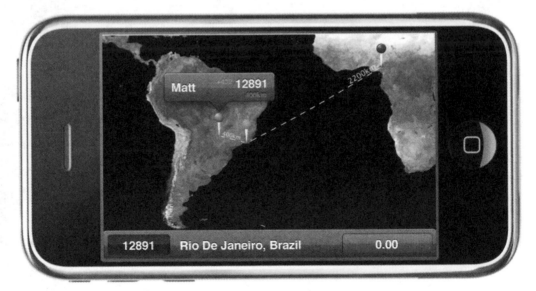

Figure 8-1. *Swipe Interactive's second iPhone game, Pole2Pole*

Multiplayer Networking Options

When I started to develop Quick Draw, I aimed to build an application that allowed players from anywhere in the world, whether they're connected through wireless, 3G, or even slower speed mobile Internet connections, to be able to play together. Figure 8-2 shows the login screen to join the Quick Draw network. The first port of call was therefore to get an underlying device-to-device communication system working, through which messages could be sent quickly and reliably between devices. We managed to achieve this only after going through many different methods, the most important of which I will be discussing in this section.

Figure 8-2. *The login screen for Swipe Interactive's first iPhone game, Quick Draw*

Communication Is Key

Most of the methods I cover here will involve a server through which the devices must communicate in order to transmit or retrieve the information they require, as illustrated in Figure 8-3. This means that in order to develop a game utilizing these communication methods, you will also need some knowledge of how to get a server to handle the information you send to it. This can be achieved in many ways, whether you write simple scripts accessible over a web server or whether you run a more complex gaming server (I will touch on this idea later). In this chapter, I will show how to use a simple HTTP GET method implementation based around PHP scripts to demonstrate communication with a server, but of course there are many solutions to this type of problem. The method you choose will depend on your programming background and personal preference.

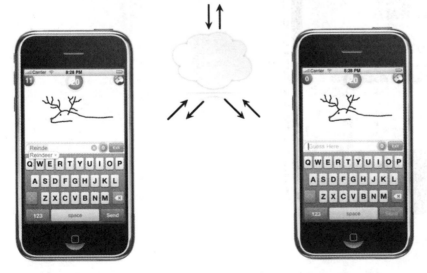

Figure 8-3. All messages between devices in Quick Draw are transferred through a multiuser server.

URL Requests

The first attempt I made to communicate with servers over the Internet from the iPhone was to use the simple NSString method initWithContentsOfURL: to load information from a URL. For example, Listing 8-1 shows a simple process of loading and updating scores from a URL.

Listing 8-1. *Loading Data Synchronously from a URL*

```
-(NSInteger)retrieveScoreForUser:(NSString *)usr {

  NSString *urlStr = [NSString stringWithFormat:
                      @"%@/score.php?u=%@",server,usr];
  NSURL *scoreURL = [NSURL URLWithString:urlStr];
  NSString *returnStr = [NSString stringWithContentsOfURL:scoreURL];
  // perform some validation on returnStr if necessary

  return [returnStr integerValue];

}


-(void)updateScoreForUser:(NSString *)usr withScore:(NSInteger)scr {

  NSString *urlStr = [NSString stringWithFormat:
                      @"%@/updateScore.php?u=%@&s=%i",server,usr,scr];
  NSURL *scoreURL = [NSURL URLWithString:urlStr];
  NSString *returnStr = [NSString stringWithContentsOfURL:scoreURL];

  // perform some validation on returnStr if necessary

}
```

This method of reading and writing to and from servers is acceptable for some situations, but it is fundamentally flawed for responsive gaming. The main problem with NSString's stringWithContentsOfURL: is that it loads the content of the URL **synchronously**, meaning that it blocks the current program loop until it finishes loading. This is clearly not ideal, because your application will stop responding for the duration of URL request, which itself can take some time to complete.

In order to run nonblocking, or **asynchronous**, URL requests, you can use NSURLConnection class methods. When using NSURLConnection to make URL requests, the actual request is handled in the background, allowing the rest of the program to continue running. When data is obtained, or even when the request fails, a chosen delegate object is notified to handle the data. Listing 8-2 shows a method that initiates the retrieval of information from a web page (here a simple PHP page, *score.php*) using NSURLConnection. Listing 8-3 shows the associated delegate methods.

Listing 8-2. *Using NSURLConnection to Load a Web Page*

```
-(void)retrieveScoreForUser:(NSString *)user {

  NSString *urlStr =
    [NSString stringWithFormat:@"%@/score.php?u=%@",server,user];
  NSURL *scoreURL = [NSURL URLWithString:urlStr];
  NSURLRequest *scoreRequest =
    [NSURLRequest requestWithURL:scoreURL
              cachePolicy:NSURLRequestReloadIgnoringLocalAndRemoteCacheData
              timeoutInterval:10.0];
  theConnection = [[NSURLConnection alloc] initWithRequest:scoreRequest
                                               delegate:self];

  if (theConnection) {
    theData=[[NSMutableData data] retain];
    // theData is an instance variable
  } else {
    // failed to make connection
  }

}
```

Listing 8-3. *Delegate Methods for NSURLConnection*

```
-(void)connection:(NSURLConnection *)connection
  didReceiveResponse:(NSURLResponse *)response {

  [theData setLength:0];

}

-(void)connection:(NSURLConnection *)con didFailWithError:(NSError *)err {

  NSLog(@"Can't connect - %@", [err localizedFailureReason]);
  [con release];
  [theData release];

}

- (void)connection:(NSURLConnection *)con didReceiveData:(NSData *)data {

  [theData appendData:data];

}

- (void)connectionDidFinishLoading:(NSURLConnection *)connection {

  NSString *responseStr
```

```
    = [NSString stringWithFormat:@"%s",[theData mutableBytes]];
// some validation on responseStr if necessary

    score = [responseStr integerValue];

    [connection release];
    [theData release];

}
```

The nonblocking behavior of NSURLConnection is clearly an improvement over using NSString's blocking stringWithContentsOfURL: method, and it can produce good results for games where information doesn't need to be transferred between devices and a server very often. You will find, however, that when you need to transfer several messages per second, such as the drawing information I needed to transmit between devices in Quick Draw, you need a more efficient solution.

This brings me to the subject of working with sockets, which will be the topic of the next section.

Socket Connections

You can use socket connections to provide an open connection between a device and a server, thereby removing the need to create a connection from scratch each time something needs to be sent or retrieved. When using sockets, a remote open socket is required for you to connect to, which to be of any use would have to be attached to an application that handles the gaming messages. To handle the gaming messages required in Swipe Interactive's Quick Draw and Pole2Pole games, I built a multiuser server, so in this chapter I will describe the socket connections as being between the device and a server. Developing one of these servers from scratch can be quite a difficult task and is not a subject that I can cover in this chapter. If you find yourself needing a multiuser server, then you can find many resources available on the topic online.

Creating socket connections on the iPhone requires some more involved code than was needed for the previous methods of communicating, and as such, there are some concepts and functions included in this chapter for which you will need to look further than the iPhone SDK documentation to find detailed explanations of. The result of this extra work, however, will mean that you can communicate your gaming messages quickly and easily, resulting in much faster gaming.

You can start by creating a socket connection to a known address and port using the Core Foundation CFSocket class, as shown in the SocketController class in Listing 8-4.

Listing 8-4. *Connecting a Socket*

```
#import <netinet/in.h>
#import <sys/socket.h>
#import <arpa/inet.h>
```

```
@implementation SocketController

-(CFSocketRef)initSocket {

  CFSocketContext context = {
    .version = 0,
    .info = self,
    .retain = NULL,
    .release = NULL,
    .copyDescription = NULL
  };

  CFSocketRef socket = CFSocketCreate(
    kCFAllocatorDefault,
    PF_INET,
    SOCK_STREAM,
    IPPROTO_TCP,
    kCFSocketDataCallBack^kCFSocketConnectCallBack, // callBackTypes
    socketCallBack, // callBack function
    &context
  );

  uint16_t port = 12345;

  struct sockaddr_in addr4;

  memset(&addr4, 0, sizeof(addr4));
  addr4.sin_family = AF_INET;
  addr4.sin_len = sizeof(addr4);
  addr4.sin_port = htons(port);

  const char *ipaddress = "12.34.56.78";

  inet_aton(ipaddress, &addr4.sin_addr);

  NSData *address = [NSData dataWithBytes:&addr4 length:sizeof(addr4)];

  CFSocketConnectToAddress(socket, (CFDataRef)address, -1);

  CFRunLoopSourceRef source;
  source = CFSocketCreateRunLoopSource(NULL, socket, 1);
  CFRunLoopAddSource(CFRunLoopGetCurrent(), source, kCFRunLoopDefaultMode);
  CFRelease(source);

  return socket;

}

@end
```

The initSocket method in Listing 8-4 sets up the socket connection to a remote port (in this case I'm using the address 12.34.56.78 and port 12345) and assigns a callback function called socketCallback to handle socket events. An important feature of the callback function is that you can choose which socket events will result in the callback function being called. You can see that I have chosen to have the callback function called when events of type kCFSocketDataCallBack *or* kCFSocketConnectCallBack occur, which (respectively) correspond to data being received by the socket and a new connection being made by the socket. You can find further details on these types, and the others available, in the iPhone SDK documentation.

You now need to set up the callback function to handle the socket's connection status and incoming data callbacks. Note that in order to be able to call SocketController class methods from within socketCallback, .info is set as self in the socket context in Listing 8-4. This means that the SocketController property self is always passed to socketCallBack as the info parameter, allowing access back to the class methods. Listing 8-5 shows an example of a socket callback function.

Listing 8-5. *Socket Callback Function to Deal with Socket Connection and Incoming Data*

```
static void socketCallBack( CFSocketRef s, CFSocketCallBackType type,
  CFDataRef address, const void *dataIn, void *info )
{
  SocketController *socketController = (SocketController *) info;

  if(type==kCFSocketConnectCallBack) {

    if(dataIn) {

      SInt32 error = *((SInt32*)dataIn) ;
      printf("error code %d\n",error);

    }

    return;
  }

  if(type == kCFSocketDataCallBack) {

    unsigned char *dataBytes;
    dataBytes = [(NSMutableData *)dataIn mutableBytes];

    [socketController dealWithData:dataBytes];
    // deal with data in dataBytes

  }

}
```

Now that you know how to open socket connection between the device and server and any incoming data is being dealt with in a method of your choice, only one thing is left to do to complete the communication cycle: send a message to the server. Communicating a message to the server doesn't require anything more than telling the already-open socket to send a message by calling CFSocketSendData, as described in Listing 8-6. You can use the return value of CFSocketSendData to validate the send operation, because it returns the following values on success or failure:

- Returns 0: Successfully sent data

- Returns –1: Socket error

- Returns –2: Socket timeout (timeout set by fourth parameter of CFSocketSendData)

Listing 8-6. *Sending a Message Through a Connected Socket*

```
-(void)sendToServerMessage:(NSString *)message {

    sendStrUTF = [message UTF8String];
    NSData *dataOut = [NSData dataWithBytes:sendStrUTF
                                    length:strlen(sendStrUTF)];
    CFSocketError error = CFSocketSendData(socket, NULL,
                            (CFDataRef)dataOut, 0);
    // validate error's value

}
```

Through the methods described in this section, you should now have all the tools needed to communicate between devices and servers. With some clever programming on the server side, whether it be in the form of simple web pages attached to databases or complete multiuser servers, it is possible to use the methods described thus far to develop multiplayer gaming applications on the iPhone.

Say "Bonjour" to Local Network Gaming

The built-in wireless connectivity on the iPhone means that it is perfect for developing multiplayer games that run over the local network, a feature that is built into Swipe Interactive's second iPhone game, Pole2Pole, as shown in Figure 8-4. The first question you may ask when looking at the methods covered so far is, where is the server for the device to connect to? Clearly, having to set up and run a gaming server on the local network in order to be able to play is not an option, and having the devices connect to a remote server on the Internet defeats the point of trying to harness the high-speed wireless connections. Therefore, the obvious solution is to have the devices connect directly to one another, but how do the devices know where to look on the network for another device ready to play? This is where Bonjour comes in.

Figure 8-4. *Pole2Pole uses Bonjour in its WiFi multiplayer mode to allow network play.*

What Is Bonjour?

Bonjour is Apple's solution to zero-configuration networking over IP. Any application running a Bonjour service on a network can be discovered quickly by another application searching for a service of the same type on that network, allowing the two remote applications to interact with one another without any prior knowledge of each other's existence.

When applying this to iPhone gaming, Bonjour means that a device on the network can be running a service unique to that game while using Bonjour to advertise the service to other devices over the network. Meanwhile, another device on the network browses for the game service and, thanks to Bonjour, will quickly discover the first device available to connect with. After using the information being broadcast by Bonjour to resolve the details of the remote service, the devices can connect to each other and start to communicate the necessary gaming information.

Setting Up the Socket

The first step in setting up a service is to open a socket to the network. We don't know where to connect this socket to yet, so clearly it won't be connected to a particular remote address and port as before. This means that there are some changes to be made to the `initSocket` method we described in Listing 8-4. These changes are as follows:

- The callback type in `CFSocketCreate()` must be `kCFSocketAcceptCallBack` so that the socket callback function is called when a connection is made.

- Because of the way Bonjour works, the socket must be allowed to reuse local addresses. This is set by adding the following couple of lines:

```
int yes = 1;
setsockopt( CFSocketGetNative(socket),
                        SOL_SOCKET,
                        SO_REUSEADDR,
                        (void *)&yes,
                         sizeof(yes) );
```

- The socket should set itself up on any available port rather than a particular one as before. To get the device to choose an available port for you, you should simply set addr4.sin_port = 0.

- The socket address should be set as follows:

```
addr4.sin_addr.s_addr = htonl(INADDR_ANY);
CFSocketSetAddress(socket, (CFDataRef)address4);
```

These changes result in the new initSocket class, as shown in Listing 8-7, with the updated lines shown in bold.

Listing 8-7. *Connecting a Socket for Use with Bonjour*

```
- (CFSocketRef) initSocket {

  CFSocketContext context = {
    .version = 0,
    .info = self,
    .retain = NULL,
    .release = NULL,
    .copyDescription = NULL
  };

  CFSocketRef socket = CFSocketCreate(
    kCFAllocatorDefault,
    PF_INET,
    SOCK_STREAM,
    IPPROTO_TCP,
    kCFSocketAcceptCallBack, // callBackTypes
    socketCallBack, // callBack function
    &context
  );

  struct sockaddr_in addr4;

  memset(&addr4, 0, sizeof(addr4));
  addr4.sin_family = AF_INET;
  addr4.sin_len = sizeof(addr4);
```

```
        addr4.sin_port = 0;
        addr4.sin_addr.s_addr = htonl(INADDR_ANY);

        int yes = 1;
        setsockopt(CFSocketGetNative(socket), SOL_SOCKET, SO_REUSEADDR,
                        (void *)&yes, sizeof(yes));

        NSData *address4 = [NSData dataWithBytes:&addr4 length:sizeof(addr4)];
        CFSocketSetAddress(socket, (CFDataRef)address4);

        CFRunLoopSourceRef source;
        source = CFSocketCreateRunLoopSource(NULL, socket, 1);
        CFRunLoopAddSource(CFRunLoopGetCurrent(), source, kCFRunLoopDefaultMode);
        CFRelease(source);

        return socket;

}
```

Now that the socket is set up, you need to make sure you can send and receive data
through any connections made to it. For this, it is necessary to use two NSStream subclasses,
NSInputStream and NSOutputStream. The streams are linked to the socket when a connection is made to it, by using the callback function socketCallBack, as described in Listing 8-8.

Listing 8-8. *Socket Callback Function to Deal with Accepting Connections*

```
#import <CFNetwork/CFSocketStream.h>

static void socketCallBack( CFSocketRef s, CFSocketCallBackType type,
  CFDataRef address, const void *dataIn, void *info )
{
  SocketController *socketController = (SocketController *) info;

  if (kCFSocketAcceptCallBack == type) {

    CFSocketNativeHandle nativeSocketHandle =
                                *(CFSocketNativeHandle *)dataIn;
    CFReadStreamRef readStream = NULL;
    CFWriteStreamRef writeStream = NULL;
    CFStreamCreatePairWithSocket(kCFAllocatorDefault, nativeSocketHandle,
      &readStream, &writeStream);

    if (readStream && writeStream) {

      CFReadStreamSetProperty(readStream,
        kCFStreamPropertyShouldCloseNativeSocket, kCFBooleanTrue);
      CFWriteStreamSetProperty(writeStream,
        kCFStreamPropertyShouldCloseNativeSocket, kCFBooleanTrue);
```

```
    [socketController
      didAcceptConnectionWithinputStream:(NSInputStream *)readStream
                           outputStream:(NSOutputStream *)writeStream];

  } else {

    close(nativeSocketHandle);

  }

  if (readStream) CFRelease(readStream);
  if (writeStream) CFRelease(writeStream);

 }

}
```

In Listing 8-8 I've called a method didAcceptConnectionWithInputStream:outputStream:, which will assign the respective input and output streams to NSInputStream and NSOutputStream objects in the SocketController class so that I can use them elsewhere in the class. You also want to open the streams, as well as add them to the current run loop and assign delegates so that you can interact with them asynchronously. Listing 8-9 shows the code for this.

Listing 8-9. *Methods to Set NSStreams Up to Handle Stream Events Asynchronously*

```
- (void)didAcceptConnectionWithinputStream:(NSInputStream *)istr
  outputStream:(NSOutputStream *)ostr {

  // inStream and outStream are NSInputStream and
  // NSOutputStream instance variables

  inStream = istr;
  [inStream retain];

  outStream = ostr;
  [outStream retain];

  [self openStreams];

}

-(void)openStreams {

  inStream.delegate = self;
  [inStream scheduleInRunLoop:[NSRunLoop currentRunLoop]
                  forMode:NSDefaultRunLoopMode];
```

```
[inStream open];

outStream.delegate = self;
[outStream scheduleInRunLoop:[NSRunLoop currentRunLoop]
                   forMode:NSDefaultRunLoopMode];
[outStream open];

}
```

NSNetService and Publishing

Once everything is ready to accept a connection and send/receive data through that connection, all that remains to be done is publish the fact that a service is available to the network, as illustrated by Figure 8-5. Before I go into the details on how to achieve this, it's worth first briefly discussing some terms relating to NSNetService:

- type: The service type, containing both the service name and the transport layer, is prefixed by an underscore character and suffixed with a period. The type is used when browsing for services. For example, if the type is set to _mytype._tcp., then it will be discovered only by a device browsing for services of that identical type.

- domain: This determines the domain the service should run on. To use the default domain, set it to an empty string: @"".

- name: This is the user-friendly name ("Joe Bloggs' iPod," for example) under which the service will identify itself over the network, and it must be unique. To use the default device name, set it to an empty string: @"".

Figure 8-5. *The device publishes its availability as a service to the network.*

Listing 8-10 shows how to publish a service over the network using the NSNetService class and sets the service type to _mygame._tcp..

Listing 8-10. *Publishing a Service Using Bonjour*

```
-(void)publishService {
  // find the socket's assigned port
  NSData *addr = [(NSData *)CFSocketCopyAddress(socketRef) autorelease];
  struct sockaddr_in addr4;
  memcpy(&addr4, [addr bytes], [addr length]);
  uint16_t port = ntohs(addr4.sin_port);

  // set up and publish the service
  service = [[NSNetService alloc] initWithDomain:@""
                                            type:@"_mygame._tcp."
                                            name:@""
                                            port:port];

  if(service) {

    [service scheduleInRunLoop:[NSRunLoop currentRunLoop]
                       forMode:NSRunLoopCommonModes];
    [service setDelegate:self];
    [service publish];

  }

}
```

Once publish is called, the application will attempt to advertise the service as available on the network. You can check the success (or failure) of this by using the delegate methods netServiceDidPublish: and netService:didNotPublish:.

Browsing for Services with NSNetServiceBrowser

Now that we have a published service, we need a remote device to discover it and connect to it, as illustrated in Figure 8-6. In order to start searching for a remotely published service, we need to use the NSNetServiceBrowser class, which can be set up as shown in the initServiceBrowser method described in Listing 8-11. Again, the service browser is added to the run loop and assigned a delegate so it can operate asynchronously.

Listing 8-11. *Starting a Service Browser with NSNetServiceBrowser*

```
-(void)initServiceBrowser {

  serviceBrowser = [[NSNetServiceBrowser alloc] init];
  [serviceBrowser scheduleInRunLoop:[NSRunLoop currentRunLoop]
                            forMode:NSRunLoopCommonModes];
  [serviceBrowser setDelegate:self];
  [serviceBrowser searchForServicesOfType:@"_mygame._tcp." inDomain:@""];

}
```

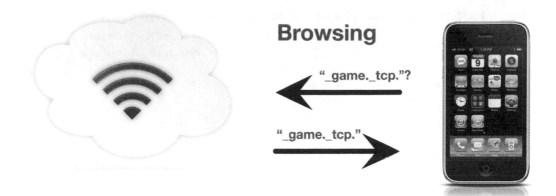

Figure 8-6. *The device uses the NSNetServiceBrowser class to discover services on the network of the requested type.*

The service browser will now begin searching for services of the requested type on the network and report back to the NSNetServiceBrowser delegate methods. Once a service is found on the network, the delegate method netServiceBrowser:didFindService: moreComing: is called. One option once a service is found, and perhaps the most appropriate when considering gaming, is to store the service in an array and display a list of available services to the user for their selection. This is the method I used in Pole2Pole, as illustrated in Figure 8-7. Also, it is worth noting that the most user-friendly option when wanting to display a service on the screen is showing its name property. Listing 8-12 shows adding a found service to a preexisting array and outputting its name to the log.

Figure 8-7. *Pole2Pole uses a UITableView to display the discovered NSNetServices.*

Listing 8-12. *NSNetServiceBrowser Delegate Method Called When a Service Is Discovered*

```
- (void)netServiceBrowser:(NSNetServiceBrowser *)netServiceBrowser
  didFindService:(NSNetService *)netService moreComing:(BOOL)moreComing {

    // netServices could be an NSMutableArray instance variable
    [netServices addObject:netService];

    // output friendly name to log
    NSLog(@"Found service named '%@'",[netService name]);

}
```

Once you have decided which service you'd like to connect to, the service must be resolved so a connection can be made between the two devices, as illustrated in Figure 8-8.

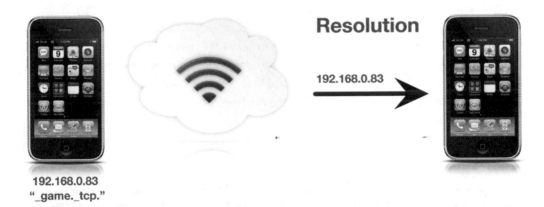

Figure 8-8. *The service is resolved, so the devices can start communicating with each other.*

By setting the delegate of an NSNetService and calling resolveWithTimeout:, as shown in Listing 8-13, the service is resolved asynchronously.

Listing 8-13. *Resolving an NSNetService*

```
-(void)resolveService:(NSNetService *)resolve {

    [resolve setDelegate:self];
    [resolve resolveWithTimeout:0.0]; // zero timeout to never time out

}
```

The delegate method netServiceDidResolveAddress: is called upon resolution, as shown in Listing 8-14, where you can then connect to the resolved service by using getInputStream:outputStream:, which provides references to the NSInputStream and NSOutputStream objects for the connection.

Listing 8-14. *NSNetService Delegate Method Called upon for Service Resolution*

```
- (void)netServiceDidResolveAddress:(NSNetService *)netService {

  if (![netService getInputStream:&inStream outputStream:&outStream]) {
    // failed to connect
    return;
  }

  [self openStreams];

}
```

NOTE

In Listing 8-14, `[self openStreams]` refers to the method described in Listing 8-9.

Sending and Receiving Data

You've now got a system that allows two devices running on the same network to quickly find, resolve, and connect to each other with only trivial interactions required from the user. The only thing left is to actually send and receive data over the socket connection, which is slightly different from before because now you are using NSNetStream instances. Any events received by the streams will trigger the delegate method `stream:handleEvent:`, from which you can interact with the current stream in a way that's dependent on the type of event. Listing 8-15 shows how to read the data from the stream using NSInputStream's `read:maxLength:` method.

Listing 8-15. *Reading Data from NSStream*

```
- (void) stream:(NSStream*)stream handleEvent:(NSStreamEvent)eventCode {

  switch(eventCode) {

    case NSStreamEventHasBytesAvailable:
    {
      if (stream == inStream) {
        uint8_t msgIn;
        unsigned int len = 0;
        len = [inStream read:&msgIn maxLength:sizeof(uint8_t)];
        if(!len) {
          if ([stream streamStatus] != NSStreamStatusAtEnd) {
            // error reading data
          }
        } else {
          // message received
```

```
        }
    }
    break;
}


}

}
```

There are, of course, other `NSStreamEvent` types, which would be useful in a working application and include the following:

- `NSStreamEventOpenCompleted`: The stream has opened successfully.

- `NSStreamEventEndEncountered`: The end of the stream has been reached.

- `NSStreamEventHasSpaceAvailable`: There is space available on the stream to write to.

Writing to the outgoing stream is a simple operation; calling `write:maxLength:` will put the data in the queue for transmission over the connection. Listing 8-16 shows the sending of data as an example.

Listing 8-16. *Writing to an NSOutputStream Object*

```
-(void)send:(const uint8_t)message {

  if([outStream hasSpaceAvailable])
    NSInteger bytesWritten =
      [outStream write:(const uint8_t *)message
            maxLength: sizeof(const uint8_t)];

  if(bytesWritten == -1) {
    // error writing to stream
  }

}
```

I hope that from the procedures I've described in this section, you now understand how to set up a socket that can receive and accept an incoming connection and then publish this as an available service. I have also worked through how to browse for available services on the network, resolve them to connect to them, and then write to and read from the data stream associated with them. These tools should be very useful in building networking applications, resulting in some great multiplayer games.

Drawing to Screen

An interesting topic that I came across early on while developing Quick Draw was that of how to draw to the screen—in my case, at the position of a user's touch. There is a lot of information in the iPhone SDK documentation on how to retrieve points from touches on the screen, so that part was easy, but it took some time when trying to work out how I was meant to draw to the screen. As it turns out, it's very simple to draw to a UIView, as long as you stick to the golden rule of performing drawing operations only inside the drawRect: method. Listing 8-17 shows the code required to build a simple finger-painting application, using a CGPath to record the points to draw.

Listing 8-17. *Drawing at Touch Location*

```
#import <UIKit/UIKit.h>

@interface DrawingView : UIView {

  CGMutablePathRef drawingPath;

}

@end

@implementation DrawingView

-(void)awakeFromNib {

  drawingPath = CGPathCreateMutable();

}

-(void)touchesMoved:(NSSet *)touches withEvent:(UIEvent *)event {

  UITouch * touch = [[event touchesForView:self] anyObject];

  CGPoint location = [touch locationInView:self];
  CGPoint previousLocation = [touch previousLocationInView:self];

  CGPathMoveToPoint (drawingPath, nil,
    previousLocation.x, previousLocation.y);
  CGPathAddLineToPoint (drawingPath, nil, location.x, location.y);
  [self setNeedsDisplay];

}
```

```objc
-(void)touchesBegan:(NSSet *)touches withEvent:(UIEvent *)event {

  UITouch * touch = [[event touchesForView:self] anyObject];

  CGPoint location = [touch locationInView:self];

  CGPathMoveToPoint (drawingPath, nil, location.x, location.y);
  CGPathAddLineToPoint (drawingPath, nil, location.x, location.y);

  [self setNeedsDisplay];

}

-(void)drawRect:(CGRect)rect {

  CGContextRef context = UIGraphicsGetCurrentContext();

  CGContextSetLineWidth(context,1.0);
  CGContextSetRGBStrokeColor(context, 1.0, 0.0, 0.0, 1.0);

  CGContextAddPath(context,drawingPath);
  CGContextStrokePath(context);

}

-(void)dealloc {

  CGPathRelease(drawingPath);
  [super dealloc];

}

@end
```

Listing 8-17 shows that the drawing code is all inside drawRect: and is updated by calling
setNeedsDisplay for the UIView. The touchesBegan: and touchesMoved: methods simply
add extra lines to the CGMutablePath, which are drawn to the screen on the next drawRect:
call.

Tic-Tac-Toe, an Example

I have not yet used the topics discussed in this chapter in a practical demonstration, so I will now show you how to use what I have covered so far to write a local network game. The game is a network version of the classic tic-tac-toe game, where two players on the same network will be able to find and play each other. I won't be showing how to develop much of the game logic, such as automatically detecting who has won, because this is meant more as a demonstration of using Bonjour to achieve network communication between devices.

First, you need to set up a new project to work with, so in Xcode create a view-based application, and name it TicTacToe. This will create several files that form the basis of a Cocoa Touch application, the most important of which, for our purposes, include the *TicTacToeViewController.h*, *TicTacToeViewController.m*, and *TicTacToeViewController.xib* files.

The next step is to place a UITableView in the main UIView that has been set up in the application's *xib* and into which you will load the available games found on the network. To do this, open the file *TicTacToeViewController.xib* and place a UITableView from the object library into the UIView present in the *xib*. In order to make this UITableView useful, you should also link both its data source and delegate outlets to the file's owner, TicTacToeViewController, as well as naming it servicesTable and linking it to an outlet of TicTacToeViewController called servicesTable. You should end up with a setup similar to the one shown in Figure 8-9.

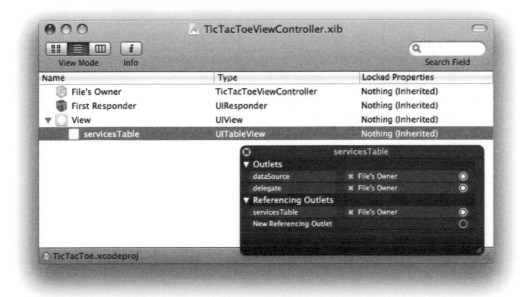

Figure 8-9. *TicTacToeViewController.xib showing outlets for servicesTable*

Now we need to place the required code into *TicTacToeViewController.h* and *TicTacToeViewController.m*. The full file listings for these files are shown in Listing 8-18 and Listing 8-19, respectively.

In *TicTacToeViewController.m*, you will notice that the class `Cell` is used for the tic-tac-toe playing cells. To include this class in your application, create a new `UIView` subclass called *Cell.m*, which will also create the file *Cell.h*. The full file listings for *Cell.h* and *Cell.m* are shown in Listing 8-20 and Listing 8-21, respectively.

NOTE

Sections of the code required for this application have already been listed in this chapter. Where there are blocks of code that I have already discussed, I'll simply reference the relevant listing.

Listing 8-18. *TicTacToeViewController.h*

```
#import <UIKit/UIKit.h>
#import <netinet/in.h>
#import <sys/socket.h>
#import <CFNetwork/CFSocketStream.h>

@interface TicTacToeViewController : UIViewController {

  UIView *overlay;

  BOOL myTurn;

  CFSocketRef socketRef;
  NSNetService *service;
  NSNetService *currentService;
  NSNetServiceBrowser *serviceBrowser;
  NSInputStream *inStream;
  NSOutputStream *outStream;
  NSString *ownName;
  NSMutableArray *services;

  IBOutlet UITableView *servicesTable;
}

-(CFSocketRef)initSocket;
-(void)publishService;
-(void)initServiceBrowser;
-(void)openStreams;
-(void)didAcceptConnectionWithinputStream:(NSInputStream *)istr
outputStream:(NSOutputStream *)ostr;
-(BOOL)send:(const uint8_t)message;
```

```
-(BOOL)tappedCell:(NSInteger)cellNumber;
-(void)endGame;
-(void)clearCells;
-(void)endGameButton;
-(void)clearCellsButton;
-(void)stopService;
-(void)stopBrowsing;
-(void)stopStreams;
-(void)closeSocket;

@property (nonatomic, retain) IBOutlet UITableView *servicesTable;

@end
```

Listing 8-19. *TicTacToeViewController.m*

```
#import "TicTacToeViewController.h"
#import "Cell.h"

@implementation TicTacToeViewController

@synthesize servicesTable;

#pragma mark init
- (void)viewDidLoad {

  myTurn = NO;

  // use UIView as game grid overlay for simplicity
  overlay = [[UIView alloc] initWithFrame:self.view.bounds];
  [overlay setBackgroundColor:[UIColor colorWithWhite:1.0 alpha:1.0]];

  // set up 3x3 grid of Cells
  int i,j;
  for(j=0;j<3;j++) {
    for(i=0;i<3;i++) {
      Cell *cell = [[Cell alloc] initWithHPos:i vPos:j sender:self];
      [overlay addSubview:cell];
      [cell release];
    }
  }

  // set up buttons to control game status
  UIButton *endGameB = [UIButton buttonWithType:UIButtonTypeRoundedRect];
  [endGameB setTitle:@"Leave Game" forState:UIControlStateNormal];
  [endGameB setFrame:CGRectMake(10, 330, 100, 30)];
  [endGameB addTarget:self action:@selector(endGameButton)
    forControlEvents:UIControlEventTouchUpInside];
  [overlay addSubview:endGameB];
```

```
    UIButton *resetGameB = [UIButton buttonWithType:UIButtonTypeRoundedRect];
    [resetGameB setTitle:@"New Game" forState:UIControlStateNormal];
    [resetGameB setFrame:CGRectMake(210, 330, 100, 30)];
    [resetGameB addTarget:self action:@selector(clearCellsButton)
        forControlEvents:UIControlEventTouchUpInside];
    [overlay addSubview:resetGameB];

    [self.view addSubview:overlay];

    // hide game view
    [overlay setHidden:YES];

    // array for keeping discovered services in
    services = [[NSMutableArray array] retain];

    // set up socket, service and service browser
    socketRef = [self initSocket];
    [self publishService];
    [self initServiceBrowser];

    [super viewDidLoad];

}

#pragma mark Socket setup and callBack

// Include socketCallBack function from Listing 8-8
// Please note that you must replace the line
//   SocketController *socketController = (SocketController *) info;
// with
//   TicTacToeViewController *socketController =
//                                 (TicTacToeViewController *) info;

// Include initSocket method from Listing 8-7

#pragma mark NSNetService publisher and browser

// Include publishService method from Listing 8-10

// Include initServiceBrowser method from Listing 8-11

#pragma mark NSNetServiceBrowser delegate methods
```

```objc
- (void)netServiceBrowser:(NSNetServiceBrowser *)netServiceBrowser
didFindService:(NSNetService *)netService moreComing:(BOOL)moreComing {

  if(![[netService name] isEqualToString:ownName]) {
    [services addObject:netService];
    [servicesTable reloadData];
  }

}

- (void)netServiceBrowser:(NSNetServiceBrowser *)netServiceBrowser
        didRemoveService:(NSNetService *)netService
              moreComing:(BOOL)moreServicesComing {

  [services removeObject:netService];
  [servicesTable reloadData];

}

#pragma mark NSNetService delegate methods

- (void)netServiceDidPublish:(NSNetService *)sender {

  // store own name for later
  ownName = [sender name];

}

- (void)netServiceDidResolveAddress:(NSNetService *)netService {

  if (![netService getInputStream:&inStream outputStream:&outStream]) {
    // failed to connect
    return;
  }
  currentService = netService;
  [self openStreams];

  myTurn = YES;

}

#pragma mark NSStream methods

// Include openStreams and didAcceptConnectionWithInputStream:outputStream:
// methods from Listing 8-9
```

```
-(BOOL)send:(const uint8_t)message {

  if (outStream && [outStream hasSpaceAvailable])
    if([outStream write:(const uint8_t *)&message
            maxLength:sizeof(const uint8_t)] != -1) return YES;
  return NO;

}

- (void) stream:(NSStream*)stream handleEvent:(NSStreamEvent)eventCode {

  switch(eventCode) {
    case NSStreamEventOpenCompleted:
      // show game view
      [overlay setHidden:NO];

      // hide servicesTable view
      [servicesTable setHidden: YES];
      break;

    case NSStreamEventHasBytesAvailable:
    { // braces to stop compiler complaining
      if (stream == inStream) {

        uint8_t b;
        unsigned int len = 0;
        len = [inStream read:&b maxLength:sizeof(uint8_t)];
        if(!len) {
          if ([stream streamStatus] != NSStreamStatusAtEnd) {
            // error reading data
          }
        } else {
          if(b<10) {
            // cell tapped by opponent
            [(Cell *)[overlay viewWithTag:b] remoteTap];
            myTurn = YES;
          } else if(b==10) {
            // use message '10' to indicate end of game
            [self endGame];
          } else if(b==11) {
            // use message '11' to reset game
            [self clearCells];
          }
        }
      }
      break;
    }
```

```
      case NSStreamEventEndEncountered:
        // opponent disconnected, end the game
        [self endGame];

        break;
    }
}

#pragma mark Game control methods

-(BOOL)tappedCell:(NSInteger)cellNumber {

  if(myTurn) {
    // send message to indicate choice of cell
    if([self send:(const uint8_t)cellNumber]) {
      myTurn = NO;
      return YES;
    }
  }
  return NO;

}

-(void)endGame {

  [self stopStreams];
  [self clearCells];
  // hide game view
  [overlay setHidden: YES];
  myTurn = NO;

  // show servicesTable view
  [servicesTable setHidden: NO];

}

-(void)clearCells {

 // clear each cell
 NSInteger cell;
 for(cell=1;cell<=9;cell++) [(Cell *)[overlay viewWithTag:cell] clearCell];

}

#pragma mark Button press methods
-(void)endGameButton {
```

```objc
    [self endGame];
    // send message to end game
    [self send:(const uint8_t)10];

}

-(void)clearCellsButton {

    [self clearCells];
    // send message to clear cells
    [self send:(const uint8_t)11];

}

#pragma mark UITableView delegate methods
- (NSInteger)numberOfSectionsInTableView:(UITableView *)tableView {

    return 1;

}

- (NSString *)tableView:(UITableView *)tableView
titleForHeaderInSection:(NSInteger)section {

    NSString *title;
    switch (section) {
      case 0:
        title = @"Available Games";
        break;
    }

    return title;

}

- (NSInteger)tableView:(UITableView *)tableView
numberOfRowsInSection:(NSInteger)section {

    return [services count];

}

- (UITableViewCell *)tableView:(UITableView *)tableView
cellForRowAtIndexPath:(NSIndexPath *)indexPath {
```

```objc
  NSString *kCellIdentifier = @"TableRow";
  UITableViewCell *cell = [tableView
    dequeueReusableCellWithIdentifier:kCellIdentifier];

  if (cell == nil) {
    cell = [[[UITableViewCell alloc] initWithFrame:CGRectZero
                            reuseIdentifier:kCellIdentifier] autorelease];
  }

  // put service name as cell text
  cell.text = [[services objectAtIndex:indexPath.row] name];
  cell.accessoryView = nil;

  return cell;

}


- (void)tableView:(UITableView *)tableView
didSelectRowAtIndexPath:(NSIndexPath *)indexPath {

  // user chose a service from table - start resolving it
  NSNetService *resolveService = [services objectAtIndex:indexPath.row];
  [resolveService setDelegate:self];
  [resolveService resolveWithTimeout:0.0];
  [[tableView cellForRowAtIndexPath:indexPath] setSelected:NO];

}

#pragma mark cleaning up

-(void)stopService {

  [service stop];
  [service removeFromRunLoop:[NSRunLoop currentRunLoop]
                    forMode:NSRunLoopCommonModes];
  [service release];
  service = nil;

}

-(void)stopBrowsing {

  [serviceBrowser stop];
  [serviceBrowser release];
  serviceBrowser = nil;

}
```

```objc
-(void)stopStreams {

  [inStream removeFromRunLoop:[NSRunLoop currentRunLoop]
                     forMode:NSDefaultRunLoopMode];
  [inStream release];
  inStream = nil;

  [outStream removeFromRunLoop:[NSRunLoop currentRunLoop]
                      forMode:NSDefaultRunLoopMode];
  [outStream release];
  outStream = nil;

  [currentService stop];
  currentService = nil;

}

-(void)closeSocket {

  if (socketRef) {
    CFSocketInvalidate(socketRef);
    CFRelease(socketRef);
    socketRef = NULL;
  }

}

- (void)dealloc {

  [self stopService];
  [self stopBrowsing];
  [self stopStreams];
  [self closeSocket];
  [services release];
  [overlay release];
  [super dealloc];

}

@end
```

Listing 8-20. *Cell.h*

```
#import "TicTacToeViewController.h"

@interface Cell : UIView {

  TicTacToeViewController *viewController;
  BOOL cellTappedRemote;
  BOOL cellTappedLocal;

}

-(id)initWithHPos:(NSInteger)i vPos:(NSInteger)j
  sender:(TicTacToeViewController *)sender;
-(void)remoteTap;
-(void)clearCell;

@end
```

Listing 8-21. *Cell.m*

```
#import "Cell.h"

@implementation Cell

-(id)initWithHPos:(NSInteger)i vPos:(NSInteger)j
  sender:(TicTacToeViewController *)sender {

  viewController = sender;

  [self initWithFrame:CGRectMake(i*100 + 10, j*100 + 10, 100, 100)];

  self.multipleTouchEnabled = NO;
  [self setBackgroundColor:[UIColor colorWithWhite:1.0 alpha:1.0]];

  // UIView tag used to identify cell
  self.tag = j*3 + i + 1;

  cellTappedLocal = NO;
  cellTappedRemote = NO;

  return self;

}
```

```
-(void)remoteTap {

  cellTappedRemote = YES;
  [self setNeedsDisplay];

}

-(void)clearCell {
  cellTappedLocal = NO;
  cellTappedRemote = NO;
  [self setNeedsDisplay];
}

- (void) touchesEnded:(NSSet*)touches withEvent:(UIEvent*)event {

  if(!cellTappedLocal && !cellTappedRemote)
    if([viewController tappedCell:[self tag]]) {
      cellTappedLocal = YES;
      [self setNeedsDisplay];
    }

}

- (void)drawRect:(CGRect)rect {

  // Draw box around cell so we can see it
  CGContextRef context = UIGraphicsGetCurrentContext();
  CGContextSetLineWidth(context,1.0);
  CGContextSetRGBStrokeColor(context, 1.0, 0.0, 0.0, 1.0);
  CGContextSetLineCap(context, kCGLineCapRound);
  CGContextAddRect(context, CGRectMake(1, 1, 98, 98));
  CGContextStrokePath(context);

  // put relevant mark in cell if tapped
  if(cellTappedLocal) {

    [[NSString stringWithString:@"X"]
        drawInRect:self.bounds
          withFont:[UIFont boldSystemFontOfSize:100.0]
      lineBreakMode:0
          alignment:UITextAlignmentCenter];

  } else if (cellTappedRemote) {
```

```
    [[NSString stringWithString:@"0"]
        drawInRect:self.bounds
          withFont:[UIFont boldSystemFontOfSize:100.0]
     lineBreakMode:0
         alignment:UITextAlignmentCenter];

  }

}

- (void)dealloc {
  [super dealloc];
}

@end
```

This application should provide some insight into how best to use the powerful networking capabilities of the iPhone—together with the methods I have covered in this chapter—to build your own multiplayer games. If you are unfamiliar with C, Objective-C, or both, then some of the topics covered here may be hard to grasp in their entirety at first, but if you can follow the majority of the methods explained in this chapter, there is not much more you need to know on the device side in order to get a multiplayer game up and running.

The nature of networking means that when developing applications that rely on network or Internet communications, you must be sure that problems such as network outages, dropped or incomplete packets, or even slow transfer rates can be encountered without causing issues in your application. If you bear this in mind throughout development, making sure you have every situation covered, then you will no doubt end up with much more stable games that work regardless of the users' connection quality.

Summary

By reading this chapter, you now know far more than I did when I began programming for the iPhone, just a few months before Swipe Interactive's first release, Quick Draw. This puts you in an excellent position for becoming a developer of one of the increasingly exciting applications that are appearing in the App Store every day.

Keep a lookout for many more iPhone projects from Swipe Interactive, and I look forward to seeing your applications released into the App Store soon.

Index